MAFIA
SUMMIT

ALSO BY GIL REAVILL

Aftermath, Inc.: Cleaning Up After the CSI Goes Home
Dirty (film script by Chris Fisher, Gil Reavill, and Eric Saks)

MAFIA SUMMIT

J. Edgar Hoover, the Kennedy Brothers, and

the Meeting That Unmasked the Mob

GIL REAVILL

THOMAS DUNNE BOOKS ⚏ St. Martin's Press, New York

THOMAS DUNNE BOOKS.
An imprint of St. Martin's Press.

MAFIA SUMMIT. Copyright © 2013 by Gil Reavill. All rights reserved. Printed in the United States of America. For information, address St. Martin's Press, 175 Fifth Avenue, New York, N.Y. 10010.

www.thomasdunnebooks.com
www.stmartins.com

Design by Steven Seighman

Library of Congress Cataloging-in-Publication Data

Reavill, Gil, 1953–
   Mafia summit : J. Edgar Hoover, the Kennedy Brothers, and the meeting that unmasked the mob / Gil Reavill.—1st ed.
       p. cm.
   Includes bibliographical references.
   ISBN 978-0-312-65775-8 (hbk.)
   ISBN 978-1-250-02110-6 (e-book)
   1. Mafia—United States—History—20th century.   2. Organized crime—United States—History—20th century.   3. Organized crime—United States—Prevention—History.   4. Hoover, J. Edgar (John Edgar), 1895–1972.   5. Kennedy, Robert F., 1925–1968.   I. Title.
   HV6446.R43 2012
   364.1060973—dc23

eISBN 9781250021106

2012038009

First Edition: January 2013

10   9   8   7   6   5   4   3   2

In memory of my father, Acton Reavill,
who set me on my path in life as a young child, taking me to Al
Capone's hideout in northern Wisconsin, and to Little Bohemia lodge,
where he showed me the bullet holes from John Dillinger's shoot-out
with the Feds

CONTENTS

CAST OF CHARACTERS

GOVERNMENT

Joseph Amato: Federal Bureau of Narcotics agent; member of the original "Italian Squad" based in New York City

Joseph Benenati: New York State Police Sergeant Investigator, Sidney Barracks

Edgar Croswell: New York State Police Sergeant Investigator, Vestal Barracks

J. Edgar Hoover: director, Federal Bureau of Investigation

Irving R. Kaufman: jurist, United States District Court for the Southern District of New York

Estes Kefauver: U.S. senator, chairman of Senate hearings on organized crime, presidential candidate

John F. Kennedy: U.S. senator, Rackets Committee member, afterward President of the United States

Robert F. Kennedy: chief counsel, Senate Rackets Committee, afterward Attorney General of the United States

Vince Vasisko: New York State Police Trooper, Vestal Barracks

Milton Wessel: special prosecutor, U.S. Justice Department

Paul Williams: U.S. Attorney for the Southern District of New York

ORGANIZED CRIME

Albert Anastasia: Commission member, Mafia boss of the Brooklyn waterfront; his 1957 murder precipitated the Apalachin summit

Joe Barbara: host of Apalachin summit

Joe Bonanno: Commission member, boss of one of New York City's five Mafia families

Russell Bufalino: Scranton area mob front man; cohost of Apalachin summit

Frank Costello: influential head of New York underworld; gambler, slot-machine king; known as "Prime Minister" for his political connections and mediation skills

Carmine Galante: narcotics trafficker, hit man in the 1943 Carlo Tresca murder, his 1956 traffic stop outside Binghamton helped police connect summit host Barbara with organized crime figures

Carlo Gambino: boss-in-waiting, heir to the Anastasia crime empire

Vito Genovese: Mafia don based in Manhattan; chief motivator for the Apalachin summit

Sam Giancana: Commission member, Chicago mob boss

Meyer Lansky: Jewish mob boss; spearheaded organized crime push into Cuban casinos

Charles Luciano: mob boss exiled to Sicily

Steven Magaddino: Buffalo crime boss and Commission member; Apalachin summit held in his territory

Carlos Marcello: New Orleans mob boss and Commission member

John C. Montana: mob front man in Buffalo area; chosen as Buffalo's "Man of the Year" in 1956

Willie Moretti: New Jersey mobster, ally and cousin of Frank Costello.

Joe Profaci: Commission member, boss of one of New York City's five Mafia families; the "Olive Oil King"

Arnold Rothstein: gambler extraordinaire, narcotics trafficker; murdered in 1928

Santo Trafficante Jr.: Tampa mob boss, smuggler, Havana casino operator

Santo Volpe: mob boss in the Scranton area; mentor to Joe Barbara

What a field day for the heat . . .
—STEPHEN STILLS
"FOR WHAT IT'S WORTH"

PROLOGUE

McFall Road, Apalachin, New York

OUT OF ALL THE CARS parked alongside McFall Road in the tiny New York hamlet of Apalachin, the Chrysler Crown Imperial limousine stood out. Not just an automobile, but a statement of wealth and prestige, expressed in an ornate chrome grill and a set of sweeping tail fins. A fat, shiny, outlandish vehicle, a perfect signifier for 1950s America.

Midday on a foggy, rainy Thursday, November 14, 1957. Through his field glasses from fifty yards away, Sergeant Edgar Croswell of the New York State Police surveilled not only the big Imperial, but also a dozen similar late-model land boats around it, as well as the hilltop estate where they were parked.

Sergeant Croswell always had a sharp eye for cars. When his youngest son Bob was a child, Croswell taught him to recognize automobiles as a kind of parlor trick—a six-year-old able to nail the difference between a Ford Custom, say, and a Galaxie, rattling off the make, model, and year like a savant.

Back in the 1920s, Walter Chrysler founded the Imperial line to compete with GM's Cadillac and Ford's Lincoln. Though it never quite measured up, selling only a single car for every ten Cadillacs, the model had its adherents. In later days, the Imperial found itself banned from demolition derbies, its X-frame construction so solid that it was virtually unbeatable.

The forty-four-year-old Croswell drove a Buick himself, but the Imperial sparked his interest. The current-year's model, brand spanking new. The big sedan took its place among a whole fleet of Caddies and Continentals and Lincoln Premieres, parked in the spacious driveway lot in front of a four-bay garage, left alongside the road or pulled into a field next to a rustic field-stone ranch house.

With Croswell that day were his state police partner, Trooper Vincent R. Vasisko, and a pair of revenue agents from Treasury's Alcohol and Tobacco Tax Unit, Art Ruston and Ken Brown.

Croswell turned to his cohorts and ticked off the state plates visible from his post.

"New Jersey, Pennsylvania, New Jersey, New York, New York, Ohio, Illinois," he said. Some of the license plates, he noticed, had special low numbers, usually indicating owners of influence.

"Those aren't salesmen cars," Vasisko said.

"No," Croswell said. "Let's get the numbers down as fast as we can."

The lawmen moved forward, taking plate numbers. Lots of cars, but no people. The driveway, yards, and fields around the compound appeared curiously devoid of life. Where was everybody?

The fieldstone house on McFall Road—really a collection of buildings, a compound of sorts, with a main residence, a summer pavilion, a garage, and outbuildings—belonged to Joseph Barbara Sr., who presented himself to the world as an upstanding citizen, the area distributor for the lucrative Canada Dry line of beverage products.

But Joseph Barbara defined the old police term "hinky." Croswell knew Barbara had been buying up sugar—massive amounts, really, 30,000 pounds a month for the past year. That much sugar meant illegal stills.

Counterintuitive as it was, moonshining had not ended with Prohibition. By avoiding excise taxes, illicit alcohol production could prove enormously lucrative, not as golden as it had been during the Volstead Act, but even so a steady earner.

Unsure exactly what was going on at the McFall Road estate, but thinking it might have something to do with moonshining, Croswell called in the revenuers.

Sergeant Croswell served as a senior investigator with the BCI, the Bureau of Criminal Investigation, which was the State Police equivalent of a detective bureau. Over a decade previous, during World War II, upon his first encounter with Joe Barbara, Croswell opened a mental file on the man, the informal kind of data-set all lawmen keep continually up-to-date, on the hinkiness of whatever kind that crops up within their territory.

Every once in a while, at least a couple times a month, Croswell would drive up to Barbara's impressive Apalachin compound, ten miles west of Binghamton. His personally motivated ten-year surveillance campaign, wholly unmandated by his superiors in the State Police, had come to this: a single cruiser parked at the property line of the Barbara estate, near a driveway parked thick with expensive limousines that, by all rights of logic and cop intuition, should not have been anywhere near backwoods Southern Tier New York.

The squadron of big cars, bespeaking power and privilege, ranged against the single unmarked police car with its force of four. Croswell started to feel a little lonely up there on top of the hill. He made an executive decision, got on his radio, and put the word out to his fellow state police.

Black-and-whites began pulling out of barracks in Binghamton and the neighboring towns of Waverly and Horseheads, cutting off the approaches to Apalachin. In all, seventeen additional troopers answered the call, men Croswell had worked with often before, their names readily familiar to him: Lieutenant Kenneth Weidenborner, Sergeant Joseph Benenati, Trooper Joseph D. Smith, Trooper Richard C. Geer, Trooper Howard Teneyck.

The state police threw a net around the Barbara estate, cutting off not only McFall Road but also East River Road to the north, McFadden Road to the west, Pennsylvania Avenue to the east, and Rhodes Road to the south. Whoever or whatever was there at Barbara's—moonshiners, or something more sinister—was boxed in, with cops blocking any and all possible exit ways from the area.

Croswell hoped he was right in alerting the troops. All he had to go on was a homeowner's extensive arrest record, a strangely out-of-place collection of big cars, and a few other indications that some sort of illicit gathering was going down on McFall Road.

A fish truck emerged from the Barbara place and rattled up the road. The quartet of lawmen let it pass. The driver, local merchant Bartolo Guccia, had just taken an order for three pounds of porgies and a pound of mackerel at the kitchen of the big stone house. Guccia, a sallow little man with an old-world Italian accent, proceeded past the cops, but then pulled up and came back. He waved jauntily at Croswell and Vasisko and returned to the Barbara compound.

Almost at the same moment, a crew of a dozen men in sharp suits ("fourteen-karat hoodlums," Croswell mentally tagged them, "like a collection of George Rafts") rounded the corner of the screened-in summer pavilion on the Barbara estate. As though they were cartoon characters, the men stopped comically short upon seeing the staties taking down plate numbers along the road.

Cops and quarry eyed each other, the same thought occurring to both groups: who were these guys?

Through the binoculars, Croswell noted the heavy gold watches on almost every man's wrist. He could pick out their diamond jewelry, rings, stickpins, and studs, sparkling in the washed-out light of the autumn noon.

Guccia reached the compound garage. Croswell heard words being exchanged but could not make out what was being said.

"Roadblock," was what the fishmonger said to the mob boys. "State police! They're stopping everybody!"

The gangsters scattered.

Croswell watched the rout through his binoculars. "They're running," he told Vasisko. But his partner could see that for himself.

Figures poured out of the house, climbing into the cars or fleeing on foot across the fields, heading toward the surrounding woods. The sergeant tracked them, keeping his eyes glued to his field glasses, swiveling from the grounds to the forests and back to the property.

"This is going to be a bad day for a whole lot of people," Croswell murmured, utilizing his usual dry-as-dust understatement to characterize what would prove to be a turning point in the long and tortured history of American law enforcement's battle against organized crime.

What State Police Sergeant Edgar Croswell had stumbled into, with a curious combination of accident and brilliant, cop-savvy intent, would come to be known as the nation's most notorious Mafia gathering ever, the Apalachin summit. Assembled at Joseph Barbara's country house was virtually the entire leadership spectrum of an American racketeering underworld that raked in billions of dollars per year.

These were bosses, underbosses, and made men, powerful figures in organized crime. Almost every one of them carried arrest records heinous enough to make any lawman sit up and take notice. Stated a prosecutor who assembled legal cases against those involved: "Never before had there been such a collection of jailbirds, murderers free on technicalities and big wheels in gambling and dope rackets."

This book relates the story of the Apalachin summit, why the mobsters gathered, and what took place in the brief time before their meeting was interrupted by police. It also chronicles the bloody mob wars that led up to the gathering, as well as the bitter law enforcement turf battles that followed it.

The account has been told before only in snatches, within other contexts, always incompletely, and at times erroneously. This new telling uses fresh material obtained from the principals involved, as well as documents from official sources and government files.

Only a single warning shot was fired at Apalachin, no blood spilled, no gunfights as the mobsters fought their way out past the roadblock. The legal charges stemming from the summit were likewise anticlimactic. Sixty gangsters were detained out of the hundred-plus attending the meeting. The Federal conspiracy convictions of twenty of the participants were reversed upon appeal.

So as a bust, Apalachin was something of a bust. A few perjury raps, some contempt of court jailings—on the face of it, that's the sum total of what came out of the roundup. A wet firecracker.

But the judicial win-loss record is deceiving. The resulting exposure dosed the Mafia with its least favorite poison: publicity. "I don't know what is going to happen in the courts," Ed Croswell said after the sweep. "But the New York State Police action threw the mobsters up in the air, where everyone could take a shot at them."

In Apalachin's aftermath relentless government action bore down on the mob, and there were no fewer than a dozen separate probes looking into the affair, police investigations, legislative hearings, grand juries. For years after the November 1957 gathering, subpoenas rained down like confetti, and mobsters could do little more than trudge from hearing to hearing, repeating their sad Fifth Amendment catechisms.

And there's this: Apalachin also triggered the interest of the one man the underworld would come to recognize as its chief nemesis, Robert Francis Kennedy.

To judge just how much of a disaster the summit was for its participants, hear the words of a man who lost everything because of it. "I should have broken both my legs," said mob boss Vito Genovese, something of an expert on broken legs, "before I accepted that invitation [to Apalachin]."

The summit's importance far exceeds its zeroed-out body count and fizzle in the courts. The gathering and its repercussions not only changed organized crime, but transformed law enforcement. Unlike the murderous mob wars that led up to Apalachin, the subsequent governmental infighting was bloodless. But it was no less fierce. Two giants, representing two competing visions of America, clashed and wrestled and hammered at each other like a couple of Norse gods.

Robert Kennedy, brother of a senator who would be president, afterward attorney general in that brother's administration, faced off with J. Edgar Hoover, director of the Federal Bureau of Investigation, the sclerotic administrator of the nation's premier law enforcement arm, long-ensconced, hugely powerful and, before Bobby came along, virtually unchallengeable. The FBI and the Justice Department itself were altered irrevocably by their battles.

So there were two Edgars involved here, Hoover and Croswell, and they approached their jobs in very different ways, differences that were instructive on a larger scale. They both interacted with Bobby Kennedy, too, and the dissimilarities in their dealings with him held deeper meaning also.

Kennedy saw the danger of the mob the way Croswell did, not only in terms of crime but in terms of corruption, the bad infiltrating and polluting the good, with organized crime a virus entering the bloodstream of labor unions, police, and political parties. RFK warned that an "invisible government" threatened to take over our own, buying off public officials.

The problem was epidemic and not limited to this or that city. Organized crime corrupted mayors, police chiefs, legislators, judges. In the immortal words of Richard Nixon: "Sure there are dishonest men in local government. But there are dishonest men in national government, too." The mob suborned scores of them.

The consequences of Apalachin were felt not only institutionally, but in individual lives. New York City crime lord Vito Genovese summoned his underworld associates from all over the country to come together at Joe Barbara's stone ranch house. In the harsh light of his post-Apalachin notoriety, Genovese found himself targeted by a government drug sting, convicted of trafficking in heroin, and sent to federal prison, where he would remain until his death.

Also as a result of the summit, FBI director J. Edgar Hoover, the nation's celebrated top crime fighter, revealed himself to be a self-inflated charlatan. The bust-up of the Mafia gathering exposed the inordinately sensitive Hoover to public ridicule. For all the puff pieces in newspapers over the years, for all the fawning newsreel hagiography and laudatory movies about mythic "G-men," it became clear that Hoover had simply fallen down on the job.

Until Apalachin, the FBI director had spent his entire professional life dismissing the very existence of the Mafia, terming it, in one of his milder imprecations, "baloney." In the wake of the summit, Hoover embarked upon a crash catch-up program of illegal electronic surveillance on the underworld that thoroughly trashed civil liberties but helped frustrate the Mafia's stubborn cult of secrecy.

Hoover, Robert Kennedy, and the mob. Apalachin began the beguine that led to an extended three-partnered dance.

"Summit," the word, comes from the Latin *summum,* meaning "the highest point." In 1950, at the beginning of the Cold War, Winston Churchill coined the contemporary sense of summit as "a meeting among leaders." It's a fitting description for a gathering of mob bosses trying to sort out tangled allegiances and bloody consequences, not of a cold war but a very hot one.

It's fitting in a couple of other ways, too, since Apalachin represented a summit, a high point for the mob, whose reach and influence would never again attain pre-1957 heights. In a sense, it also marked a high point for J. Edgar Hoover, who would see his power gradually wane from that junction forward until his death in 1972.

Hoover first encountered the word "Apalachin" only after the event, on the morning of November 15, 1957. 65 HOODLUMS SEIZED IN A RAID AND RUN OUT OF UPSTATE NEW YORK VILLAGE, read the headline in *The New York Times.*

The summit revealed an intelligence failure of the first magnitude. Not to put too fine a point on it, Hoover had been caught with his pants down. The director, who liked to portray his beloved Bureau (and himself) as hugely competent, proved clueless in the wake of the biggest mob gathering in history.

The definitive reference guide on the FBI passes this judgment: "Dating from the Apalachin incident, the FBI had become enmeshed in controversy as questions were increasingly raised both about FBI director Hoover's adamant denial that the Mafia existed and the FBI's seeming failure to recognize organized crime as a national problem."

Here's Rudolph Guiliani, ex–New York City mayor, former racketbuster:

By and large, no one had really ripped off the veil and seen that this was not just a couple of isolated hoods, but a vast national organization. Apalachin gave the first demonstrative, solid evidence that this was a very large criminal conspiracy. Before Apalachin, there was a debate as to whether the Mafia actually existed. There was no sense of this national operation that had been put together and that had really been operating since 1931. What they got until 1957 was almost—not quite, but almost—immunity from Federal investigation and prosecution.

Or, as Mafia expert Thomas Reppetto put it, more succinctly: "Apalachin forced the federal government to move."

Though proof of actual criminal activity at the summit remained elusive, the incident led to new legislative initiatives that would eventually (after a process of a quarter century) snap the spine of the mob in America. Organized crime persists. But law enforcement pressure that began as a result of Apalachin dismantled the classic national leadership structure that had guided the Mafia throughout its high-water years during the middle of the twentieth century.

As a backdrop, the Apalachin summit presents the well-cushioned, brightly enameled America of the 1950s, a period with a deceptively simple reputation, a time of "I Like Ike" and Sputnik, gleaming on the surface with the polish of a Chrysler Imperial limousine, but which upon closer inspection reveals darker rumblings beneath the surface of the national psyche.

Bit players in the Apalachin saga include a lineup of fifties-worthy figures, not only Joltin' Joe DiMaggio but also the cop who busted jazz great Charlie Parker, the judge who executed the Rosenbergs, and the gangster who sold singer Billie Holiday her dope.

The multiple meanings of the summit reverberate even now, over a half century later, lessons about the arrogance of government and the hubris of gangsters. But at the core of Apalachin there is a bedrock-basic story, one of the oldest known, a hero's tale: the always heartening, always startling phenomenon of a good man in the right place at the right time doing the right thing.

Somehow, this essential truth has faded. In the months immediately after the gathering, amid a welter of government investigations into the event, journalists emphasized the *omerta*-spawned inscrutability of the mob. APALACHIN STILL AN UNRESOLVED MYSTERY, headlined the *New York Times* on December 22, 1957. And again, more than a year later, on April 5, 1959: APALACHIN STORY IS STILL A DEEP MYSTERY.

Writers rushed in to offer solutions to the "mystery" of Apalachin. A survey of the literature reveals an array of alternative (and quite simply wrong) theories. A book on the alliance between the Sicilian and American Mafias states definitively the Italians were responsible for informing the

New York State Police about the gathering. A history of the Federal Bureau of Narcotics claims that the FBN agents knew about the meet all along and were thus responsible for Croswell's action.

Another account, purporting to be the direct testament of Charles Luciano, confidently maintains that the great mob chieftain, exiled in Italy, sabotaged the summit. Hank Messick's *Lansky*, predictably, quotes "underworld sources" as saying criminal mastermind Meyer Lansky informed Croswell of the meeting. No shred of documentary evidence is presented to back up any of these theories.

It seems inevitable. Write a mob book, reveal that it was your particular subject who engineered the bust-up of the Apalachin summit. It was an inside job. The cops were tipped. The mob, itself a wide-ranging conspiracy, naturally attracts conspiracy theorists. Demonology requires snaky, diabolical cleverness on the part of the foe. Somehow, some way, the mob itself just *had* to be involved in the disruption of the summit.

Direct testimony of the principals involved indicates none of this is so. No one in law enforcement had any kind of advance notice. People on both sides of the badge, those behind it and those confronted by it, were equally surprised that day.

If evidence doesn't suffice, logic does. Say the conspiracy theorists are right. Grant that the police knew beforehand what was going on at Joe Barbara's place, that the gathering included such marquee names as Genovese, Gambino, Profaci, Magaddino, and Bonanno, as well as others at the top of the organized crime hierarchy, scores of mobsters in all.

Given that advance knowledge, would Sergeant Ed Croswell have trundled up McFall Road in a solitary car with a single fellow trooper and a pair of revenue agents?

Anyone who believes that has little knowledge of police tactics, which tend toward overkill in the extreme. Tipped off, the authorities would never have sent a warrantless, ad hoc gang of four under the command of a single sergeant. They would have mobilized a whole army and gone in, as the phrase has it, like gangbusters.

"I don't even like to hear it called a 'raid,'" Croswell said in the aftermath. "There were no plans to raid Joe Barbara's big stone ranch house. We didn't start out with a raiding party."

Yet the idea of a preplanned operation off an informant's tip somehow persists. In his comprehensive and mostly excellent *Mafia Encyclopedia*, Carl Sifakis writes, "It becomes almost impossible to reject insider foul play." Sifakis states that a cabal of Meyer Lansky, Frank Costello, and Carlo

Gambino "tipped off the authorities about the meeting." How, exactly, would the trio of mobsters have accomplished this? Especially since Gambino himself was picked up at the summit?

Likewise, Paul Lunde's *Organized Crime*: "It is difficult to believe that the fiasco of Apalachin was not orchestrated by Luciano." Or Jay Maeder of the New York *Daily News*: "Some observers wondered if perhaps some anonymous prankster had picked up a phone and dropped a dime on Vito Genovese."

All this brings to mind Virginia Mayo's sneer to Jimmy Cagney in the classic gangster movie *White Heat*: "It's always 'somebody tipped them,' it's never 'the cops are smart.'"

It takes a little picking apart, but this is one historical "mystery" that turns out to be fairly transparent. We know what happened at Apalachin. Over the years, the story has been meted out in bits and pieces by the people involved. More evidence has been scattered willy-nilly across the historical record, waiting only upon being collected and smoothed into a comprehensive narrative.

The simple truth is actually a much more compelling story, a more arresting tale, one might say, than any insider tip-off. An exhaustive search of police archives, contemporary first-person testimony, as well as the voluminous reports of more than a dozen government investigative agencies summon up a clear picture, and the truth of the Apalachin summit is revealed.

A solitary lawman, acting at times in concert with cohorts, certainly, but doggedly following through on his own singular initiative with energy, intelligence, and courage, struck the most damaging blow to organized crime in America's history. He made for an unlikely hero. It was *High Noon* on the Susquehanna.

Ed Croswell was right. November 14, 1957 was a bad day for a whole lot of people. But the events leading up to it were a great deal worse. If there was no bloodletting at Apalachin, slayings and mayhem preceded the meetup like a rolling, miasmic fog, a corpse-strewn run of violence that led, in a blood trail, to Joseph Barbara's stone house.

Ignorant armies clashed by night. Gangsters targeted their enemies, died themselves in execution-style killings, made war on each other for advantage in dominance and succession. The mobsters fought over gambling profits from the huge new tourist casinos in Cuba. They got themselves tangled in the million-dollar-a-day trade in smuggled heroin.

In fact, Cuba and heroin stitch themselves deep into the fabric of organized crime in the fifties, intertwined threads in the weave. With so much money coming in, it was impossible for the dogs not to snarl over it and tear out the occasional throat. Then, after the killings, it was time to kiss and make up. Perhaps at a comfortable stone manor house in the countryside of rural New York.

Two mobsters figure prominently in the run-up to the summit, a pair of crime lords who circled each other for years, looking for weaknesses, gauging opportunities. Albert Anastasia and Vito Genovese, both based in New York City, battled for supremacy in the dog-eat-dog underworld of the Mafia. The summit at Joe Barbara's grew out of their war. The story of Apalachin begins, as so many mob stories do, with the spilling of blood.

PART I
Albert and Vito

1

Murder on Fifteenth Street

CARLO TRESCA IS A NAME not much remembered today, but in the first half of the last century he was widely known, a leading light of the American left, when in response to the Great Depression the nation turned to progressive, even radical, ideologies. One writer recalled Tresca as a "labor spellbinder," citing his ability to whip up a crowd of workers with fiery oratory.

In January 1943, Tresca found himself in the middle of a fight to determine the future of his beloved homeland, Italy. The Allied invasion of Sicily—the initial thrust in the battle to break the Axis in half—remained six months in the future. But it was already clear to anyone with a modicum of awareness that the days were numbered for Benito Mussolini's fascist ruling order. Tresca adamantly demanded that the still-aborning postwar Italian government be free of both former fascists and eager-to-dominate communists.

Tresca habitually found himself in the middle of public political fights. A thin-faced firebrand born in the Abruzzo in 1879, he wore a Trotsky-like beard and, after moving to America in 1904, helped organize strikes for the Wobblies, the International Workers of the World. Tresca's personal politics matured like a rogue Chianti, beginning with nationalism, proceeding through socialism, finally to arrive at a vinegary style of anarchism. His newspaper, *Il Martello* (the Hammer), had carried on the battle against Mussolini since 1920. The Spanish Civil War and the Russo-German non-aggression pact had soured him on Stalin and the communists.

While agitating against Mussolini and the fascists as well as against Stalin and the communists, Tresca also fought the mob. He vehemently opposed organized crime's infiltration of trade unions. Since the days of the Black Hand, the original Italian crime syndicate, Tresca had battled the mob in his adopted home of America.

Tresca's enemies were legion. In 1931, Mussolini put the rabble-rouser on his "death list." The man had been repeatedly beaten, threatened, and targeted for assassination. The first try was in 1909 by a razor-wielding assailant in Pittsburgh, who missed Tresca's throat but slashed through his cheek and jaw.

Tresca didn't quit. An odd alliance occurred in WWII Italy. In the prewar years Mussolini had mounted an impressive assault on the entrenched Mafia, in Sicily and elsewhere in Italy, shattering its century-old hold in many parts of the country, hounding its soldiers into exile.

Yet, in the early 1940s, one of the powerful figures in Il Duce's orbit was an Italian-American mafioso named Vito Genovese. And it was this man—the same fedora-wearing figure Ed Croswell would spot inside a Chrysler Imperial limo at Apalachin—whom Carlo Tresca decided deserved special attention.

Born near Naples in 1897, Vito Genovese emigrated with his family in 1913 to the Lower East Side. There he formed a friendship that would shape his life, meeting one Salvatore Lucania, who as Lucky Luciano would come to be known as the premier organizer of organized crime in America. The same age, Lucky and Vito represented the classic mob combination of brains and brawn, respectively.

As a young turk in the twenties' and thirties' mob, Genovese cut a violent swath across New York City and its environs. His rap sheet reads like a true gangster résumé: homicide, disorderly person, burglary, homicide, carrying a dangerous weapon, homicide. These were only the crimes that came to police notice—there were others, infamous and bloody. The judicial dispositions of the arrests were equally interesting: discharged, dismissed, discharged, discharged, dismissed, discharged.

In 1936, in flight from the heat over one of these murders, Genovese decamped for the homeland, settling in Nola, near Naples. He prospered. He helped lay the groundwork for the Marseilles-Cuba-Montreal "triangle trade" in heroin smuggling. He cultivated contacts in Fascist leadership circles in Italy. His legitimate bona fides developed to the degree that he became part owner of several factories, power plants, and a castle in Campania.

None of this sat well with Carlo Tresca. He had a run-in with Genovese in 1935, when the mobster wanted to open a fascist-friendly club for Italian seamen in New York City. Tresca, an avowed antifascist, put the kibosh on the plan. Later, when he heard of Genovese's activities in Italy, Tresca reasoned that the only way the gangster could be accepted by higher-ups was through ignorance of his past. He fired off a series of letters to the government, detailing Vito's unsavory background in America.

Vito Genovese was not a man to be trifled with, especially not by a left-leaning anarchist journalist with multiple political axes to grind. According to an anonymous informant, Genovese had the following conversation with Il Duce at a 1942 Christmas party in Rome.

"Carlo Tresca is an archenemy of mine," Mussolini said to Genovese.

"Mine, too," Genovese said, agreeing with the dictator that Tresca had bothered too many powerful people for too long.

"If there is anything you can do to rid us of him," Mussolini said, "I would do anything in the world for you."

Some two weeks after this exchange, on the evening of Monday, January 11, 1943, Tresca worked late at the *Il Martello* office on the third floor of a six-story commercial building at 96 Fifth Avenue in Manhattan, on the southwest corner of Fifteenth Street. He had finished a busy day, huddling with associates, discussing plans to disrupt a meeting of the Office of War Information the following Thursday, seeing writer John Dos Passos for lunch, meeting with a job seeker, an engraver, staffers at the newspaper.

At around nine p.m., a lawyer named Giuseppe Calabi arrived at the *Il Martello* offices. He and Tresca had a committee meeting planned, but the other members didn't show up, so the editor suggested the two men go for a meal at a nearby bar. They left the building via a Fifteenth Street exit and turned toward Fifth Avenue.

Wartime gas rationing and blackout rules meant the cross street was very dark. As Tresca and Calabi headed east, a gunman stepped out of the shadows behind them and fired—a single shot, then three more in quick succession.

Two bullets hit Tresca, either of which would have been fatal, one tearing through his left lung and one penetrating the right side of his face to lodge in his spine. He dropped to the pavement, his legs cocked awkwardly, feet splaying to the curb. Witnesses—two workers from the nearby Norwegian consulate—reported a black Ford sedan pulling away down Fifteenth after the shooting.

Carlo Tresca, activist, anarchist, friend to the workingman, was pronounced dead on arrival at St. Vincent's Hospital, four blocks from the murder scene.

That should have been that. A man with many enemies gunned down on the street, an anarchist killed amid the kind of lawless chaos he himself advocated. The list of likely suspects was long.

But the murder of Carlo Tresca would become a tiny ringing bell, vibrating, dinging, pealing, setting off sympathetic tremors, triggering expanding circles of effect that passed through the echelons of American law enforcement until it arrived, years later, within the patient, long-memoried reach of Sergeant Edgar Croswell.

"La Marese," they called them—the Mafia soldiers and bosses from Castellammare del Golfo, Sicily. If Italy is the boot kicking the Sicilian football, then Castellammare is the northwest tip of the ball.

A rough declension played itself out among Italians in the mob in America, dividing them into two camps. There were the Castellammarese, from the insular, secretive commune in Sicily, and then there were immigrants with backgrounds in and around Naples, the provinces of Calabria and Campania.

It wasn't black and white, and there were exceptions hailing from all over Italy, but generally the division held true. The styles could be said to be different, too. La Marese and Neapolitan, the heart and the head, the fiery emotional and the coolly rational. Again, nothing set in stone, just a vague stereotype, both true and untrue in the way of all stereotypes.

The opposing clans banged and bloodied each other in the fabled Castellammarese War at the dawn of the 1930s, a revenge-fest that left sixty gangsters dead.

In the heat of battle, factions proved fluid and situational. Mobsters regularly killed their allies and made alliances with their enemies. Younger, more assimilated gangsters used the war to further their ambitions, displacing the older, more traditional "Mustache Petes" of the first immigrant generation. When the smoke of the Castellammarese War cleared, clearly the mobster who benefited most was the Sicilian organizational genius, Charles "Lucky" Luciano.

Luciano ushered the Mafia into a new era. The mob evolved from an ethnic-based society preying on immigrant enclaves into a well-oiled syndicate reaping illicit profits from nearly every sector of the American economy. Luciano forged a pan-ethnic alliance with Jewish gangster Meyer Lansky. Borders were crossed, divisions were abandoned, and organized crime went national.

Another casualty of the Castellammarese War in-fighting was the old "honored society" tradition that forbade any involvement in narcotics and prostitution. The gangland battles foreshadowed the end of Prohibition in 1933 and, like any forward-thinking corporate boss, Luciano realized new revenue streams had to be developed. Dope and sex fit the bill.

By the fifties, the division of the mob along geographical lines had increasingly faded, but still held on as an inherited vestige. The Sicilians Joe Bonanno, Joe Profaci, Steven Magaddino, and Frank Garafalo lined up as La Marese, while Vito Genovese, Frank Costello, and Albert Anastasia had roots in Naples and Calabria.

Also numbering among La Marese in 1943 was a deadly thirty-three-year-old cigar-chomping killer named Carmine Galante. Born in Italian Harlem of Castellammarese parents, Galante—known all his adult life as "Lilo," slang for cigar—acted as close ally and underboss to Joe Bonanno. Galante was also, as it happened, certifiably unhinged.

Prison psychologists at Sing Sing once got hold of Carmine Galante, ran him through a battery of personality tests, and diagnosed their prisoner—big surprise to those who knew him—as a psychopath. "He had a mental age of 14-and-a-half and an IQ of 90," read the assessment, diagnosing the subject as a "neuropathic, psychopathic personality, emotionally dull, and indifferent."

Whenever he was out of prison and on the bricks, Lilo proved himself eminently useful to his superiors as a torpedo, racking up more than eighty contract killings. He was vengeful and spiteful in the extreme. Even after his old mob enemy Frank Costello died, his tomb wasn't safe from Galante, who dynamited the crypt.

When, in 1943, as a courtesy to Mussolini—but also for his own purposes—Vito Genovese was looking for a killer to take out the trouble-making journalist Carlo Tresca, naturally Lilo's name came up.

At eight o'clock on the night Tresca was murdered, Galante, just released after an eight-year stretch in prison for the armed robbery of a brewery, visited his parole officer, Sidney Gross, in the state offices at 80 Centre Street in Manhattan. When Galante left Gross, he picked up a tail, Fred Berson, another parole officer, who followed Lilo to ascertain if the ex-convict was violating his parole by associating with known criminals. Galante crossed Centre, proceeded down Worth Street, but instead of entering the subway climbed into a black sedan. Berson noted the license plate, IC 9272.

Straight from the parole office to murder. An hour and a half later, Galante was the shooter who stepped out of the Fifteenth Street darkness to nail Carlo Tresca with bullets to the head and chest. He was the one who had lain in wait for the anarchist outside the offices of *Il Martello*. With him were his La Marese allies, Frank Garafalo and Joseph Di Palermo, along with a wheelman named Sebastiano Domingo.

When Tresca and his lawyer friend Calabi stepped into the street and headed off toward their ill-fated supper, Galante was there in the shadows.

"Which one?" Galante hissed to Garafalo. "Which one do I do?"

"Kill the son of a bitch with the whiskers," Garafalo told him, and Lilo did.

It could only be called bad luck to have a parole officer tail when heading off to commit murder. Galante was perplexed when, the next night, upon coming out of a candy store at 246 Elizabeth Street with Di Palermo, he was picked up by police. Sure, he had just shot some poor sucker, but hadn't he gotten away clean?

Not quite. A couple hours after the killing, a patrolman named Saul Greenberg happened upon a black Ford sedan while walking his beat. The car was parked on Fifteenth Street only blocks from the murder scene, outside the entrance to the Seventh Avenue subway, its car doors left flung open, key in the ignition.

License plate IC 9272. The same car parole officer Berson had seen Galante entering just before Carlo Tresca was gunned down.

The police held Galante, first as a material witness and then for a parole violation, while they investigated the assassination on Fifteenth Street. They kept him in limbo for over a year, with District Attorney Frank Hogan repeatedly promising to present the case to a grand jury.

It never happened. The assistant district attorney assigned to prosecuting Galante, Louis Pagnucco, had a history of fascist sympathies and was presumably no great admirer of Tresca (Pagnucco's college thesis extolled the "courageous leadership of Mussolini"). An FBI agent in the New York field office memo'd Hoover that, even with solid evidence of Galante's guilt, political pressure had evidently derailed the prosecution.

In December 1944, the New York authorities released Galante from jail.

The assassination of Carlo Tresca faded in the rearview, lost amid the flurry of war news, memorialized by a few of his left-wing associates, perhaps, but largely just one more notch on Carmine Galante's gun.

A few people remembered. A state police sergeant in upstate New York, for example, a cop who was becoming increasingly suspicious of mob activity in his territory. So it happened that on October 18, 1956, more than thirteen years after the Tresca killing, the memory of his murder set off a chain of events that would lead, a little more than a year later, to the bust-up of the Apalachin summit.

New York State Route 17 cuts diagonally across the Southern Tier, a region of farms and hills along the border of Pennsylvania. Some one hundred miles east of Binghamton, the road picks up the Susquehanna and follows its valley. That specific stretch has always been something of a speed trap, with a confusion of varying speed limits along its length.

On this busy four-lane highway that cool, dry, pleasant fall day in October 1956, outside Windsor, New York, a state police trooper named F. W. Leibe clocked a speeding Oldsmobile sporting New Jersey plates (HA 9J9), heading east, traveling at 65 miles per hour in a 50 mph zone.

Leibe snapped on the bubble lights of his black-and-white and pulled the vehicle over. Inside the Olds sat three men. The driver presented a license that identified him as Joseph Di Palermo of 246 Elizabeth Street, New York City. But something did not sit right with Leibe. The physical description on the license did not match the man sitting in the driver's seat, a broad-shouldered gent of about forty with thinning hair and a cigar in his mouth.

When state police stopped cars on the highway in the fifties, running a drivers license represented quite a process, much slower and more arduous than the scanning of a bar code as is the current procedure. Inquiring on a plate or license meant a radio call to a central dispatcher, who had to enter the information manually into a Teletype terminal.

If the dispatcher believed highway personnel were running too many licenses, a "phone the station" call would go out and the uniformed officers were told to knock it off. A call to the station at times required finding a pay phone or stopping at a friendly farmer's house.

In addition, 1950s drivers licenses didn't have photos, so all a patrolman had to go on, in order to decide if the person on the license was actually the citizen in question, was information on height and eye color. Despite the difficulties, Trooper Leibe detected problems.

"This is not your license, sir," Leibe said, invoking the studied politesse of his state police training.

"Oh, I guess I looked in the wrong coat and grabbed the wrong one," the driver said. He made a vain show of going through the pockets of the other coats in the car.

"I don't have mine with me," he finally said to Leibe. "I must have left it at home. But look, I'm in a hurry. Can't we make a deal?"

Trooper Leibe didn't like the looks of the men in the car. His hand strayed down to the gun in his holster. "Get out of the car," he said to the driver. "You're coming with me."

To Joseph Di Palermo, Leibe said, "You follow me to the station."

The driver in the Olds hesitated for an agonizing moment. The highway was crowded and the scene was public. Maybe at another time—in a dark street, say—he might have tried something. Not here, not now.

"Okay," the driver said. He turned to Di Palermo. "You know what to do." Palermo did indeed. He neglected, of course, to follow the trooper. He and the other two occupants of the car, Frank Garafalo and John Bonventre, sped away.

Leibe brought his charge to the Five-Mile Point state police substation east of Binghamton. There, the man identified himself to the sergeant in charge—one Edgar Croswell—as Carmine Galante.

Galante. Di Palermo. Hadn't he heard those names before, Croswell thought, or read them in the numerous circulars that the NYPD and the Bureau of Narcotics sent out?

A name arose in Croswell's memory, almost unbidden, a street murder victim from many years ago. Tressler? Trevas? Something Italian.

Tresca.

The man standing before him at the Five-Mile station was impatient, upset, staying just on the safe side of belligerent. "Look," Lilo Galante said, "this is a lot of crap. So I don't have my license with me. So I pay my fine. Let's get it over with. I can make a lot of trouble, you know."

A not-so-veiled threat. Croswell did not allow Galante to see his hackles rise, only continued in his usual carefully measured way. "I'm sorry, sir," he said. "I'm afraid you'll have to remain here until we find out about your driver's license. It's just routine, but that's the rule."

Lilo had that "why-I-oughtta" look in his eyes, but there was nothing he could do. Croswell had him searched, turning out his pockets to reveal a cash cache of $1,815, most of it in hundred-dollar bills.

It is a distinct habit of mobsters to carry paper money not in a wallet but rolled up and secured by a rubber band. That way, whenever they felt the need to flense off a few notes, their money was handy. The practice lent a virtue of display, too, a thick cylinder of bills denoting wealth and demanding respect. Croswell recognized this quirk, and identified it in the mobster money roll of his lead-foot suspect.

Croswell left Galante cooling out in a detention cell and went to work. He got on the teletype, querying his brethren in the NYPD, the Jersey State

Police, the Bureau of Narcotics, and the FBI for the jackets on Carmine Galante and Joseph Di Palermo. The search eventually turned up Galante's violent past, including verification of his alleged association with the Tresca killing.

With his fellow state police officers, Croswell conducted a telephone canvass of area motels and hotels. A few hours after he sent Galante off to chill, a positive hit came up. Galante, Di Palermo, and the two other occupants in the pulled-over Olds—Frank Garafalo and John Bonventre—had registered for the previous night, October 17, 1956, at the Arlington Hotel in Binghamton. According to the preliminary search Croswell had done, all were high-profile New York mobsters.

Croswell called the Arlington to verify. "Could you tell me who paid the bill?"

A beat of silence while the hotel clerk checked.

"Joseph Barbara," came the voice over the phone. "Paying in the name of the Canada Dry Bottling Company."

There had been other clues, other hints over the years that Joe Barbara was not the legitimate businessman he pretended to be. There had been run-ins between Croswell and Barbara before. The state police sergeant always kept an eye on the owner of the big stone house on McFall Road.

But here was something different. Here was proof that the local man was mobbed up, connected at the highest levels. Tresca to Galante to Barbara. Connect the dots.

Sometimes you can gauge the size of a fish by the ripples set off when you pull him in. And with Galante, there were ripples aplenty. For a routine traffic stop, the reaction was all out of proportion.

The first feelers came via Albany, where state senators and assemblymen, Democratic and Republican both, fielded phone calls from a series of highly paid, well-connected New York lawyers. Can't something be done for poor Carmine Galante? Maybe a call to state police higher-ups, rein in this cop Croswell?

The legislators took one look at Lilo's glow-in-the-dark criminal record and begged off. Thanks for contacting us, mister attorney, sir, but no thanks. We can't do anything for your guy. We may be politicians, but we're not stupid.

When the Albany end-run two-step didn't work, Galante's backers in the mob fell back on good old-fashioned bribery. But they chose only the finest emissaries. Nine days after Lilo's arrest, Chief of Detectives Captain Christopher Gleitsmann and Detective Sergeant Peter Policastro of the West

New York, New Jersey police department visited Croswell at the Five-Mile substation. After some just-us-cops small talk, they got down to business.

"What about this Galante case?" Captain Gleitsmann asked.

Croswell responded cautiously. "Well, what about the Galante case?"

"He comes from my town, you know," the captain said. "He's not a bad guy."

Only in the morally relative universe of West New York, just across the Hudson from Manhattan, could Lilo Galante be described as "not bad." West New York was long a haunt of mobsters, with Genovese, Lucchese, and Bonanno family interests all well represented there. The local DeCaval-cante crime clan, which controlled West New York, would send three of its bosses to the Apalachin summit, and eventually serve as one of the models for Tony Soprano's family on the HBO series.

The detective captain from West New York wasn't getting anywhere with Croswell. "I've been sent by my commissioner, Modarelli. I'm not sup-posed to use his name, but you should know."

That commissioner would be Ernest W. Modarelli, director of public safety in West New York. Croswell's stony silence only prompted Gleits-mann to blunder on, a rush of words.

"Galante runs the Abco Vending Company, and is a very close friend of the commissioner," Gleitsmann said. So close, in fact, that Galante's Abco Vending had a direct telephone line between it and police headquarters.

"We'd like to see Galante excused," Captain Gleitsmann said. "It wasn't really a bad violation. We'll pay the maximum fine. Can't we get him out of a jail sentence?"

In answer, Croswell pulled out Galante's rap sheet and pushed it across the desk toward Gleitsmann, who only glanced at it.

"Look," the West New York cop said, putting a meaningful emphasis on his words, "there'll be considerations."

"The answer is definitely no," Croswell said.

Gleitsmann stuck his hand up, forefinger extended.

"Is that supposed to mean a thousand dollars?"

"Yes," Gleitsmann said. "And if you think I'm kidding, here it is." He hauled a money roll out of his pocket, twenties, fifties, hundreds, rolled together mob-style with a rubber band. "If that isn't enough, I'll have to use your phone for a few minutes." A thousand dollars. That amount equalled almost two months of Croswell's state police salary back then. But it didn't tempt the cop.

Ed Croswell's wife Nathalie once described him as "a man with two moods, angry and 'blah.'" Captain Gleitsmann had provoked the non-blah mood.

"Now don't be foolish," Gleitsmann said hurriedly. "We cops should take the opportunities that come our way. We should decide whether a case gets quashed."

Croswell rose from his chair. "Put the money back into your pocket," he said. "Get out of here, fast."

In the publicity surrounding the Apalachin summit, interest in the Galante traffic stop blew up big. THE SPEEDING TICKET OF THE DECADE ran a headline in Albany's *Knickerbocker News*. Galante could have paid his fine, done his time, and kept the whole affair off the radar. His notoriety—and Ed Croswell's long memory—prevented that.

From the time of the Galante arrest forward, Croswell's interest in Lilo's friend Joseph Barbara shifted into high gear. He searched police records, looked into the business practices of Barbara's beverage company, and generally went from keeping a lazy eye on the man to training a sharp one. All because the name "Carmine Galante" had set off alarm bells in Croswell's mind, linked to a WWII-era murder.

Ding, ding, ding. A tiny bell, expanding ripples. The assassination of a left-wing anti-Mafia journalist that Vito Genovese once engineered as a favor to a dictator would come back to bite the Mafia boss. Many years later, what should have been Genovese's shining moment at the Apalachin summit was destroyed by a state police sergeant who just happened to remember what they did to Carlo Tresca on Fifteenth Street that dark night in 1943.

Irony of ironies. Resting in his grave, the Italian anarchist must have sported a thin smile. In the events surrounding Apalachin, there would be more of that—more laughter from corpses, more irony, more intricate, far-reaching connections. And, especially, more murder.

2

The Rise of Joe Barbara

THE TALL, PALE SERGEANT who confronted Lilo Galante in the state police substation was born in Woodstock, New York in 1913. Around the time Edgar Dewitt Croswell came into the world, his father Percy quit farming to join the Binnewater Lake Ice Company, an ice and cold-storage business run by his brother-in-law (and his son's namesake), Edgar Shultis.

Later in life, Ed Croswell occasionally reminisced to his coworkers about childhood excursions into the icehouse, the cool darkness contrasting with the summer heat outside. A fellow sergeant on the state police joked the icehouse must have been where Ed got the ice water in his veins.

Born in Woodstock, yes, but by no stretch of the imagination a child of the Woodstock generation. The Croswell family moved to Kingston, the first capital of the state, a former canal town ninety miles north of New York City on the western bank of the Hudson. Many of the sidewalks of Manhattan were fashioned from Kingston bluestone. Anthracite coal from the mines of northeastern Pennsylvania used to journey via the Delaware and Hudson Canal, which had its terminus in Kingston.

The waterway was long gone by Ed Croswell's time, hauling its last load in 1904. Hard hit by the Depression, Kingston nevertheless allowed the Croswell family a solid, middle-class prosperity. Taciturn even as a child, Ed naturally gravitated toward official work where, he felt, he could help people. He served first in the Kingston Fire Department, then as a Kingston patrolman, then did a stretch as an investigator for the Sears department store chain.

"They thought the world of him at Sears, he could have stayed there for life," said one of his bosses around this time, Kingston Police Chief Charles

Phinney, who mentored Croswell when he worked as a patrol officer on the city force. "Everyone liked him, because of his personality and efficiency."

Not a garrulous man, Croswell nevertheless enjoyed a good joke, with a sharply edged sense of humor that tended toward the sarcastic and dry. It was difficult to get the best of him. Croswell did not suffer fools gladly. If his superiors ever queried him on factual material that they could have easily found in the files, he could get irritated, dismissive.

"I never like stupid questions," he would say.

He joined the State Police as a road trooper in 1940, eventually winding up in the Bureau of Criminal Investigation and rising to the rank of sergeant investigator. Croswell's straight-shooter makeup placed official corruption of any kind squarely in the crosshairs. In 1946, his superiors credited him with breaking up a bribery conspiracy ring. Three years later, he arrested the head of the Binghamton vice squad, also for bribery. He was the superego, personified.

For a long time, the superego drove a Buick. Cars always held a fascination for Croswell as a prime marker of social prestige. In his life he forever aspired to a luxury model, a Cadillac or Lincoln, but could not yet afford one on his $6,000 sergeant's salary. He took the wages of sin as a personal affront.

About gangsters, he said, "I was always annoyed by them, and their sleek cars, and fancy clothes, and flashy diamonds, sneering at the police, as if we didn't exist or blundered around not knowing what we were doing."

On the road as a trooper during the war, Croswell triggered a chain of events that led to him running up against just such a man. The encounter would have enormous consequences for them both.

May 1944. It would be the first time Ed met Joe.

As he headed down a rural two-lane near Binghamton, Croswell drove up on an illegally parked truck. He pulled alongside, and just then the driver emerged from the woods. Seeing the statie, he leaped into the cab of the truck and turned over the engine, as if to hightail it out of there.

Trooper Croswell summoned the driver out for a talk. He could have sent him on his way with a warning, writing off the walk into the woods as a rest break, but something didn't sit right. When he poked around in the underbrush a little, he discovered two five-gallon jerry cans of gasoline. The driver readily confessed to siphoning off the fuel from the beverage truck and stashing it in the woods, planning to come back later and pick it up.

Wartime rationing rules meant fuel was at a premium, and also meant the driver's actions ran afoul of those rules. Croswell had only recently been assigned to the Troop C substation in Vestal, so after arresting the driver, he took him there. The truck, a big two-ton rig, proved to be registered in the fleet of a company called Mission Beverages in nearby Endicott. Croswell phoned Mission, laid out the circumstances of the bust, and set in to wait for the driver's boss to come by the substation.

When he did, the encounter did not quite go as Croswell expected. Instead of an employer grateful to be informed of an instance of employee theft, he found himself confronted by a sputtering, angry fireplug of a man with black hair and a round, rather babyish face.

"I'm Barbara," he said, pronouncing the name Italian style, bar-BEAR-uh.

Croswell gestured toward where the Mission Beverages driver cooled his heels. "This gentleman says he is employed by you."

"Yeah, that's my man," said Joe Barbara Sr., his words heavily accented. "Why did you arrest him? He ain't done nothing wrong!"

Croswell felt puzzled. *What was he getting so upset about?* But he remained bland. "Your driver was stealing your gas," he said. "Fuel is hard to get these days."

Examining the man standing before him, the trooper felt his spider-sense tingle when he noticed a bulge at Barbara's hip.

"Are you carrying a gun, sir?" he asked.

"Sure, I carry a pistol," Barbara said. "I got a permit for it."

"May I see it?"

"The pistol or the permit?" Barbara asked.

"How about both?" Croswell said. Barbara produced the document and a .32 caliber Smith & Wesson revolver. Croswell examined them. The pistol was loaded and, in a sense, so was the permit, in that it was signed by a powerful local judge named Thomas A. McClary. The document listed the address of Barbara's place of business, Mission Beverages, at 7 Badger Avenue in Endicott, alongside the Erie Railroad tracks.

Barbara continued in his truculent manner. "Now you release my man, see? He ain't stole nothing. You let him go right away."

Not a request, a command. Just the kind of behavior that ran against Croswell's grain. Something was clearly off about the big butterball asshole standing before him. He restrained himself from acting on his immediate impulse to back the man against the substation's wall, flush out his pockets, and give him a good rousting. He simply returned gun and gun permit to the friend-of-a-judge beverage man, released his driver, and bid them both to go on their way.

But Barbara left a bad taste in Croswell's mouth. That initial 1944 encounter led him, over the next few weeks, to work the horn, calling the state police's criminal identification division, the Federal Bureau of Investigation and, because Joe Barbara's spoor led back to the Pittston-Scranton-Wilkes-Barre area, the Pennsylvania State Police. Checking arrest records, prison files, investigative reports.

What he found bore out his initial judgment. The trooper's search for dirt turned up whole graveyards' worth of it. From then on, Ed Croswell was married to Joe Barbara as sure as if the two had been wed in a church. But right at the start, his surveillance campaign quite literally almost got Croswell torn apart.

What came in across the wire was murder, mayhem, and moonshining.

Born in Mafia-dominated Castellammare del Golfo, Sicily, in 1905, Joseph Mario Barbara immigrated with his parents from Italy to America when he was sixteen. He stayed in New York City only a short while. Then, like a number of fresh-off-the-boat Italian immigrants, Joe Barbara relocated to Endicott, one of the factory-heavy Triple Cities of the Southern Tier, the other two being Johnson City and Binghamton.

The shoe industry of the area had faded somewhat from the palmy days when it had shod the Union army during the Civil War, but there were still jobs to be had. Ellis Island officials told of Italian immigrants hitting shore with only a single sentence in English: "Which way E-J?" They meant the E-J shoe factory of the Endicott-Johnson Corporation, headed by an innovative capitalist named George F. Johnson, known to all simply as "George F."

After rising through the workingman ranks in the company, George F became half owner in 1899. He gradually developed a wide-ranging program of worker-friendly benefits and policies that made E-J, as he tirelessly publicized it, "the Home of the Square Deal." He sponsored churches, libraries, theaters, swimming pools, and parks, free for his workers to use. Profit-sharing, health care, and home financing for company-built residences were also part of the package.

No wonder impoverished immigrant leather workers were attracted to the place. Nothing remotely like it existed in the Old World. Commentators labeled it "welfare capitalism," noting that for all its altruistic patina, it also worked to head off trade unions and labor organizing.

The company, and the Johnson family, dominated the local economy. E-J built tanneries, factories, and ancillary firms throughout the Triple Cities area, a few principalities of which were actually renamed to bear the company stamp: Lestershire became Johnson City, and Hooper became Endwell, named after a line of E-J shoes.

When young Joe Barbara showed up in Endicott in 1921, he landed in the warm embrace of George F. Everything was taken care of for the new-comer. He could work a factory job, learn English, take time to get his bearings in his new American surroundings.

Barbara had other friends around, too, apart from his labor-coddling, wolf-in-sheep's-clothing factory-owning boss. The Triple Cities were the turf of a powerful La Marese mafioso from Buffalo, Steven Magaddino.

Barbara became a U.S. citizen and a made man in the same year, 1927. His nickname was the Joe the Barber, a tribute to all the close shaves he had gotten himself out of. As a sideline, he opened a second-floor brothel on Washington Avenue in Endicott, his first official foray into the kind of criminality that would become a hallmark of his life.

Fifty miles south of Binghamton, across the state line in Pennsylvania, another Triple-Cities area attracted hordes of Italian immigrants. Pittston-Scranton-Wilkes-Barre was, not coincidentally, also Magaddino territory. No welfare capitalism there. Mines provided high-quality anthracite coal for the stoves and factories of New York City, a hundred and twenty miles southeast. For workers, life in the coal fields of northeastern Pennsylvania was nasty, brutish, and short.

The mine owners had always displayed a muscular disdain for labor organizing. They needed a steady supply of goons to keep the miners in line and the unions on the ropes. Relocating from Endicott in 1928, Joe Barbara drifted south to help out.

There his troubles began. Or perhaps what occurred should not be described as troubles, really, since Joe escaped cleanly from a series of violent scrapes with the law. More accurately, in northeastern Pennsylvania during his mid-twenties, Joe Barbara's true colors began to show.

The five-year stretch he spent in the south, before he returned to Endicott in 1933, transformed Barbara from a knockaround thug into a well-heeled, well-dressed *goomba* who could masquerade as a respectable businessman. Moon-faced as he was, Barbara came to bear a resemblance to the Dick Tracy villain Flattop Jones, coarse-featured, uni-browed, thick.

That crucial half decade in Pennsylvania, 1928 to 1933, also spanned the duration of the Castellammarese mob war, as well as the sputtering tail-end of Prohibition. Joe made his bones in both. He became an enthusiastic and extremely prosperous operator of illicit stills, producing corn sugar alcohol in the countryside around Scranton, Pittston, and Wilkes-Barre. As such, he was a creature not only of Steven Magaddino but of local mob boss Santo Volpe, his mentor, the self-proclaimed "king of the night."

A longtime Capone associate, a former independent coal mine operator with many bloody union battles behind him, Santo acted as the violent and crafty ruler of the Scranton-area rackets. "The Fox," they called him, in tribute to his last name, which meant fox or bitch in Italian.

Born in Sicily, Volpe came to the States in 1906, tearing a fearsome criminal organization out of the coal fields of northeastern Pennsylvania. Labor unrest was virulent. Heads needed to be knocked together. Volpe found a way. Settling on Wyoming Avenue in West Pittston, he became an unrivaled power in the area, rising to such a level of respectability that he sat on the board of directors of a local bank. His Scranton friends called him Sandy.

Scranton itself, of course, is nowadays widely known from the television series, *The Office,* as the headquarters town for the Dunder Mifflin Paper Company. But the city of Joe Barbara's time was not quite so fey. The whole area retained some of the wild-and-wooly atmosphere of the coal-mining days, still experiencing widespread labor unrest, extortion, and political corruption.

The Mafia spilled into the area from New York City, finding it ripe for the usual plagues of the working man: loan-sharking, union racketeering, and gambling. After the First World War, garment industry jobbers began to locate there, exploiting a ready labor pool to churn out overflow orders from the City's burgeoning rag trade. The concentration of sweatshops earned Scranton, Pittston, and Wilkes-Barre the label of the "Garment Corridor." More immigrant workers, more opportunities for Mafia skim.

By that time in America there lived two million Sicilians by birth or parentage, the vast majority of whom—it must be said—were law-abiding. Using the rough estimate of 5,000 as the total Mafia membership, not all of whom were of strictly Sicilian background, the ratio delivers up a tiny quarter-percent criminal class within the larger Sicilian demographic. Yet in the popular press, at least, if not the popular imagination, an aura of criminality hung heavily over anyone with a Sicilian background.

The Sicilian Joe Barbara settled in Old Forge, a township to the southwest of Scranton. He started with Volpe as a bodyguard-driver. In January 1931, Pennsylvania State Police arrested him as a suspect in a murder charge. Records of the killing disclose that an Italian immigrant named Calomero Calogare arrived in Pittston on December 31, 1930. Four days later, around eight p.m., Calogare proceeded along Railroad Street, an ill-lit industrial thoroughfare running near the tracks of the Delaware, Lackawanna, and Western Railroad.

Two men followed Calogare down Railroad Street that night. When they overtook him, one of the killers fired five or six shots, several of which struck the victim. Pennsylvania State Police from a barracks just across the Susquehanna River in Wyoming, Pennsylvania, arrived at the scene, but the shooters were long gone.

Calogare managed a deathbed statement to police, accusing Tony Morreale of the crime, citing bad blood between himself and mob boss Santo Volpe. Tony Morreale, with brothers Carmel and Joseph (also known as "Colorado Joe") all lived at the same address. Joe Barbara, a close friend of the brothers, made frequent visits to their boarding house.

When police picked up Tony, he provided an odd alibi, claiming that at the time of the murder he was working at an Old Forge still operated by Barbara. I'm not guilty of murder, officers, just of moonshining. Police arrested Barbara on suspicion of being the second man who followed Calogare down Railroad Street that night.

But Joe Barbara's luck—or his reputation for violence—saved him. Witnesses failed to come forth with a positive ID, which forced the court authorities to discharge Joe Barbara the day after police detained him.

Later the next year, Joe Barbara busted his cherry once again, this time with an arrest in New York City. The occasion was yet another gala gathering of mobsters, a celebration of sorts, commemorating the ice-pick murder of Pittsburgh mob boss John Bazzano.

On the night of August 7, 1932, Bazzano's murderers lured him to an abandoned storefront near the Brooklyn docks and killed the gang leader there. Police discovered his mutilated body the next day, inside a burlap sack dumped at Centre and Hicks Streets in Brooklyn. Investigators counted twenty-two stab wounds. For good measure, Bazzano had been strangled with a rope, his tongue cut out, and his lips taped shut.

The killing turned out to be an early test for the Commission, the ruling panel of bosses put together by Charles Luciano and designed to prevent random headline-grabbing violence between the mob families. Bazzano's elaborate death had been authorized by the newly formed Commission as a punitive measure. It thus represented the first sign of a new world order in organized crime.

Bazzano had to be killed because, in a move unsanctioned by the Commission, he himself had killed. Three Volpe brothers, his former bootlegging partners, were shot to death on July 29 in an ambush at the Roma Coffee Shop on Wylie Avenue in Pittsburgh. Santo Volpe was a cousin to the victims. At his behest, the Commission met, condemned the triple murder as a rogue hit, and ordained that the murderer be executed forthwith. Bazzano's death meant Lucky Luciano's vaunted Commission was serious about preventing unauthorized hits within the ranks.

A successful meting out of justice, mob-style, meant it was time to celebrate. The mobsters convened at a midtown Manhattan hotel. Brooklyn crime boss Albert Anastasia headed the guest list, which included Santo Volpe, of course, as well as a collection of mafiosi from Buffalo, Brooklyn, and Pittsburgh. Among the party favors, a $20,000 pot to be divided among the four hit men who aced Bazzano.

In a foreshadowing of Apalachin, the NYPD busted the party before it ever got going. Barbara was in town, and just a week earlier had earned a weapons rap for possession of a revolver, but his charmed life in the courts continued, and the arraignment judge dismissed the charge.

Since the Castellammarese War still raged, Joe needed to replace his iron fairly quickly. A month after his bust, the war ended in a fusillade of gunshots, when Salvatore Maranzano died, as did Bazzano, at the hands of a quartet of assassins.

Barbara was not quite done yet. On February 21, 1933, he was again arrested by Scranton police on suspicion of murder. At some point between the hours of ten and midnight on February 15, killers unknown had strangled Samuel Wichner, a racketeer involved in bootlegging, highjacking, and blackmailing.

The crime wasn't uncovered until the next evening, when a patrolman found a Ford coupe belonging to the victim parked on the 400 block of Scranton's Meridian Avenue—once again, alongside the tracks of the Delaware, Lackawanna, and Western, Barbara's favorite killing ground. The body had been stuffed into the coupe's trunk.

Judging by forensic evidence, crude in those days, the actual murder took place elsewhere, somewhere indoors. Wichner's pulped-up face showed signs of a vicious beating. He had struggled with his murderers, who pummeled him at least partially unconscious before they applied a slip-noose about his neck and saw it cinch tight until he died.

Left in place on the corpse in the trunk was the classic Mafia hogtie, a cruel method of death by which the victim is made to strangle himself. Two pieces of number nine sash-cord, each twelve feet in length. One was noosed about the neck and half-hitched at the arms, then run under the knees, where it was knotted and brought down about the ankles. The second cord started at the feet and wrapped tightly around the body.

Police analysis showed that the fatal ligature had been affixed before the killers crammed the victim, minus hat and coat, into the rear compartment of his own Ford, which was driven to Scranton and abandoned.

A witness said the two men who left the Wichner vehicle entered a black Buick sedan that had followed them to the spot. The subsequent investigation showed Barbara's signature all over the crime. During that period, he drove a black Buick.

The night before the murder, Joe had invited Wichner to his own house in Old Forge, promising a conference with Santo Volpe. The king of the night and another mobster, Angelo Valente, were slated to be Wichner's silent partners in a new bootlegging venture.

"Come back tomorrow night at 9:30," Barbara told Wichner after the meeting. "Don't let anyone know where you're going to be, not even your wife."

Barbara was oddly insistent about the last point. Wichner must have sensed something wrong, since he did indeed tell his wife he was headed out to meet Joe Barbara the night he died. After the discovery of her husband's body, Wichner's wife recounted his plans to police, who arrested Barbara on suspicion of murder.

The rap never even made it to arraignment. At an appearance in police court, a magistrate officially discharged Joe the day after his arrest, ruling there was insufficient evidence to charge him.

All this was ancient history by 1944, when Ed Croswell first began looking into the pistol-packing beverage man who wanted his gas-stealing driver set free. Could such a legit business owner, operator of a hugely lucrative bottling plant, who held an 83 percent ownership stake in the company, possibly be the same thug who a decade in the past had slipped the leash on a couple of homicides?

The Endicott version of Joseph Barbara presented a smooth, lawful facade to the outside world. The man possessed a liquor license, and Croswell knew the vigorous vetting by the State Liquor Authority (SLA) necessary to land one of those. There seemed to be a disconnect there.

One of the remarkable facts about the Apalachin summit participants would be the number who had dismissed murder raps on their records, eighteen unprosecuted homicides in all. Two or three could be written off as dumb luck. But the sheer number spoke of something else. Political corruption.

For an average citizen, an arrest on a homicide charge ranked as an earth-shattering event, something from which they would not readily recover. For the boys at Apalachin, murder charges seemed to be just another day at the office.

Croswell, though, viewed Joe Barbara's seamy past quite seriously. He had taken the measure of the man, and knew what he had within his jurisdiction: a hoodlum, a wise guy, a mobster. So what if Barbara could pull the wool over the investigators at the SLA? Croswell knew for certain the guy was all wrong. He'd just have to dig deeper.

He went through local murders, this time not in the Scranton area but closer to home, around Binghamton. One thing that turned up was an old mob killing that occurred in Endicott soon after Barbara moved back there from Old Forge in 1933.

The Fourth of July is a perfect day for murder. Amid the bottle rockets' red glare and firecrackers bursting in air, random gunfire can easily go unnoticed. No one witnessed the shooting of Barbara's old friend from Scranton, Joseph "Colorado Joe" Morreale, but police found his bullet-riddled body in a ditch in Endicott on Independence Day evening, 1934.

Nobody had been charged in the crime, but digging through the records, Croswell turned up a ten-year-old investigative report that pointed to Barbara. It was like the guy was leaving a trail, not of bread crumbs but of bodies, that led straight to his door.

Croswell watched and waited and watched some more. He began making forays, every month or so, taking his own unmarked car up to what later press reports would label Joe Barbara's "barony" on McFall Road. He didn't make a big deal about it, just drove past the stone ranch house, proceeded a quarter mile to where the dirt road dead-ended at a collapsed bridge over Apalachin Creek, then turned around and drove back past the compound again.

With a cop's eye, Croswell assessed the barony. He noted that the trees and shrubs had been cleared within pistol range of the house. The driveway looked like a boulevard, with a paved parking area, and the backyard resembled a small, nicely groomed golf course. Three motel-style guest cottages were located on the property. Spotlights lit the grounds at night. A half dozen large dogs patrolled the place. Joe had the couple hundred feet of McFall near the house paved with asphalt to keep the dust down.

Croswell stopped once to take a few photographs, a move that almost snapped back at him badly. The guard dogs weren't in evidence that day, until suddenly they were. Standing a distance away from his Buick, pointing his camera toward the compound, Croswell was surprised by two snarling boxers who bounded out from behind the garage. The missus of the manor, Josephine Barbara, showed herself at the door. She didn't look happy or welcoming.

"Hello, ma'am," Croswell called out, while she held the dogs at bay. "I'm a representative of *House & Garden* magazine. I'm in the area, looking for fine houses that might be suitable for inclusion in our publication."

Josephine melted. Her turnaround was almost comical. She shooed the boxers inside and told Croswell to take all the pictures he wanted.

The darkly pretty Josephine Vivona was an Endicott girl whom Joe Barbara married in June 1933, when he ducked back north from Pennsylvania to escape the heat after the Wichner murder.

Rummaging through old crime reports, Croswell noticed something: Ten a.m. on the morning of the Barbara-Vivona wedding, June 26, 1933, two armed gangsters robbed the payroll of the Gotham Shoe Company, 26 Park Avenue in Binghamton. The duo got away with $4,775.

Witnesses said the men drove a Buick, license plate 2L4520, registered to a fictitious address in Brooklyn. The getaway car was discovered abandoned, its engine still running, a mile from the scene. Other witnesses saw a Chrysler sedan bearing Pennsylvania plates 69Z12 pick up two men near where the Buick had been dropped off. The Chrysler checked out to be registered in the name of Joseph Barbara, 717 S. Main Street, Old Forge, Pennsylvania.

Disbelieving what he read, Croswell gradually realized from the interview notes of the investigators, as well as from the make of the getaway car and descriptions of the perpetrators, that all evidence indicated Barbara was one of the stick-up artists. Get me to the church on time, but let me stop off and make a little unauthorized payroll withdrawal on the way. That was one approach to building up a nest egg when embarking upon matrimony.

Touching up old friends was another. Santo Volpe set Joe up with a wedding gift "loan" of $65,000 to open the Endicott bottling plant, part of a larger mob strategy, ordained by Lansky, Luciano, and others, to infiltrate legit businesses.

Barbara started Endicott Beverage in 1934 and a few years later formed Mission Beverage, the same company whose truck, parked on a back road near Binghamton, led to Croswell's initial interest in Barbara. When Joe

Barbara became a franchisee with the thriving and determinedly legitimate Canada Dry conglomerate, Mission and Endicott Beverage merged to
form Canada Dry Bottling Company of Endicott, Incorporated.

Carefully preening his businessman camouflage, Barbara and his wife
settled into what looked to be an ordinary upper middle-class lifestyle,
with the requisite two boys and a girl, Joseph Junior, Peter, and Angela. The
family lived in a stucco house on Loder Avenue in Endicott until their new
prosperity allowed them to move, in 1948, to the stone house on the hill
above Apalachin.

Scamming the system, Joe Barbara arranged the paper purchase of a
herd of cattle from an area farmer, in order that his estate qualify for rural
electrical service. Though Joe joined the Elks Lodge, the Sons of Italy, and the
Mutual Aid Society, the newcomers didn't exactly mix with the Apalachin
locals. The half-mile-long McFall Road, ostensibly a public thoroughfare,
in reality acted as the Barbaras' private driveway.

The women definitely monopolized the looks in the family. Joe Junior, a
mini-me version of his round-featured father, played high school football.
But Angela—Angie—and her mother both had a well-coiffed, Ava Gardner
air about them.

Everyone spoiled Angie, brothers and parents both. She tooled around
town in a convertible and received a $5,000 mink stole when she graduated
from Union-Endicott High School in June 1957. All in all, an upscale existence, especially when compared with the folks in the village at the bottom
of the hill.

"It's hard to remember we live in Apalachin," Josephine would say later.
"I'm a native of Endicott. We don't go out much. We're not affiliated with
the town at all. We live for the family."

No outsider penetrated the Barbara domain except, occasionally, Ed
Croswell. He would soon enough have reason to find out just exactly what
kind of "family" Josephine Barbara was talking about.

3

Albert Anastasia's Waterfront

THE WATERFRONT OF NEW YORK harbor embraced all five New York City boroughs, slipped across the river to New Jersey and north to Yonkers, and comprised 771 miles of river and bay shoreline, over half of which was developed with piers, wharves, boat-basins, docks, dry docks, berths, anchorages, and warehouses, the sieve through which the world's commerce had long been strained.

At the dawn of the 1950s, the Port of New York was still the world's largest, though it was losing ground fast, with container shipping and interstate trucking about to give it a beating from which it would never recover.

Bankers and gangsters adhere to the same principle: the time to dip one's beak, slice off a piece, take a percentage is whenever material changes hands during transfers, exchanges, transit points. The waterfront of New York represented acres of those kinds of opportunities, a tantalizing territory to be plundered by the mob.

Bananas from Central America, pig iron from Germany, textiles from Britain, a flow of goods worth millions every month, year in and year out, fat, recklessly unprotected, ripe for thievery and highjacking. Passenger traffic from the bustling transatlantic lines, in those days before Pan Am, represented another opportunity for smuggling, graft, and random venality.

The Mafia families of New York were in essence all waterfront gangs. They began their histories harborside, they were succored there, and they remained tied to the docks as surely as any freighter. The mobs carved up the waterfront like a group of schoolboys divvying up a candy bar, or perhaps more like swine muscling each other at the trough. Ethnic rivalries prevailed, with turf assigned according to accent and area of origin.

The piers on the west side of Manhattan, running from the Battery all the way north to the 60s, were largely Irish: parceled out and controlled by mobsters such as Mickey Bowers (57th to 42nd Streets), Tim O'Mara (42nd to 14th Streets) and John M. Dunn (everything below 14th).

Alex Di Brizzi and Charlie Yanowsky ruled Staten Island and Jersey City, respectively. The waterfront was a dangerous place to be boss, with Dunn getting the electric chair and Yanowsky murdered with an ice pick, both in 1949.

Brooklyn, though, the richest plum of all, Brooklyn was reserved for the Italians, from the old Erie and Atlantic basins of Red Hook, south to the Bush Terminal, north past the bridges to the Navy Yard. The Italian fiefdom maintained its own beachhead across the East River in Manhattan, controlling the Fulton Fish Market and environs, but Brooklyn remained the mothership, the mother lode. Half of all New York longshoremen, some 4,000 of them, lived and worked in Brooklyn, mostly in Red Hook.

There existed multiple ways to make bank on the waterfront. Outright theft was one, plundering the drafts in the holds of the big freighters. Labor racketeering was another, controlling who worked and who didn't among the longshoremen, charging those who did a kickback fee for the privilege.

Also lucrative were loan-sharking and bookmaking services to the workers, extorting payments from the big shipping companies to ensure their freight got unloaded in a timely manner, as well as insurance scams, arson and homicide for hire.

By the 1950s, it all added up to a handsome mob payday, to the tune of some $350 million a year, more than a third of a billion dollars in annual skim from the Port of New York, deposited into the pockets, swelling the coffers, and fattening the rubber-banded money rolls of the underworld.

The Italians could thank none other than local boy Al Capone for their dominance of the Brooklyn waterfront. Notorious for his control of the Chicago rackets, Capone was in fact a Brooklyn boy born and bred. Chased out of town in 1921 by a clash with a local Irish mobster, Capone relocated to the rich killing fields of Chicago.

He returned to Brooklyn on Christmas four years later to take care of a bit of unfinished business. The ostensible reason for the trip was banal, almost quaint. Capone's only child, the sickly eight-year-old Albert, suffered a mastoid infection in his left ear. During that preantibiotic era, such an illness could often result in a complete loss of hearing. In December 1925, a twenty-six-year-old Capone brought Albert to New York for surgery by a New York specialist.

That was his cover story, anyway. He also came east to consult with Frankie Yale, the Mafia boss of the Red Hook waterfront and Capone's mentor during his coming-of-age in Brooklyn (Capone often joked that he received "a Yale education"). Yale was then locked in a bitter rivalry with mobsters of the White Hand gang: the Irish White Hand against the Italian Black Hand in a battle over control of the rich dockside rackets.

Brooklyn's Adonis Social and Athletic Club didn't quite live up to the gaudiness of its name, nor to its founding ideal of brotherhood between Italian and Irish dockworkers, articulated in the club's charter at incorporation in 1917. A ramshackle Gowanus speakeasy at 152 Twentieth Street, lodged between the Red Hook docks and the vast Green-Wood Cemetery, the place was well known as a bastion of Frankie Yale.

Yale's White Hand enemies, five men led by Richard Lonergan, planned a brazen visit to the Adonis during the joint's annual Christmas party. They showed up at 2 a.m., December 26, 1925, not realizing they had walked into a trap.

Capone, his cousin Sylvester Agoglia, and two other associates lay in wait inside the Adonis. Masquerading as employees—Capone had worked as a bouncer during his Brooklyn days—the Chicago imports went unrecognized by the normally wary Lonergan. Fueled by plentiful alcohol, the White Hand boss began making an obnoxious, loudmouth spectacle of himself, slurring the Adonis customers as "dagos."

He got his. Agoglia kicked off the melee by splitting open Lonergan's head with a meat cleaver. Capone doused the lights and the Italians began blasting away at the Irish. Even with a cleaver hit to the skull, Lonergan managed to stagger to his feet. Capone followed him toward the front door of the Adonis to deliver two shots, one to the head and the other to the spine. Lonergan fell forward into Twentieth Street, collapsing at the curb in the front of the club.

There the Irish crime boss of Brooklyn was found two hours later by Richard Marano, a beat cop who had been warned earlier to stay out of the Adonis. The death of Lonergan (killed along with two of his pals that night), effectively meant the end of the White Hand in Brooklyn, delivering control of the lucrative waterfront rackets into the hands of the Italians.

For Capone, the Adonis Club massacre was only an afterthought, just a last backhand favor extended to his hometown Mafia pals. But the killings turned out to have a huge impact on the New York underworld.

The eventual heir of the territory Al Capone secured, the criminal colossus who stood astride the Brooklyn waterfront in the fifties was mob boss Albert Anastasia. By that time somewhat gone to middle-aged fat, in his youth Anastasia ranked as one of the most notorious killers in all of gangland.

Born in the village of Tropea, the sunny red-onion capital of Italy, Anastasia numbered among nine brothers in a hard-luck family, fatherless early on. Enlisting as a deckhand in the merchant marine, he jumped ship on the docks of Brooklyn, where he joined thousands of other recent Italian immigrants in Red Hook scrapping for a living.

Albert scrapped harder than most. As a kid with a wavy-haired pompadour rising from an acne-pitted forehead, he was well known on the waterfront for his violent rages. It helped that he had a pair of brothers nearby to back him up, Tony and Gerry, a gang of three all destined for the life of crime. A fourth brother somehow managed to head in another direction to become a priest.

The main stem of the Brooklyn docks was Columbia Street, running along the waterfront, scene of the "shape-up," the daily marshalling of longshoremen, picked for work crews by foremen favoring those willing to kick back a portion of their wages to the mob. With all the jostling and elbowing for advantage along the Columbia Street piers, a pair of ready fists could come in handy, a knife or an ice pick even handier, a revolver handiest of all.

A few blocks inland from the waterfront, Red Hook's Little Italy centered around Pioneer Street, a dense, flavorful stretch of tenements, produce markets, and taverns where, for a time, the up-and-coming Anastasia found a home. There, he was still known by his given name of Umberto. Longshoremen and "shenangoes"—low-paid day workers—lived and worked and drank and gambled all within a tight, five-block radius of the docks. They comprised Umberto's clientele or, to see it another way, his prey.

Muscle and force and weaponry were always Anastasia's tools for getting what he wanted. He pulled his first murder rap when he was seventeen. In the late '20s and 1930s, he had a premier role in the mob's storied unit of enforcers, nicknamed "Murder, Inc." by the newspapers. The underworld elite needed a way to take care of people who needed taken care of. Murder, Inc. provided the way, a service company with homicide as its only product.

Anastasia acted as Murder, Inc.'s COO alongside Jewish gangster and labor racketeer Louis Buchalter as CEO. The loose-knit network of enforcers carried out hundreds of murders, contract hits ordained by higher-ups. The killing of Dutch Schultz, the rogue beer baron who challenged the mob's leadership, served as a high-profile example of Murder, Inc.'s work.

In 1935, Schultz had gone to Luciano and proposed an insane plan to assassinate New York's racket-busting district attorney, Thomas Dewey. Dewey was breathing hard down everyone's neck, but especially on Schultz, coming after him with tax evasion charges. But killing a sitting D.A. represented a move that even the sanguinary leadership of the mob recognized as reckless.

The loose cannon could not be allowed to roll around on deck any longer. Luciano gave the contract to kill Dutch Schultz to Anastasia, who passed it to Buchalter, who designated the actual shooters for the job, Charles Workman and Mendy Weiss. Schultz was shot in the john of a Newark beer joint, hit by a spray of bullets that—several times removed—was directed by Albert Anastasia.

It's an old story in the mob, when the muscle rises to become the boss, the torpedo transforming itself into the battleship. Al Capone acted as a gunsel, brought in from New York to back up Johnny Torrio, before taking control as king of the Chicago rackets himself. Four of the leading mob bosses from the fifties—Anastasia, Ben Siegel, Vito Genovese, and Joe Adonis—secured their leadership positions in 1931 by pouring bullets into their doomed former chief, Joe Masseria.

The second in command oftentimes wound up taking command.* Thus it happened with Anastasia. At the dawn of the fifties, Albert was officially an underboss in the Brooklyn gangland hierarchy, beneath Vincent Mangano. A rare Mustache Pete who survived the fallout from the Castellammarese War, Mangano was one of the original generation of mob bosses who did not, in point of fact, wear a mustache.

Uneasy sat the crown, though, on a boss who had Anastasia as an underling. The Brooklyn mob kept a front organization called the City Demo-

---

* The practice continued for decades. When John Gotti wanted to take out his boss, Paul Castellano, he made sure he hit Big Paul's bodyguard and longtime subordinate, Tommy Bilotti, at the same time. Otherwise, Bilotti would have been a prime candidate to step into Castellano's shoes, which Gotti wanted to fill himself.

cratic Club (C.D.C.), located in a building Mangano owned on Clinton Street in Red Hook. The announced purpose of the C.D.C. was high-minded: to promote the civic interests of Italian-Americans in the neighborhood. In truth, the place acted as a classic mob social club for Mangano and his boys.

Mangano and Anastasia appeared often at the Clinton Street place, where they tangled repeatedly, frequently overheard having heated arguments. Several times, the fights turned physical, and Anastasia had to be peeled off of his sixty-three-year-old boss. Within the underworld, the two men were both known by the nickname of "The Executioner." They were both hot-blooded. The only question was whose blood ran hotter.

It was Albert's. At 9:55 a.m. on April 19, 1951, a Sheepshead Bay boat owner named Mary Gooch called police to report a dead body hidden in tall grass at Bergen Beach, south of Avenue Y near East Seventy-second Street, Brooklyn. The body in the swamp had no ID and was stripped of its pants, but still displayed a gold tie clasp fastened neatly in place. In the right-side pocket of the dead man's shirt were two pairs of blood-spattered glasses. Police invoked underworld parlance to suggest that the deceased had been "taken for a ride."

That area of the Jamaica Bay neighborhood had a reputation as a mob dumping ground—Gooch had also discovered another body in nearly the same place the previous year, a police officer's strangled wife whose murder had never been solved.

A search of fingerprint files identified the dead man as Philip Mangano, Vincent Mangano's brother, his second in command. When detectives went around to the C.D.C. to interview Vincent regarding Philip's killing, the boss could not be located. No sign of Vincent Mangano was ever seen again, and police dated his death on the same day as his brother's.

The Mangano crime family thus underwent a regime change, taking on a new name as of April 19, 1951, becoming the Anastasia crime family. The 1950s were a golden age for crime reporting, and the new boss of Brooklyn proved to be good copy. Harry T. Feeney, a crime reporter for the *New York World-Telegram,* took Albert's "Executioner" nickname and ran with it, labeling him "The Lord High Executioner," from the Gilbert and Sullivan character in *The Mikado.*

Behold the Lord High Executioner!
A personage of noble rank and title
A dignified and potent officer,
Whose functions are particularly vital!

The popular press loved colorful mob nicknames, epithets, *noms de pavé*. Many of them existed most vividly only in the overheated minds of reporters. It doesn't take much imagination to figure out what would have happened if a supplicant showed up at City Democratic one day and called out to Anastasia, "Hey, Lord High Executioner!" Ben Siegel was always "Bugsy," a name he hated. Charles Luciano disliked "Lucky."

Albert's union official brother Anthony Anastasio (he retained the family "o" ending to his surname, unlike his older sibling) went by "Tough Tony." From childhood Carmine Galante was Lilo, but Albert liked to call him "Wacky." (When a man such as Anastasia labels you wacky, it might be time for a mental health checkup.)

Nicknames were useful on the street, serving as tribal identifiers, known only to insiders. Calling Fulton Fish Market kingpin Joseph Lanza by his handle of "Socks" demonstrated a streetwise knowledge. Knowing that the moniker came not from the item of clothing, but from Lanza's predilection for fisticuffs, meant you were clued in all the more.

Harry Feeney was widely credited with coming up with the tag, "Murder, Inc." He had a second nickname for Anastasia, too, like Lord High Executioner, another educated reference: "The Mad Hatter." Albert got tagged with that one, from the *Alice in Wonderland* character, because he customarily wore a hat and was, well, quite obviously mad.

But those names were only for mooks who read the newspapers. Anastasia's real handle, the only one that had any currency within the mob, was "Don Umberto," Umberto being his given Christian name and "Don" being a sign of respect. The usage traditionally signaled a member of the Italian nobility, a prince or duke. In the American underworld, "don" took on a different shade of meaning.

Boss.

If you wanted to know about Albert Anastasia, ask Budd Schulberg. Or watch Schulberg and Elia Kazan's epic crime movie, *On the Waterfront*. Anastasia is there, enshrined in cinematic glory, present in the larger-than-life character of the waterfront mob boss "Johnny Friendly."

Here's Lee J. Cobb as Friendly with Marlon Brando as Terry Malloy:

JOHNNY
Listen kid, I'm a soft touch, too. Ask any rummy on the dock if I'm not good for a fin any time they put the arm on me.

(then more harshly)
But my old lady raised us ten kids on a stinkin' watchman's pension.
When I was sixteen I had to beg for work in the hold. I didn't work
my way up out of there for nuthin'.

TERRY
(sorry to have aroused Johnny—who speaks loud and with fright-
ening force when stung)
I know, Johnny, I know . . .

JOHHNY
Takin' over this local, you know, it took a little doin'. Some pretty
tough fellas were in the way.

Albert Anastasia, in other words, was the kind of guy who prevented
other guys like Terry Malloy from being contenders.

All the "tough fellas" Anastasia encountered died along the way. In the
late twenties, for the murder of a fellow longshoreman, he was convicted,
sentenced to death, and remanded to Sing Sing prison, but gained a re-
prieve and a re-trial. The four witnesses in the original trial disappeared,
never to be heard from in court or otherwise, and Albert had successfully
cheated the electric chair.

Schulberg based his script for *On the Waterfront* on a series of muck-
raking articles in the soon-to-be-defunct *New York Sun* newspaper by reporter Malcolm "Mike" Johnson. The series, originally running on the *Sun*'s
front page in twenty-four parts over 1948–49, won the Pulitzer Prize for
local reporting as it tore the lid off Port of New York gangland racketeering.
Many of the characters in the film were based on real figures, most prominently Father Barry, taken from the life story of Jesuit crusader Father John
M. "Pete" Corridan.

Corridan organized primarily on the docks of the Irish West Side, and
much of Schulberg's research centered there, including memorable pub
crawls from Chelsea north to Hell's Kitchen, drinking with his longshoremen sources.

The Italians who controlled the Brooklyn docks, on the other hand,
proved immune to penetration by outsiders, including film writers. When
it came time to choose the setting of the waterfront labor drama, Schulberg
and Kazan went not with the West Side, certainly not with Brooklyn, but with
Hoboken, New Jersey, out of "concerns for the safety of the cast and crew."

Nevertheless, Johnny Friendly clearly has elements of Albert Anastasia in him, mixed in with Albert's labor union official brother, Anthony, and such other waterfront bosses as Bowers, O'Mara, and Dunn. Mike Johnson's original *Sun* articles fingered Anastasia by name:

The East River piers and the tough South Brooklyn docks are controlled by the notorious Albert Anastasia, a gunman arrested five times for murder. He once spent eighteen months in the death house, until he won a new trial and acquittal. Anastasia, once named as a director in Murder, Inc., the organization of hired killers, continues to rule the Brooklyn waterfront, his bailiwick for years . . .

Named in the papers or not, revealed as a crime boss or not, Anastasia further entrenched himself as the *Sun*'s crusading series came and went. By the time *On the Waterfront,* the film version of the *Sun* stories, premiered in 1954, he had eliminated the Mangano brothers to become the unchallenged boss of his crime family. Johnny Friendly reigned supreme in Brooklyn, on the waterfront and in the tabloids.

Elia Kazan, who directed the film, said the mob was ever-present on the Hoboken waterfront: "There were gangsters watching me shoot the picture." Kazan also made a related point, which comes out in the movie, of how much genuine allegiance mobsters such as Anastasia commanded in the neighborhood. A stroll down Pioneer Street with the Lord High Executioner would not see people diving for cover, but would rather be an occasion for obsequious greetings, if not an outright stampede of lips aimed at Albert's backside.

Part of this was simple human nature. He from whom all largesse flows was necessarily a popular figure. But it's easy to forget, with the hindsight emphasis on Anastasia's killing career, that he was also, oddly enough, well liked. Terry Malloy feels respect and even affection for Johnny Friendly. "Friendly is the guy who takes him to ball games and who is his boss and who supports him," Kazan says. "Terry and Johnny Friendly liked each other."

Those days, in the early to mid-1950s, represented a superb time to be boss. Something new came under the sun during that time, an age-old, mystical-miraculous potion remade and reintroduced, which in turn rendered Anastasia's position as lord of the waterfront many times more valuable than it had been before. It turned out the docks offered a golden opportunity that went far beyond labor racketeering, extortion, loan-sharking, pilferage, and bribery.

Smuggling, a practice as ancient as the sea, was always part of the waterfront equation. Now it became paramount. In the 1950s, the French Connection started to yield huge dividends. Behold the pale horse of heroin, its rider named Death, which thanks to Anastasia's connections and smuggling expertise became more and more of a moneymaker as the decade progressed.

The fat cat became fatter. Anastasia put on pounds, coming to resemble what to the police and newspapers he always swore he was, an ordinary middle-aged businessman. With his paunchy face and thinning hair, he resembled a Mr. Magoo, except in place of myopia he sported the dead eyes of a Great White. In police photographs, their blank look bled into the rest of his features.

Some time in the early fifties he took up residence far from his roots on Pioneer Street, inside a walled estate on Bluff Road in Fort Lee, New Jersey, near his fellow mob bosses Joe Adonis and Tony Bender. Along with the rest of fifties' America, the urban crime lord had gone suburban. Truth be told, though, and in common with a lot of municipalities just across a river from a metropolis, Fort Lee was a fairly loose town, with its own carpet joints and casinos, including one of Albert's hangouts, Ben Marden's Riviera.

It would turn out later that Anastasia's Jersey mansion was crammed to the rafters with electronic bugs. NYPD detectives told tales of listening in as Albert padded around in the kitchen every morning, preparing formula for his baby daughter. No one, not even the Mad-Hatter-Lord-High-Executioner-of-Murder, Incorporated, can be full-on evil all the time. After such tranquil domestic interludes, his bodyguard and driver, Anthony Coppola, would chauffeur him across the bridge into the City.

An example of Albert Anastasia's work: in 1950 Willie Sutton enjoyed notoriety as America's favorite bank robber and bust-out artist, having escaped every prison the law put him in, including Sing Sing. On March 9 of that year, Sutton masterminded a crew of five who extracted $69,933 from a Manufacturers Trust branch in Sunnyside, Queens without the benefit of withdrawal slips or, in fact, any accounts at all.

Sutton would achieve immortality with his laconic answer to the insipid question of why he robbed banks: "Because that's where the money is."

Post–Manufacturers Trust, he quietly took up residence in an apartment on Dean Street in Brooklyn, just a few blocks from police headquarters.

Two years later, at noon on February 18, 1952, Sutton had the bad luck to cross paths with a twenty-three-year-old trouser salesman named Arnold Schuster, a Coast Guard veteran who liked to read crime stories in the tabloids, who even styled himself as something of an amateur sleuth. Sitting opposite the famous bank robber on the downtown BMT train, Schuster managed to do what no beat cop, detective, or man in the street had managed to do over the course of two years.

He recognized Willie Sutton.

And the kid did more than that. He tailed him. Out of the subway at Pacific Street in Brooklyn, down Third Avenue, where Schuster ran into a couple of uniformed police officers named Donald Shea and Joseph McClellan.

"You'll probably think I'm crazy," Schuster said to the cops, "but I just saw Willie Sutton." Shea and McClellan did think he was crazy, or at least, an ordinary deluded New Yorker of the type they dealt with every day. But they followed Schuster to Sutton.

"Are you Willie Sutton?" Shea asked Willie Sutton.

"Why, no," said Willie Sutton. "My name is Gordon." He produced an automobile registration under the name of Charles Gordon.

Somehow, the guy didn't pass the sniff test. Shea left McClellan with him and headed off to find help. At the 78th Precinct station house, the patrol officer sought out an NYPD detective, Louis Weiner, and told him about the encounter. Weiner followed up, sought out "Charles Gordon," and made the biggest arrest of his career.

Under interrogation, Sutton, whose nickname was "Slick Willie," adamantly stuck to his story. He wasn't an infamous bank robber, but a simple citizen named Gordon. Only when the cops proposed fingerprinting him did Sutton come clean.

"Okay, you got me!" he said. But he bridled at being asked to strip down.

"Take your shorts down," the cops said, going for the full search.

"Hey, come on, guys, this is embarrassing," Sutton said.

When his captors insisted, they discovered a pistol hidden between Slick Willie's legs.

At first the reports of Sutton's capture left Arnold Schuster out in the cold, but he got angry when newspapers printed the false rumor of a $70,000 reward. He hired a lawyer and went to the press with his story, and soon he was celebrated by the media and NYPD alike as a citizen crime-buster.

"I want to publicly commend Arnold Schuster for the great help he gave the police force in ridding the land of one of its notorious criminals," pronounced Police Commissioner George Monaghan.

Among those hearing of Schuster's exploits was Albert Anastasia. Seeing Arnold interviewed on the TV news one night, Anastasia exploded. "I can't stand squealers," he said. Couldn't stand them to the degree he sought to wipe Schuster off the face of the earth. Anastasia had no connection with Sutton at all, had never met the man, was related to him through no family or Mafia ties. He simply could not abide informers.

Two and a half weeks after he ID'd Willie Sutton, Schuster left work at his father's clothing store, Mac's Pants, and headed home to Borough Park. He never got there. Ten doors away from his house, death came for Arthur Schuster. His killer gut-shot him first, then drilled both his eyes out. The message couldn't be missed. The mob—and Albert Anastasia—dealt harshly with people who saw too much.

So Anastasia got the last word on poor young Albert Schuster. Or perhaps not. The publicity after the murder rose to the level of hysteria. Brooklyn prosecutor Burton Turkus ranked it just behind the Lindbergh baby kidnapping in triggering public indignation.

The heat got turned on, and even though the perpetrators were never found, the whole incident upset the publicity-shunning hierarchy of the mob. The twisted poetic justice of the hit didn't much impress the other bosses. What the murder of Arnold Schuster did make them think about was what an unhinged son of a bitch they had on their hands in the person of Albert Anastasia.

"Anastasia was really off his rocker," said Charles Luciano. "He was starting to see himself like some guy in the old gangster movies."

In some imaginary scorebook of the mob somewhere, a black mark appeared alongside Anastasia's name. All bosses of his stature were allowed many more than just three strikes, so no one counted him out just yet. Nevertheless, Arnold Schuster's killing definitely went down in the tally. And the black marks against Albert were beginning to add up.

Even at the height of his power, Anastasia's world was already slipping away. The Port of New York had seen its high-water mark. At one time a billion-and-a-half dollars' worth of cargo passed through the piers, warehouses, and docks of Brooklyn in any given year, more than half of all New

York's shipping traffic. But now the freight action was migrating westward, to newer, more expansive, container-friendly facilities of Newark and Port Elizabeth, New Jersey, or north to the Port of Albany.

Perhaps new prospects, new prestige, new money made Anastasia take his eye off the ball. Maybe Arnold Schuster spun off some karmic repercussions from the grave. Perhaps it is only inevitable that the mighty will fall from whatever grand heights they achieve. For whatever reason, the seeds of Albert's downfall were already sown.

A new threat would rise to challenge Anastasia's supremacy in the mob, an old rival whose power, ambition, and Machiavellian cleverness Albert would not fully recognize until it was too late.

4

Vito Comes Home

THE ATLANTIC OCEAN was always a two-way street. Mobsters came from Italy to America, yes, but the traffic also flowed the other way, too. Willingly or not, a mafioso might find himself in midcareer abruptly relocated back to the old country, deported at the direction of the U.S. government, or in flight from criminal prosecution. Many of them slipped into *il patria* as into a warm bath. They found a welcome there, friends, opportunities.

In 1937, fleeing a murder charge in New York to settle near Naples, Vito Genovese established his place among the first of these revenants. He prospered. He became intimate with the Fascist ruling elite, to the degree that even the Mafia-phobic Mussolini elevated him as a Commendatore of the King of Italy, the country's highest civilian honor. The award recognized Genovese's contributions to building a new Fascist Party headquarters in the Nola Commune, a suburb to the west of Naples.

So close was Vito to Il Duce that when Mussolini mentioned he wished a certain muckracking Italian journalist named Tresca silenced, Genovese graciously complied.

The war proved a boon to illegalities of all sorts, and during it Genovese prospered even more. He effortlessly played both sides. After the Allied invasion of Italy in 1943, the former friend of Mussolini transformed himself into a servant of the American occupiers.

Officers of the Allied Military Government (AMG) wrote glowing letters of recommendation for Vito. "Absolutely honest," gushed one, "unselfish" read another, while a third called Genovese "trustworthy, loyal and dependable."

A car of Vito's, a 1938 Packard sedan, wound up in the possession of

Lieutenant Colonel Charles Poletti, commissioner of the AMG and therefore de facto ruler of Italy at the time. Poletti, a former lieutenant governor
of New York and briefly, for a twenty-nine-day interim, governor of the state,
accepted the car as a personal gift from Genovese. The AMG employed
Vito as a translator, seemingly unaware of the mobster's past in New York,
just as the National Fascist Party had been.

But in a foreshadowing of his troubles with a dogged, solitary law enforcement officer at Apalachin, Vito Genovese found himself confronted in
Italy with a cop who just wouldn't quit.

In spring 1944, an Intelligence Sergeant in the U.S. Army's Criminal
Investigation Division (CID) with the memorable name of Orange Dickey
probed a highly organized black market ring in and around Naples. Dickey
represented the typical American citizen-soldier of World War II. His previous experience in law enforcement was as a campus cop at the University
of Pennsylvania.

The black market gang had a distinctive M.O. The thieves would steal
U.S. Army trucks, drive them to supply depots on the Naples waterfront, have them loaded with goods, principally flour and sugar, then sell
the booty to the commodity-starved Italian citizenry at a stiff markup. To
cover their tracks, they would afterward torch the trucks. In the chaos of
post-Fascist Italy, the scam went unnoticed until June 1944, when Dickey
stumbled on a pair of the burned-out Army trucks in San Gennaro, north
of Naples.

At the scene, Dickey arrested a pair of Canadian soldiers, who told
them they had driven trucks a number of times from the Naples docks to
various outlaying districts, always with the instruction to say "Genovese sent
us" when they arrived at their prescribed destinations. For the rest of the
summer, Dickey investigated who Genovese was and how he was connected
to the black market. An informer described Vito as the head of the Mafia in
southern Italy.

On August 27, Dickey closed in. Genovese was on his home turf of Nola,
chauffeured in a Fiat 1500, visiting the local mayor's office on Via Bruno
Giordano. He had sniffed out Dickey's pursuit, and was making a break for
it. He requested from the mayor an easing of wartime travel restrictions to
be able to leave the Campania district.

"Guns were pretty obvious in the front of his belt," Dickey recalled, and
Genovese traveled with a chauffeur-bodyguard. But when the driver left to
park the car, the CID agent, backed up by a pair of quickly dragooned En-

glish soldiers, took Vito without a fight. Dickey relieved the mobster of two Italian-made automatic pistols, a 9mm Beretta and a 7.65 Victoria, and jailed him in the District One Military Police stockade in Naples.

Now that he had him, though, Dickey soon discovered that no one had any idea what to do with Genovese. Beyond that, some influential people seemed determined to spring him. Nicola Cutuli, the chief Italian *questore*, or police investigator, requested the man be released to his custody. This was tantamount to J. Edgar Hoover reaching out to a lowly cop. Dickey politely sidestepped the request and held on to Genovese.

When the CID agent busted him, the mobster had on his person the letters of recommendation from AMG brass, testifying to Genovese's sterling character. Dickey searched his apartment and found a cache of black market goods, generous supplies of cigarettes, soaps, candy, shaving cream— and a piece of paper with Nicola Cutuli's name scrawled on it. Something was rotten in Rome.

Dickey soon enough connected Vito Genovese, Commendatore of the King of Italy, with Don Vito Genovese, New York City mob boss, killer and fugitive. Requesting Genovese's jacket from the States, he found the last entry in the arrest sheet showed Vito had been indicted for homicide in Kings County, New York, on August 7, 1944.

It was an old beef, the one that had sent Genovese scurrying from New York to the safety of Italy seven years before. Genovese stood accused of the murder of Ferdinand Boccia in connection with a crooked card game in 1934. It took the Brooklyn DA ten years, but a murder rap finally came out of the killing when authorities turned up a witness.

Indictment or no indictment, nobody wanted to have anything to do with Genovese. The AMG, the United States Army, and the State Department all passed on extraditing the mobster to the States. Dickey held a hot potato and couldn't find anyone to take it off his hands.

Genovese tried to make it easy for him. He offered Dickey a bribe, $250,000, to get himself released. At that point in time, a U.S. Army sergeant's pay was $210 a month.

"Now, look, you are young," Genovese told him. "There are things you don't understand. This is the way it works. Take the money. You are set for the rest of your life. Nobody cares what you do. Why should you?"

Dickey refused the quarter million. He soldiered on, a voice crying in the wilderness, trying to get someone, anyone, interested in prosecuting the mobster he had in custody. Finally, in January 1945, the logjam suddenly seemed to clear a bit. The Brooklyn DA communicated to Dickey that extradition proceedings could move forward.

What had happened? In protective custody in Brooklyn's Raymond Street jail, Pete LaTempa, the crucial witness against Genovese in the Boccia murder case, had been taking medicine for a gallstone attack. When turnkeys doled out his drugs on January 15, LaTempa collapsed, dead from a fatal dose of sedatives slipped into the pills.

With the LaTempa gone, the case against Genovese died. The obstructionist effort to prevent Dickey from prosecuting Vito died with it. An odd circumstance, that, a mobster brought to justice only when it became clear there was no justice to be had.

On May 17, 1945, forty long weeks after Dickey had taken Genovese into custody, the two men embarked on the *S.S. James Lykes* from Bari, Italy, bound for Brooklyn.

"Kid, you are doing me the biggest favor anyone has ever done to me," Genovese told Dickey. "You are taking me home."

"I am surprised," assistant U.S. district attorney Edward Heffernan told Dickey, when the CID agent arrived with his captive in tow, handcuffed to him, in fact. "We never expected to see this boy back here."

But Dickey's gallant stand against the mob's political allies, his lonely campaign to expose Vito Genovese as the mobster he was, came to naught after the Brooklyn DA's office dismissed the Boccia homicide case. It was not only Albert Anastasia who could cheat the chair.

In releasing Genovese, Judge Samuel S. Liebowitz pronounced a blistering verdict against an erstwhile defendant who was, nevertheless, not guilty in the eyes of the law.

"By devious means," Liebowitz declared from the bench, "among which were the terrorizing of witnesses, kidnapping them, yes, even murdering those who could provide evidence against you, [Genovese] thwarted justice again and again. I cannot speak for the jury, but I believe that if there were even a shred of corroborating evidence, you would have been condemned to the chair."

Soon enough, Genovese was back on the bricks, and Orange Dickey was once again swallowed up in campus cop obscurity. Vito must have remembered him, though, as one guy who couldn't be backed down, bullied or bribed. He would meet another at Apalachin.

But a question lingered: What had Genovese really been up to all those years in exile? Sure, palling around with dictators, corrupting the Italian political system, strong-arming his way into control of black markets and electrical companies. Anything else?

As a matter of fact, there was something else, something big.

Like ships passing in the night, Vito Genovese and his old Lower East Side neighborhood ally, Charles Luciano, crossed the Atlantic Ocean in opposite directions in the mid-1940s. In summer 1945, Genovese hit his old haunts in New York City, a free man. A half year later, in February 1946, Luciano, his prison sentence for pandering commuted and a deportation order signed, left New York for Italy aboard the freighter *Laura Keene*.

From Genovese, the exiled Mafia mastermind Luciano inherited the Italian contacts, organization, and operations of a smuggling and black market racket that was doing a rollicking business. In the chaos that was postwar Italy, narcotics represented only a small sector of mob profits. But both Genovese and Luciano recognized it as a growth opportunity.

Vito left behind the framework. Lucky built upon it, and eventually a dope pipeline developed that remained viable for decades, supplying the lion's share of America's heroin. "The basic Turkey-Italy-America heroin route continued to dominate international heroin traffic for more than twenty years," notes one expert.

The mob's romance with dope began as far back as the 1920s. Arnold Rothstein, celebrated as "The Brain" and "The Big Bankroll" because of his sharp gambling practices, definitely had a darker side. Prosecutors claimed that Rothstein's gang brought two tons of narcotics into the United States in a single seven-month period in 1926. Said one AUSA in 1928, "Rothstein was the financial agent for an international drug-smuggling operation."

Among his myriad other ventures, the Big Bankroll bankrolled heroin.

With Rothstein's murder in 1928, the Brain died but the body kept pumping dope. Slowly, Italian mobsters took over from Jewish mobsters, gaining control of smuggling and distribution networks. Luciano and Genovese helped regularize financing and supply logistics.

Brooklyn boss Joe Bonanno once actually attempted to take Canadian citizenship, so enamored was he of the enormous dope profits flowing through thoroughly corrupt Montreal, Quebec, and equally crooked Hamilton, Ontario. His cousin Steven Magaddino in Buffalo facilitated the flow of drugs. By the mid-fifties, the five New York Mafia families had a Rockefeller-level monopoly on dope, controlling 90 percent of the heroin sold in the United States.

The Italian takeover of the heroin trade was not without its bumps, and was felt soon enough on the street level. "The Italians stepped on [adulterated] the H much more than the Jews, and they charged more money," said one postwar junkie. "As a matter of fact, the old-timers who used junk . . . would pass the remark many a time, 'Jesus, it's too bad the Jews ain't around to handle it again.' The Jews were much easier on everybody."

As the labs and smuggling activity migrated north to Corsica and Marseilles, the route would become infamous as the French Connection, but the road to the shooting galleries of Harlem and the Lower East Side still ran through Sicily. Palermo remained the entrepôt, the halfway point between the poppy fields of Turkey's Anatolian Plateau and the Corsican-staffed refineries of Marseilles.

Heroin derives chemically from the opium poppy, grown primarily in a four-thousand-mile-long crescent of mountainous highlands that extends from Turkey, through Iran, Afghanistan, Pakistan, and India to the "Golden Triangle" of Burma, Laos, and Thailand.

Opium itself has a long and storied history as a folk potion and recreational magic carpet. Chemists first extracted morphine from raw opium sap in 1805. Morphine's turbo-charged cousin, heroin, chemically synthesized for maximum effect upon human physiology, first appeared in 1874, and premiered commercially via the Bayer Company in 1898.

The drug's popularity waxed and waned in synch with suppression efforts and availability. Oddly enough, for related and parallel reasons, heroin and the Italian Mafia both reached a low point during the mid-twentieth century. Two decades of Mussolini's anti-Mafia campaigns broke the back of the classic criminal underground in Italy. And wartime interdiction had stemmed the smuggling of heroin to a tiny trickle.

The average purity of street heroin in the United States fell from 28 percent in 1938 to 3 percent after the war began in 1941. Supplies dried up. Legions of junkies went through involuntary withdrawal. By 1945, there were only 20,000 heroin addicts in America, by far the lowest number since the rise of the drug in the 1890s.

In that same year, the decimated remnants of the old-style Mafia in Sicily and Naples had largely lost their grip on power. Hundreds of mobsters had fled Italy, many of them winding up in America.

Thus there was a real possibility of a tipping point, a chance, in the aftermath of World War II, that both the twin scourges—smack and the Italian mob—could be effectively neutralized.

It was not to be. Postwar politics, and especially the urgent push against the communist parties in Italy and France, worked with deadly consequence to breath new life into the Mafia and the heroin trade.

Vito Genovese wasn't the only mafioso employed by Allies after liberation. In town after Italian town, the Allies appointed mob-connected mayors to preclude the alternative of appointing communists. The occupying military authorities granted Calogero Vizzini, formerly Genovese's mentor and black market partner, the mayoralty of Villaba as well as an honorary title of colonel in the United States Army. After years of being battered by Mussolini and the Fascists, the Mafia had found a new patron in the U.S. government.

"At the beginning of the Second World War, the Mafia was restricted to a few isolated and scattered groups and could have been completely wiped out," writes Italian mob expert (and Villaba native) Michele Pantaleone. "The Allied occupation and the subsequent slow restoration of democracy reinstated the Mafia with its full powers."

The postwar resurgence of heroin offers an even more cynical object lesson in the unintended consequences of mindless anticommunism. Charles Luciano had stepped seamlessly into Vito Genovese's place as a leading mob power in Allied-occupied Italy, utilizing Vizzini as well as other Genovese contacts. Vizzini was himself a *paesano* of Luciano's, who was born in a small village close to Don Calogero's home base of Villaba.

Luciano's first order of business was to reestablish a narcotics trade that had been severely curtailed during the war. At first, he relied upon an ingenious source for high-grade heroin, receiving a steady supply of product skimmed from a Turin-based pharmaceutical company. According to a 1950 report of the U.S. Bureau of Narcotics, the legally produced dope, supplied via mail order and then smuggled into the United States, amounted to some 1,500 pounds.

American pressure soon closed that source down, but Luciano developed an alternate connection. Morphine base, from Turkish opium smuggled into Lebanon and converted in Beirut, began arriving in Sicily in the late 1940s. To chemically synthesize the morphine into heroin, Luciano created a lab in Palermo, registered in the name of his cousins (under the guise of a candy factory) and operated by Vizinni.

The effort to refine heroin in Sicily, however, proved unworkable. Too many prying eyes, too many outstretched hands from local police and government figures. Five hundred miles north across the Mediterranean, Luciano discovered a more secure venue.

Marseilles had a mobbed-up reputation as the "Chicago of France," but the teeming, raucous port resembled nothing so much as Albert Anastasia's waterfront stamping grounds in Brooklyn. A smuggler's paradise, the city represents France's gateway to the south, to Africa, the Middle East and, via the Suez Canal, Asia. In Marseilles, Luciano found a perfect ally for the narcotics trade, close-knit Corsican mob families, secretive, disciplined and, best of all, schooled in the arts of drug chemistry.

The French Connection was born. Turkish opium went to Lebanon to become morphine, and in turn that morphine traveled to Marseilles to become heroin. Throughout, the mafiosi of Italy acted as the middlemen, providing logistics, transport, and financing.

Since it is highly concentrated, smuggler-friendly heroin number four, 80 to 95 percent pure diacetylmorphine, can be hidden and moved with minimal fuss. A small, bread loaf–sized kilo, for example, would be adulterated into forty pounds of street dope with a purity of 5 percent or less. Pure number four smack, in other words, can be worth ten times its weight in gold.

That's what Charlie Luciano meant when he described heroin as "a million dollars in a suitcase."

But refining morphine base into the pure drug is a fairly sophisticated technical process, demanding carefully calibrated pressurized heating. In labs sprinkled throughout Marseilles and in villas in the surrounding hills, the Corsicans proved adept at the procedure.

More to the point, they were politically bulletproof. The Corsicans prospered during war in alliance with Vichy and the Nazis. After liberation, the chameleon switched its colors, and the French intelligence bureau, the SDECE, used Corsican mobsters to break communist-led strikes on the Marseilles waterfront.

In exchange for this service—and with the Corsicans honoring a strict tradition of never disbursing their product in France itself—the SDECE covertly granted the Marseilles labs immunity from police harassment and seizure.

As it had in Sicily with its alliance with the Mafia, postwar anticommunism once again struck a deal with the devil, this time trading the souls of American addicts for a French port cleansed of Reds.

The results soon started washing up on the shores of America, more specifically, in the waterfront purlieus of Albert Anastasia (Brooklyn) and Vito Genovese (Greenwich Village and the West Side of Manhattan).

In February 1947, New York customs agents boarding the liner *John Ericsson,* docked at Pier 40 at West Fiftieth Street, discovered a hundred ounces of heroin number four on the person of a Corsican crewman, Angi

Marie Poggi. As if someone was anxious to destroy evidence, the ship later burned at the pier.

The next month, the French freighter *St. Tropez* out of Marseilles arrived at Pier 28 on the East River, Joseph Lanza territory, and thus under the control of Anastasia. Port patrol officers turned up almost thirty pounds of heroin in packets concealed in the pockets of a pair of deckhands, Negro Cesar and Rene Bruchard, and stashed in the ship's cache of dirty linen. The packaging of the *St. Tropez* dope packets, officials noted, was identical with that of the *Ericsson* seizure.

Drugs confiscated by customs officials and law enforcement, of course, are only the tip of the proverbial iceberg, with contemporary estimates putting the ratio at 100 units getting through for every unit interdicted. For over two decades, the French Connection proved amazingly durable and efficient, in a single year pushing through 4.8 tons of product from the Third World poppy fields of Turkey, Iran, and Afghanistan to the First World cities of America.

The Connection utilized multiple delivery routes to get at the American markets. Despite setbacks such as the *Ericsson* and *St. Tropez*, shipping directly to the Mafia-friendly piers of New York City always remained an option. But increasingly, the Marseilles-based smugglers turned to two other back-door entryways into the States: Cuba, controlled by the Tampa-based Trafficante mob family, and French-speaking Montreal, with a healthy immigrant population from Corsica.

If Croswell and other law enforcement officers wondered what a mobster like Carmine Galante was doing speeding along the roads of upstate New York, their brethren in the Bureau of Narcotics could have clued them in. From the early 1950s on, Galante had been acting as the liaison between the New York mob and the Corsican dope smugglers of Montreal. Galante, this friend of ours, became our man in Canada.

As any dope dealer will admit, as Al Capone learned, as mobsters down through the years have found, what to do with all the money becomes much more of a headache than the actual smuggling and distributing of the contraband. Throughout the 1950s, the American gangland take on French Connection dope spiraled up in value until it hit a million dollars a day.

All that pelf had to wind up somewhere. Ambrose Bierce once defined a hand as a human appendage habitually found in someone else's pocket. The wars of Prohibition proved that any vast new influx of cash into underworld coffers inevitably sparked vast new campaigns of violence. The money flowed and the bullets flew.

When French Connection money began to plump up the pockets of ambitious New York ganglords such as Vito Genovese and Albert Anastasia, that once again proved to be the case. Close to the end of the world war, another war ramped up, this one a nasty little street battle over the pure profits of heroin.

5

Genovese Hits Costello

HOTEL DIPLOMAT, ON WEST Forty-third Street in Manhattan, began its life as the Mother Lodge of the Benevolent and Protective Order of Elks. By 1946, when Vito Genovese and two dozen other mobsters convened in the hotel's second-floor banquet room, it had been transformed into a shabby-but-respectable Midtown hostelry. This was to be Vito's official coming-out party, announcing his return after a near decade-long absence from New York.

Nine o'clock at night on a sweltering Monday, June 24, the hottest day of the year so far. As the oldest boss at the gathering, Santo Volpe, the leader of the mob in the Pittston-Scranton-Wilkes-Barre area of northern Pennsylvania, congratulated Genovese on his release in the Boccia murder case and formally welcomed him back from exile in Italy.

A chorus of "Welcome back, Vito," and *"Dare il benvenuto, Don Vitone,"* arose from others around the banquet table. Scranton front man to the mob Russell Bufalino had come down from Pennsylvania with Volpe. Albert Anastasia was there, and another Brooklyn crime lord, the olive oil king, Joe Profaci.

Dodging a murder charge raised a mobster to an elite class. Anastasia had done so, prompting a grand jury to decry the dropping of an "ironclad case" against the puppet-master of the Brooklyn waterfront. Carmine Galante had a parole officer actually witness him climb into a murder car an hour before a killing, and still walked in the homicide of Carlo Tresca. In New York in those waning days of Tammany, more than a few killers could wear a big button that read, "I Beat a Murder Rap, Ask Me How."

At the Hotel Diplomat gathering, Genovese, fresh off his own close call with Judge Liebowitz and the Brooklyn district attorney, urged his fellow mobsters to refrain from infighting, forsake violence, and keep one foot in legitimate businesses as a way to take the heat off. An informer at the meeting later detailed the goings-on.

"We got to take a page from Joe's book," Genovese lectured the gathering, gesturing to fellow family boss Joe Profaci. "The olive oil he sells is good stuff. He doesn't fool around with any phony oil. He tries to keep it honest all the way. He even goes to church every Sunday."*

Actually, Profaci had been hauled into court several times for adulterated product, with his Mama Mia brand having peanut and cottonseed oil detected in it. But never mind. The "be like Joe" idea was easy to grasp just by looking at the conservative, overtly religious, and tightly wound mobster.

The same "cool it down" message had been going forth to the mob rank and file since Charles Luciano first organized the underworld into a federation-style hierarchy after the Castellammarese War. It had been repeated so often that it became a sort of boss bromide. Yet the killings continued. Many times, the prime movers behind the violence were the very ones counseling restraint.

Only Anastasia spoke up in opposition to Genovese, regarding the murder of an informer, which Vito refrained from endorsing. "I'm not saying I disagree with you," Anastasia said mildly, "but I'm not saying I agree with you, either."

There it was. A first stirring that Vito the Great was not unchallengeable. The 1946 Hotel Diplomat summit marked the start of a ten-year slow-motion cockfight between Genovese and Anastasia, two murderously ambitious underbosses, both with designs on more power. It was inevitable that they would clash. As in a classic western, New York City, the town big enough to contain almost any ambition, wasn't big enough for both of them.

The former allies had come up at the same time. In 1931, they had literally murdered together, standing shoulder to shoulder pumping bullets into Joe "the Boss" Masseria. Vito and Albert were now at a friendly meeting in a Midtown banquet hall. But their battle for supremacy would culminate during the long, hot summer of 1957, and eventually lead to another mob meeting in an upstate hamlet.

---

* Genovese wasn't kidding about the overtly religious Profaci, who attended St. Bernadette's in Brooklyn and had a private chapel in his basement. Three years after the Hotel Diplomat meeting, a group of Brooklyn priests and Catholic laypersons recommended to Pope Pius XII that Profaci be knighted by the church. Only intervention by Brooklyn district attorney Miles McDonald, who detailed Profaci's predilection for loan-sharking, extortion, and murder in a letter to the Pope, prevented it from happening.

The unspoken truth behind Anastasia's brusque behavior at the Diplomat gathering was that much had changed in New York during Genovese's absence in Italy. The jostling at the trough had produced a whole new order, different from the one Vito had known in 1937, when he left New York. And the primary truth of the new order was that Genovese no longer represented anyone's idea of a top dog.

Sure, let him gas on about what's what, let him glory in the fact he had just beaten a murder rap. But essentially, Vito Genovese had been busted down from underboss to captain. He had his crew and his personal fiefdom in Greenwich Village, but that was all. He still lived high, still had good money coming in from his Italian lottery racket, but even if he didn't wholly grasp the reality just yet, Genovese's position in the hierarchy of the mob had been much diminished.

If he wanted to regain his old position of power, he'd have to wait on line, because a few people stood in his way.

The New York families greeted Genovese's return from exile with a variation on what-have-you-done-for-me lately. It's the way of the world: top earners rise to the top. And Vito Genovese wasn't even near the top. Even though he had created the foundations of a lucrative heroin smuggling route, in 1946 the French Connection hadn't fully connected yet.

No, the top earner and thus the top dog of the underworld had ensconced himself in a seven-room, eighteenth-floor apartment at 115 Central Park West, in the twin-towered Majestic, across the street from the Dakota. Nothing was too good for Frank Costello, a former bootlegger and now an unrivaled slot-machine king, who surrounded himself with luxury in apartment 18F, with antique gold wall hangings and a Howard Chandler Christy "Christy Girl" portrait over the fireplace.

A suave and well-manicured man about town, five-seven and 155 pounds, Costello had stepped up when Vito Genovese and Charles Luciano disappeared into jail or decamped for Italy. He loved the luxe life, demonstrating a taste for English Oval cigarettes and upscale Manhattan restaurants. He stood in the shadows behind manager Jules Podell at the Copacabana, his name appearing on no ownership papers for New York City's famed nightclub, but nevertheless its true power.

Born Francisco Castiglia in the Calabrian mountain commune of Cassano allo Ionio, in the hills above the Gulf of Taranto, he Americanized his name after his family immigrated to Italian East Harlem when he was nine.

Repeated jailings for assault and robbery convinced Costello that street crime represented a dead end, and he became a sort of gangster Gandhi, known for never carrying a gun and eschewing violence, a principle that would lead to difficulties later.

Collecting a steady rain of cash from his 24,000 slot machines, Costello allied himself with Luciano and Meyer Lansky, rising in the crime hierarchy not only on the strength of his earnings, but also on the strength of his character. With deep and long-nurtured Tammany Hall political connections, he preferred the purring of a well-oiled machine over the childish spectacle of fireworks, and was authoritative rather than ruthless, resolving disputes with reason and diplomacy. For this he earned his "Prime Minister of the Underworld" nickname.

The Prime Minister embodied the role of the ultimate "cool it down" gangster. He longed for legitimacy. During prohibition, Costello ran his bootlegging racket like a business, with an office in the Chrysler Building and operations departmentalized into distribution, traffic, corruption, defense, and intelligence.

But Costello's cash cow was always gambling, which he considered a harmless and unavoidable human habit, evil only when it was suppressed by government. After Costello's death in 1973, his longtime lawyer, George Wolf, pointed to the national takeover of gambling by government and mainstream commercial businesses as a vindication of Costello's no-harm-no-foul viewpoint.

Peel back the sophisticated veneer a little, though, and Frank remained at heart a gangster. He and Albert Anastasia, for example, always got along well, an admitted odd couple, but one that as the years progressed formed a durable alliance. When Costello's carrots didn't work, Anastasia could be relied upon to bring out the stick. As auxiliary troops in any fight, Costello could also employ the soldiers of his cousin and longtime gambling ally Willie Moretti, a New Jersey crime boss.

Costello skipped the 1946 meeting at Hotel Diplomat. Too busy. Vito Genovese might have felt snubbed, but for the moment, Costello reigned supreme and untouchable. He brought in too much coin, had too many allies, counted too many friends in high places. Like all wise underdog challengers, Genovese lay in the cut and waited. He retreated to his Village domain, where his string of nightclubs and gay bars (the famous Stonewall Inn was one of his), provided a natural distribution network for narcotics.

They were near polar opposites, these two, Frank and Vito, the business executive-manque Prime Minister and the Machiavellian don. Frank's own bookmakers could have taken bets as to which one would come out on top. The smart money would have been on Vito.

In this particular face-off, Costello's first misstep, a near-fatal one from which all his later troubles flowed, came in 1951. A U.S. senator from Tennessee, Estes Kefauver, conducted a series of hearings on organized crime. The national television networks were just coming in, and the legislators-versus-mobsters spectacle proved to be what passed for riveting viewing in the early 1950s.

During a March 1951 hearing at the federal building in Manhattan's Foley Square, Kefauver called on Frank Costello to stop by and tell the folks what he knew about the interstate ins-and-outs of gambling in America. The obvious play, indulged in any number of gangsters called as witnesses, would be to dodge the subpoena, lay low, plead the Fifth. But Costello was gulled by his own sense of legitimacy. *What do I have to hide?*

His was probably the strangest appearance of any length by anyone in the history of American TV. Costello's lawyer, George Wolf, objected to the presence of cameras at the hearing. His client's display on national TV might be prejudicial, Wolf averred, might slur his sterling reputation. The networks hit upon a bizarre compromise. All right, they agreed, we will not show your client's face. But, unbeknownst to either Costello or his lawyer, the TV cameras shot footage anyway, focusing exclusively upon Costello's manicured hands.

Costello in fact had an appealing, open face, a little fleshy, but smooth, sophisticated, and nonthreatening. But the combination of broadcasting his voice as it detailed underworld gambling practices, while picturing his hands—restless, gesturing, fiddling obsessively with his glasses—turned out to be disastrous. The absence of the face made the proceedings feel more sinister, and the TV audience could summon up all sorts of thuggish fantasies.

"Those writhing, twisting hands were hypnotic to viewers," admitted Wolf, whose legal strategy backfired.

The whole nation sat transfixed by the Kefauver hearings, among the world's first true mass-media news events. Streets emptied, stores were deserted, and bars with TVs were packed for the afternoon broadcasts. Today, in a more savvy age, the images appear quaint, harmless. It's hard to imagine what the fuss was all about.

Why didn't the Kefauver hearings wake up the country to the dangers of organized crime? To some extent, they did. They were transfixing TV, but perhaps that fact worked to trivialize them a bit. The issue quickly died, and the Kefauver effect didn't last. America was like a sleeper, prodded once to awake, rolling over, hitting the snooze button, and going back to sleep.*

As Rudolph Giuliani analyzed the situation thirty years after the fact: "People didn't believe it—Kefauver was accused of having political ambitions." The public thought the threat of organized crime was somehow "made up by Kefauver for political reasons."

The hearings had enormous repercussions for the career of Estes Kefauver, propelling him to the forefront of presidential politics in the Democratic Party. They would also have a lasting impact on a pair of brothers from Massachusetts just beginning political careers of their own. Organized crime, the Kefauver hearings taught John and Robert Kennedy, was an issue that could drive a presidential campaign.

But appearing before Kefauver had a devastating effect on Frank Costello. Aware that things were going badly for him, he staged a walkout from the hearings. It was too late. He had become too well known to return to anonymity. Costello had popped up from the trenches of the underworld, providing a clear target for snipers from law enforcement.

Legal woes dogged Costello throughout the remainder of the fifties. His walkout prompted a contempt-of-Congress charge, for which he drew an eighteen-month prison sentence. The government attempted to strip him of his U.S. citizenship on the grounds he had lied during the naturalization process. The IRS mounted tax cases against him. Slowly, the juggernaut of justice simply ground Frank Costello down.

One by one, his friends dropped, too. Costello's New Jersey ally Willie Moretti, his mind assaulted by the effects of tertiary syphilis, had testified before Kefauver, more garrulously than was to the liking of other gangsters. In the mob, oftentimes, the squeaky wheel gets greased. On October 4, 1951, one of Moretti's lunchtime companions at Joe's Elbow Room Restaurant in Cliffside Park suddenly reached out, grasped his tie, and slammed his head backward. Another "friend" at the table pulled out a .38 and put two into Moretti's head.

Later on, mob tattletale Joe Valachi would characterize the Moretti hit as a "mercy killing," putting the poor guy out of his syph-riddled misery. And gangland mounted one of its spectacle memorials for the deceased,

---

* There had been one previous government attempt to wake the nation: Herbert Hoover's Wickersham Commission in 1929, created primarily to target a specific mobster: Alphonse Capone.

among the last of the great mob funerals. But the fact remained that Costello no longer could count on Moretti and his army of goons for muscle.

In 1956, another blow. The government deported a longtime Luciano and Costello ally, Joe Adonis. The support network of the Prime Minister collapsed. Assailed by legal problems of his own, Costello could not fully attend to succession issues. The mob abhors a vacuum. Into the gap left behind by the exiled Adonis and a preoccupied Costello stepped Vito Genovese, who had been waiting, ever since his return from Italian exile, to reclaim his rightful place at the head of the American Mafia.

By the spring of 1957, Frank Costello had served his time for contempt of Congress and was out on appeal from a tax case before the Supreme Court, with deportation still hanging over his head. He had a meet-up with his odd-fellow partner in crime, Albert Anastasia, in an Italian restaurant on West Forty-eighth Street.

Albert and Frank or, as they were known to their *paesanos,* Umberto and Francesco, summoned to mind a bear and his trainer, whereby the trainer prompts the animal to perform, but all the time the audience is thinking, some day that bear is going to eat the trainer for supper.

"Vito is bad-mouthing me," Anastasia said. "He's claiming I'm muscling in on the Cuba business."

Costello remained noncommittal. "So?"

"So I don't think Vito's worried about Cuba." Meaning Cuba simply served as a pretext for a Genovese power grab.

"I'll talk to him," Costello said.

"I don't think that would be too good an idea, Frank," Anastasia said. A shot over Frank's bow: with the indirectness that characterized mob conversational delicacy, Anastasia was telling him to stay away from Vito.

On the evening of May 2, 1957, Costello stopped in at Candler's bar for cocktails, dined out at L'Aiglon on East Fifty-fifth Street, then went on to a nightclub, Monsignore. Afterward, he returned to his Central Park West apartment. Passing through the Majestic's lobby, heading upstairs no doubt to admire his own faultless taste in interior decorating, Costello turned as he heard a voice behind him.

"This one's for you, Frank," the voice said. Then a gunshot, sounding enormous in the tiled space of the lobby.

Vincent Gigante, the shooter, made a hash of the job. His needless words turned his intended victim's head, and the bullet merely creased Costello's right temple. Sent on the hit by Vito Genovese, Gigante later was acquitted in the murder attempt when Costello refused to identify him and the Majestic's doorman, who did, was proved in court to be blind in one eye.

But in another sense, Gigante's botched shot did its work very well. Frank Costello was so shaken by the assassination attempt that he retired. With his fade, a quarter century of mob prosperity and relative concord came to a close. *Pax Costello* ended.

So the 1957 shooting season opened by taking out, if not killing, the Prime Minister of the underworld. Vito Genovese's Joycean strategy of silence, exile, and cunning was finally proving effective. Eleven years after the coming-out dinner in the banquet room of Hotel Diplomat, Genovese had removed his primary rival for leadership of the mob.

Contemplating the New York underworld in the wake of Costello's retirement, Vito could see only a single remaining adversary in his run to the top: Albert Anastasia. Everyone else had been taken down by the government, was under his thumb, or was otherwise neutralized. To remove this last obstacle, Genovese required only a pretext. Maybe Cuba would do, or perhaps some reckless misstep by the Mad Hatter.

"Every dog has his day," runs the old bluesman line, "and a good dog just might have two days." Vito Genovese was looking for his second day.

6

Anastasia Gets His

CUBA. IN THE 1950S, the island nation had golden connotations for the mob.

Meyer Lansky was the first to realize the possibilities. A member of a three-person mutual admiration society that included Charlie Luciano and Ben Siegel, Lansky had a steel-trap mind for numbers. He once hired his own private math tutor to help him brush up on the finer points of high finance. As early as 1938, he envisioned Cuba as an offshore mob paradise, a tropical nexus of smuggling and gambling, a place to invest the fat profits from mainland rackets.

After Fulgencio Batista returned to power in a U.S.-backed 1952 coup, Cuba split open for mob plunder like a piece of overripe fruit. Lansky was a great good friend of Batista, who had divided his time during his years out of power between Daytona Beach, Florida, and a suite in the Waldorf. He and Lansky were as entwined as two fingers on a hand.

"They were very, very close," recalled one of Lansky's lawyers. "Like brothers." In a meeting at the Waldorf, Batista and Lansky hammered out the strategy for the mob move into Cuban casinos, which pockets were to be lined, who would get what percentage.

Until Fidel Castro came along in 1959 to spoil the party, Havana experienced a legendary boom that rivaled the "crime hotels" of Las Vegas during the same period. The jewel would be Lansky's Riviera, built on the capital's Malecón esplanade. Work began in December 1956 on the 21-floor, 440-room edifice, with an ultramodern, central-air-conditioned interior and an angled exterior that embraced a swimming pool at the edge of the sea.*

Cuba represented a brave new mob-colonized world, and Albert Anastasia wanted in. As the head of one of New York's five Mafia families, he felt himself owed a cut. Lansky had the Riviera sewed up, but there was a Hilton in the works, too, a massive skyscraper in Vedado, the old Havana neighborhood. With his usual aggressive, ham-handed style, Anastasia demanded his own place at the green-felt tables.

The person he put the squeeze upon most directly was Santo Trafficante Jr., a sharp-dressing, mild-looking Tampa mobster in aviator glasses and Brioni suits. His Sicilian-born father, Santo Trafficante Sr., became wealthy running *bolita,* the Hispanic numbers racket, operating out of Tampa's Ybor City ethnic enclave, where Italian, Cuban, and Spanish immigrants worked the cigar factories.

Trafficante *figlio* built an empire on his father's beginnings, and proved himself particularly adept as a Spanish-speaking liaison to the Cuban ruling elite. He took over a crumbling club on the outskirts of Havana, the Sans Souci, and transformed it into a world-class casino. Trafficante had another virtue that recommended him to Anastasia: he was an ace smuggler.

The coves and sandbars of Tampa Bay were always superb rum-running venues during Prohibition. Goods could be transferred from large vessels into smaller boats by workers wading the offshore shallows, far from the reach of government agents. Tampa had been transshipping illegal drugs through Cuba since the 1930s, primarily cocaine, the preferred drug of the Cuban and Hispanic leisure class.

Anastasia needed new supply routes for Marseilles heroin, which was being smuggled directly off freighters on the Brooklyn waterfront or transshipped through Montreal. But those pipelines were taking a hit. In April 1957, French authorities seized twenty kilos of prime heroin number four, fresh from the Corsican labs, off the luxury liner *SS Excambion* in Marseilles harbor.

The *Excambion* had been a fiasco. The ship, with the heroin stowed safely aboard, made the initial transit to New York without a problem, but had somehow departed again—Anastasia's man Frank Scalise himself watching in frantic disbelief—before the dope could be off-loaded. The French captain

---

* The Havana Riviera opened on December 10, 1957, a month after the Apalachin summit. It had a short run: in October 1960, the Castro government shut the country's casinos and nationalized its hotels.

discovered the cache on the return trip to France, and turned it over to the gendarmes when he got to Marseilles.

Dodging narcotics enforcement meant always developing fresh routes, different entryways into the States. In that respect, the newly developed Marseilles-Buenos Aires-Cuba-Tampa itinerary, convoluted as it was, had shown promise. And for that, Anastasia had to firm up his ties with Trafficante and the Cubans.

Anastasia could look across the East River to Manhattan and witness Vito Genovese piling up drug profits with seeming ease. Vito had the nightclubs and gay bars of the Village to dispense the dope.

The smoke had cleared from the Costello shooting on May 2, revealing a stark, high-noon landscape. It looked like it was going to be either Vito or Albert. "Peaceful coexistence"—the Cold War phrase had just been codified by Russia's Nikita Khrushchev—wasn't an option.

Albert felt backed into a corner. His moves began to have a bull-in-a-china shop feel to them. The *Excambion* seizure had dire spin-off repercussions.

The boat was one of the "Four Aces" of the American Export Lines, with 125 first-class cabins, and this type of hybrid passenger-cargo vessel had customarily been used by the mob to smuggle drugs. The difficulty there was that passenger liners docked not in Anastasia's home waterfront of Brooklyn, but on the West Side piers. Which meant dealing with Vito.

A good slice of Anastasia's capital had been invested in the heroin taken off *Excambion* by French authorities in Marseilles. Anastasia had been brought into the deal by an underboss, Frank Scalise, his man in the Bronx. Scalise, an elegant, balding, fifty-five-year-old Sicilian with a pencil mustache, refused to make Albert whole again by returning the boss's investment.

Up there loose in the Bronx, a borough away from Anastasia's home base in Brooklyn, Scalise demonstrated an independent streak. In the chaos surrounding the Castellammarese War, he was once briefly the boss of the whole Mangano family, the one that Albert had effectively taken over.

Anastasia called him "Cheech" or "Ciccio" (from the last syllable of his name in Italian, Scalici). Scalise was at that time a person of interest for police in four separate homicide investigations, and had recently ducked a U.S. Senate inquiry into narcotics trafficking. Now he was dodging Anastasia over the $50,000 lost on the *Excambion* debacle.

The play here could have gone quite differently. Anastasia could have waited for the situation to shake out, waited for Scalise to put together another deal, given him some time to make good. Caught up in his rivalry with Genovese, and never a patient man to begin with, Anastasia instead brooded about the double-cross. Specters lurked in the shadows around this deal. Vito? Charlie Luciano? Either one could have tipped off the French about the *Excambion* shipment.

Anastasia didn't wait. With all the folks looking for Scalise, and him making himself scarce, he proved surprisingly easy to find. On June 17, 1957, while the city sweltered in record-setting heat, Scalise made his usual rounds in the Bronx.

Although he kept an address on Kirby Street in the Bronx outlier enclave of City Island, the teeming Crotona-Fordham neighborhood around Arthur Avenue was Scalise's true home. He and his six brothers kept a headquarters there at Jack's Candy Store, on Crescent and Arthur, near St. Barnabas Hospital.

At around one o'clock that day, Scalise left his Bahama blue 1956 Cadillac parked in front of 630 Crescent, a block from the candy store. Wearing light-colored slacks and a yellow shirt, he strolled down 186th Street to the busy shops and restaurants of Arthur Avenue. There he stopped at Enrico Mazzare's green market, where he picked out ninety cents' worth of peaches and lettuce.

Two men double-parked a black sedan in front of the grocery. One of Albert's torpedoes, Vincent "Jimmy" Squillante, his nephew, godchild, and chief enforcer in the mob's $50-million-a-year garbage collection racket, got out of the sedan with an accomplice. Both dressed in black pants and white shirts, both wearing sunglasses, they entered the store, cornered Scalise, and tore apart his face and neck with bullets from paired .38 revolvers. There were ten shots altogether, including a last one to the victim's shoulder, which spun Frank Scalise around and finally dropped him.*

Found in the dead man's pockets, a piece of paper scrawled with a name and an address: "Santo Trafficante, 2505 Bristol Av, Tampa, Florida."

A deceased Cheech could not very well make good on his heroin debt to Anastasia. And the hit backfired on Albert in another way. Killing his underling at that precise point in time was a gift from Anastasia to his archrival, Genovese. An unsanctioned murder of a well-established mob underboss provided the pretext that Vito needed to move against his Brooklyn adver-

---

* The Scalise murder triggered another. Frank's brother Joe swore revenge, so on September 7 (nine weeks before the Apalachin summit), Squillante and his accomplices killed Joe Scalise as well, dismembering his body and packing off the remains in mob-controlled garbage trucks.

sary. He could present Albert as out of control, a loose cannon, an indiscriminate killer. This was Anastasia's tabloid reputation, so the accusation would stick.

Willie Moretti, Joe Adonis, Frank Costello, then the Scalise brothers. The chessboard had become littered with knocked-over pieces. The two players, Vito and Albert, moved toward their endgame.

During the fall of 1957, Ed Croswell pursued his routine duties as a state police investigator. These were un-momentous in the extreme, involving the painstaking tracking of the numerous niggling details that, while they rarely make the movies or TV shows, actually comprise the bulk of a detective's professional life.

Croswell conducted theft and larceny investigations, canvassed for witnesses in cases of violence or assault, interviewed crime victims, fielded reports of gambling or prostitution activity. A lot of it was screamingly mundane stuff. He rarely felt the need to carry a weapon.

Via the Carmine Galante speeding arrest, Croswell had made the connection between Joe Barbara and major organized crime figures. But keeping an eye on Barbara was only one of a myriad of activities that made up Croswell's personal to-do list. It was by no means at the forefront of his duties.

Events that fall were moving inexorably to place a busy state police investigator on a collision course with the highest levels of the American organized crime hierarchy. A seemingly minor part of his job—keeping track of a beverage distributor with unsavory associates—would blow up huge, all because of a murder that occurred in New York City, a hundred and seventy five miles away from Croswell's jurisdiction.

October 25, 1957, the Friday of his death, began for Albert Anastasia in his Fort Lee home, just across the George Washington Bridge from New York City. The place boasted a seven-foot fence topped with barbed wire. Its owner left the gates at the early hour of 7 a.m., driven in a blue Oldsmobile hardtop sedan by his twenty-nine-year-old bodyguard, Anthony "Coppy" Coppola.

According to time-ticket records, the two parked at the Corvan Garage on West 54th Street a little before 9:30 a.m. From a room key found in his pocket after he died, it was clear Anastasia had met with Tampa crime boss Santo Trafficante Jr. at the Warwick Hotel on West Fifty-forth. Albert's bodyguard Coppola, who knew Trafficante well, frequently showed up at Trafficante's Cuban casino, the Sans Souci. Coppola had rented Room 1009 in the Warwick for the Tampa mob boss's use.

With Trafficante that morning, Albert renewed his campaign to secure a toehold in the Cuban casino and smuggling rackets. He presented himself to Santo as a labor facilitator, with decades of experience as a union man. His brother Tony, a veteran labor racketeer from the Brooklyn docks, could help. He promised to utilize that know-how to smooth out any troubles with workers at the Havana Hilton, then just going up.

Anastasia pulled out all the stops. Meyer Lansky came up from Cuba to meet with him, but had left two days before. While the "Little Man" was still around, Anastasia brought in Yankee great Joe DiMaggio to the Warwick, as a sort of dog-and-pony show to wow Lansky and Trafficante. The plan was for Joltin' Joe to act as a greeter at the Hilton. It probably never would have come to pass, but the desperate Anastasia was willing to go to great lengths in his pursuit of a piece of the Cuban gold rush.

That morning, his last day on earth, Anastasia kept pushing. "Everybody's getting rich down there in Havana except me," he said.

Trafficante, inscrutable, pointed out that Albert had an interest in the Oriental Park Racetrack in Havana.

"What about the casinos?" Anastasia wanted to know. "That's where the money is."

Suddenly, Trafficante appeared to cave. After all the back-and-forth, he admitted that the Brooklyn boss deserved a piece of the Hilton. The two men hammered out a deal that seemed to give Anastasia some of what he wanted. It was odd, after being stymied for a full week, that the negotiations finally turned his way.

Albert wasn't about to question it. As the two men parted, Anastasia had the last word: "I'm the boss, I know this business best. I'll decide who's going to do what."

Trafficante left the Warwick immediately after seeing Anastasia. In a hurry, the doorman at the hotel remembered. He boarded a flight for Tampa at Idewild, then flew on to Havana.

A couple blocks from the Warwick and two and a half blocks from the Corvan Garage, the thirty-one-story Park Sheraton Hotel anchored the stretch of Seventh Avenue between West Fifty-fifth and Fifty-sixth streets, just down the avenue from Carnegie Hall.

The hotel opened as the Park Central at the height of the Roaring Twenties, and already possessed an impeccable underworld pedigree. Arnold Rothstein, head of the Jewish mob, gambler extraordinaire, got himself gut-shot in Room 349 of the Park Central on November 4, 1928. He died the next day.

By October 25, 1957, Rothstein's murder had faded to a dim memory.

There was no need for a mob boss to indulge in a superstitious avoidance of the hotel. Albert often frequented the place for his morning shave and trim. At fifteen minutes after ten, his business with Trafficante completed, Anastasia showed up at Grasso's Barber Shop off the lobby in the Park Sheraton. Coppola absented himself, taking the air on the avenue, though Anastasia was normally obsessive about security.

Joe Bocchino, the barber who worked from chair number four, dusted off its cream-leather seat for Albert. The shop itself was pure city. The BMT subway rumbled underneath the premises, and the chairs all faced a mirrored wall, behind which ran the north-side sidewalk of Fifty-fifth Street.

Albert had a full head of coarse hair, thick in back. Except for his white shirt, he was all in brown, suit, tie, and shoes ("Never trust a man in a brown suit," runs the old folk wisdom). He eased himself into chair number four. Although Anastasia customarily tucked a .32 revolver into his waistband when going out and around town, it wasn't there that day.

"Haircut," he said. Albert's last recorded word. He closed his eyes and relaxed. The shop was a full-service emporium, and Anastasia was an important man. Grasso's employed a crowd: four barbers, three shoeblacks, and a manicurist. Other customers sat for service, including, just a few feet away in chair number five, Albert's hit-man godson, Jimmy Squillante, fresh off the killing of Frank Scalise. Though it is often suggested that Anastasia was unprotected by bodyguards that morning, Squillante's presence indicated the opposite.

The manicurist, Jean Wineberger, pulled up a chair to work on the mob boss's nails. Jimmy the bootblack, who operated the shop's shoeshine concession, applied polish to his client's brogued, cap-seam Oxfords.

Dispatched by Carlo Gambino at the behest of Vito Genovese, contracted through Joe Profaci, the Gallo brothers, Joey and Larry, also happened to be in Midtown that day, also happened to be on Fifty-fifth Street, and also headed toward the Park Sheraton.

On their approach, the sibling killers walked directly past Anastasia, just a few feet away from him but concealed by the mirror-covered wall of the barbershop. They turned right off the sidewalk into the hotel's entrance, passed through two sets of glass doors, and proceeded along a corridor with a bank of elevators. Their advance once again concealed behind a wall of mirrors, the Gallos pulled up handkerchiefs to veil the lower part of their faces. Making a 180-degree turn around a corner, they entered the barbershop.

Arthur Grasso, the shop's owner, stood at his post in the cashier's booth to the right of the door. "Keep your mouth shut if you don't want your head blown off," Larry Gallo said to him.

Grasso complied.

Seeing what the sleepy-eyed Albert did not—pistols in the hands of masked thugs—the barber, manicurist, and shoeshine boy all dove to the side. Both shooters opened fire at once, Larry Gallo using a .38, Joey a .32.

At 10:17, as five bits of lead slammed into Anastasia's left palm, left wrist, right hip, neck and the back of his skull, he entered a split-second realm of illusion. He clawed at his waistband for the pistol that wasn't there. Lurching to his feet, busting the footrest of the barber's chair in which he was sitting, Anastasia lunged not at his killers but at their reflections in the mirrored wall in front of him. He dragged down a glass shelf of hair products as he fell dead. One of the bullets tumbled through his clothing to wind up in his boxer shorts.

Along with the smell of cordite and the overwhelming stench of bay rum (from a bottle the staggering Anastasia shattered), a faint tang of irony could be detected hanging in the air that morning, because the dead man had so gloried in killing throughout his long career as an enforcer, waterfront thug, labor racketeer, extortionist, and mob boss.

"Death took the Executioner," read the lead sentence in Meyer Berger's *New York Times* article on the slaying. HE DIED IN THE CHAIR AFTER ALL, noted the cheeky headline in the *Daily News*.

The Gallos fled out of the shop into the lobby, past the elevator bank in the corridor. But the doors through which they entered the hotel had locked after they passed through them. Larry ditched his .38 in the corridor. The brothers turned back through the lobby and exited out onto Fifty-fifth Street.

Outside, the duo split up. Joey headed to the south entrance of the BMT, where he dumped his .32 in a trash basket. The killers faded into the numberless crowds of Midtown. Both weapons proved untraceable, and the murder remained, officially at least, unsolved. Later, though, the Gallos boasted about it, labeling themselves a "barbershop quartet."

In the immediate aftermath of the hit, Jimmy Squillante muttered, "Let me out of here," and vanished into the same Midtown streets that swallowed the Gallos. The rest of the witnesses stayed for the arrival of police, but were of little use. They were able to talk about what happened, but could not describe the assassins much beyond "one a little taller, the other a little shorter."

All investigators really needed to know lay right there on the floor of Grasso's, the shuffled-off mortal coil of Albert Anastasia, his blood pooled and darkening beside him, his body negligently half-covered by a barber's smock. Bystanders in the crowded lobby of the hotel gave up little in the way of useful information. Likewise the absent Coppola, who was, he explained, taking the sun outside on Fifty-fifth Street when his boss got drilled.

Coppola, a wise guy in more ways than one, demonstrated the mobster equivalent of an idiot savant trick. He had memorized how to say "I don't know nothing" in nineteen different languages. Literally. It was a joke, sure, but he really did know the words, and trotted them out to the detectives investigating the murder.

In the immediate aftermath of the Anastasia hit, the barbershop at the Park Sheraton turned all its chairs around, so that they now faced the door instead of the mirrored wall of illusion.

Comedy is what's left after tragedy exits: Legendary comic Henny Youngman purchased chair number four as a souvenir, installing it as a conversation piece in the living room of his Manhattan apartment. A few months later, the comedian Buddy Hackett bought Anastasia's Bluff Road mansion in Fort Lee.

Not many tears were shed over Albert Anastasia's death, but there were some. Upon hearing of his former ally's demise, Frank Costello wept. But the emeritus leader of the mob, retired and reduced to an advisory role in Mafia affairs, found himself powerless to exact revenge.

7

Genovese Calls a Confab

AS WAS THE CASE WITH DENTISTS, say, or Shriners, every once in a while mobsters liked to flock, assembling periodically at get-togethers and conventions. The history of organized crime in America was studded with meetings, summits, conferences, and secret conclaves.

The mob always displayed an odd mix of secrecy and gregariousness. Since most people were understandably hesitant to fraternize much with gangsters, the gangsters themselves resorted to birds-of-a-feather gatherings, both to consult and socialize, forming an exclusive club, the only one that would have them as members. Highlighting the combined business and social purpose of the gang summits, many of them took place in the winter holiday season or, in one case, near the wedding date of one of the principals.

The first national meeting of the Mafia occurred in December 1928, convened at Cleveland's Hotel Statler to recognize corn sugar baron Joseph Porrello as the leader of that city's mob family. In a foreshadowing of Apalachin, local cops raided the meeting before any business could be conducted.

Five months later, in May 1929, top bosses gathered for the infamous Atlantic City conference, held to coincide with the recently married Meyer Lansky's honeymoon. That summit parsed out the organization of the underworld after the Castellammarese War. Then, in October 1931, the leadership again met, this time in Chicago's Congress Hotel, and codified the creation of the national Commission, a panel of bosses that mediated disputes and assured the smooth running of the national crime organization.

In December 1946, mobsters came together in Havana to reunite with Charles Luciano, then recently released from prison in America, deported to Italy, and sneaking into Cuba under a fake visa. Anastasia, Genovese, and others showed up to pay obeisance. Toplined on the agenda for the Havana Conference: the importation and distribution of heroin.

Now, in the fall of 1957, in the wake of Costello's bullet-enforced retirement and Anastasia's murder, the situation demanded that the mob come together once again. And if the situation didn't demand it, Vito Genovese did.

It was clearly Vito's moment. He needed validation for the ten long years he had put in, since his return from Italy after the war, on his laborious climb back to the top of the heap. The coming summit would represent not so much a meeting as a coronation.

The only question was where. A few obvious choices presented themselves. Sam Giancana, leader of Chicago's powerful crime cartel, had various venues around his home turf so firmly in control that there could be no question of police interference. Cleveland was likewise in the grip of an effective mob leader, John Scalish, and the town offered a convenient middle ground between Chicago and New York.

But in this as in other matters, La Marese got their way. Joe Bonanno, a Castellammarese who headed up one of New York's five Mafia families, represented a force that Vito Genovese had to reckon with. So he let Joe Bonanno have his way in the choice of venue for the site of Genovese's coronation. Vito could afford to be big-minded.

Joe Bonanno's cousin, Steven Magaddino, controlled the mob's operations in Buffalo, New York, surging just then from narcotics smuggling across the Canadian border. Magaddino had been the one who, in 1924, had smuggled Bonanno himself into the U.S. via Cuba and Tampa.

They called Magaddino "The Undertaker," not because of any violent acts in his past, but because that's what he was. He operated Magaddino Memorial Chapel in Niagara Falls as a cover for his mob activities. But there were, of course, many, many violent acts in his past. He first set up shop in Buffalo in August 1921, fleeing retaliation from a murder he committed in Avon, New Jersey.

Magaddino—wheedling, pressuring, calling in markers—engineered the final choice of venue for the summit. He craved recognition within the sprawling national network of organized crime. His connections had smoothed the way for the Marseilles-Montreal-New York City heroin trade. In service of this trade, he headquartered himself squarely on the border, first in Niagara Falls and then in Lewiston. Coffins provided an excellent cover.

"The Arm," as Magaddino's organization was called locally, had solid links with Ontario's "Pittsburgh of the North," the tough steel town of Hamilton, as well as a lockgrip on Buffalo's Laborers International Union Local 210, workers who handled much of the cross-border import-export traffic. Magaddino was the Mafia's man on the front lines.

According to an immigration agent, "Steve Magaddino runs everything in Niagara Falls but the cascades." In the basement of his Lewiston residence, Magaddino had a board of directors–sized table with twelve upholstered leather chairs pulled up around it. Perfect for Commission meetings.

Stocky and solid, resembling Khrushchev minus the wart, Magaddino at times displayed the surly resentment that a provincial outsider feels toward the cosmopolitan city dweller. He counted himself a big man and knew he had become a big earner, but somehow he hadn't gotten the recognition he deserved. Hosting the big mob summit was a plum, and Magaddino felt he merited a plum.

Bonanno finally agreed, and in the end, Vito Genovese just could not argue with all those heroin profits raining down on him. The summit would take place in the Buffalo mob boss's territory. Magaddino's turf, Magaddino's glory.

Joe Barbara was another La Marese *paesan*, a couple steps down the food chain, an underling to Magaddino. There had been previous mob gatherings at Joe the Barber's Apalachin compound. Sergeant Ed Croswell had stumbled into one the year before, when he interrogated Carmine Galante and investigated area hotel records after Lilo's speeding stop in October 1956.

Bonanno had been in attendance at that 1956 mini-conference. He knew Barbara's elegant stone compound, a remote country hideaway far from the prying eyes of police. Joe promised to fire up his new barbecue grill just for the coming summit, and mobsters liked a good cookout as much as anyone else. Somehow Galante's bad luck with local cops failed to impress itself on the Mafia leadership, which came around to the view that Apalachin was the perfect spot for another summit.

In another sense, the choice of Apalachin was simply an accident of mob geography, an alternate reality determined not by distance but by family connections, a world quite unlike that which is portrayed in conventional atlases. Mob America was a landscape where Dallas functioned as a suburb of New Orleans, Los Angeles as well as Kansas City were fiefdoms of Chicago, and Chicago itself was not the second city but the first.

Mob geography divided New York City by family, not borough. Cleveland and Pittsburgh both claimed Youngstown, Ohio, as their own. Cuba lost its status as an independent sovereign state to become an imperial colony of the mob. Las Vegas and Miami were both "open" cities, belonging to no one single family.

Like the famed Saul Steinberg cartoon map of Manhattan, showing the distortion through which New Yorkers view the world, the mob map of America displays an outsized layout springing from the obsessions and misrepresentations of a single isolated tribe. Organized crime challenged conventions in the national economy, yes, but it also twisted borders and topography.

Buffalo, in this scheme of things, possessed an importance all out of proportion to its size. The Buffalo mob sprawled into Rochester and Utica, reaching tentacles into Canada, Ohio and, most germane in terms of the Apalachin summit, penetrating into northwest Pennsylvania, the Pittston-Scranton-Wilkes-Barre area.

When Charles Luciano and his cohorts formalized the hegemony of the modern mob in 1931, the Mafia's first ruling Commission seated seven bosses. These included representatives from New York and Chicago, which could only be expected, but also the boss of another, smaller city, one which you might not necessarily suspect would warrant the honor. Steven Magaddino of Buffalo.

Magaddino's name stands out on that debut Mafia Commission among such worthies as Al Capone, Charlie Luciano, Joe Bonanno, and Joe Profaci. What was a humble lakeside cousin doing in this august company? But Magaddino of Buffalo controlled the smuggling routes from Canada, and that lent him enormous weight. Within the organization schema of organized crime, the Queen City, the City of Good Neighbors, the City of Light—all chamber of commerce nicknames for Buffalo—possessed a surprising primacy.

In this sense, strictly in terms of the 1950s mob geography, the choice of Apalachin had a logic all its own. Dope was becoming more and more the new reality of the mob, and Apalachin fell squarely within the territory of Magaddino, one of the country's leading dope smugglers. Concealed in trucks and cars rattling down from Buffalo, headed to New York City on Route 17, shipments of heroin completed the last leg of their long international journey.

From his country retreat nestled in the hills a mile above the highway, Joe the Barber could have waved fondly at them as they passed.

Before the big meeting, groundwork needed to be laid. Two separate, smaller mob convocations had prepared the way for the Apalachin summit, one in Sicily and one in New Jersey.

The first took place October 12–16, 1957, at the Grand Hotel et des Palmes in Palermo, Sicily. The principals: Joe Bonanno and his allies Frank Garafalo, Carmine Galante, John Bonventre, and Steven's brother Nino Magaddino. The Americans stayed at the A.G.I.P. Motel in Bonanno's old home turf of Castellammare del Golfo, awaiting the arrival of their counterparts the Sicilian Mafia, led by Giuseppe Genco Russo and his cousin, Santo Sorge. Watchful Italian police tailed Charles Luciano to the meeting.

The Sicilian authorities treated Bonanno, at least, like a lord, which was fitting since he was the most old-country of the American mob bosses, and still spoke the Sicilian dialect when at home. They quite literally rolled out the red carpet when Bonanno arrived at the airport, with the Italian foreign trade minister on hand to greet him. Around Castellammare del Golfo, especially, there was much kissing of rings. Still, Bonanno and company had to wait like supplicants until Sorge and Russo showed up.

When they did, the group repaired to the Hotel et des Palmes's Richard Wagner Suite, so called because the composer orchestrated *Parsifal* there. Amid lush baroque surroundings, the Americans and Sicilians hammered out a deal regarding heroin smuggling networks.

Bonanno proposed laying off the wholesale smuggling duties onto the Sicilians and Corsicans, using Montreal's Corsican immigrant community as a primary transshipment point. A recent addition to the U.S. criminal code spooked everyone involved in trafficking. Rendered into law on August 1, 1956, the Narcotic Control Act further criminalized the transport of drugs and instituted much harsher mandatory prison sentence minimums. Getting nailed with a kilo of heroin with intent to distribute, for example, meant an automatic twenty-year stretch.

Put bluntly, the Narcotics Control Act of 1956 gave the Mafia hierarchy the piss-shivers. More than any other factor—more than the new primacy of Vito Genovese, more than the division of Albert Anastasia's spoils, more than new bosses or irregularities in granting mob membership—the Narcotic Control Act (on wiretaps, "that fucking law") demanded a meet. In fact, it demanded two, not only at Hotel et des Palmes, but at Apalachin.

Bonanno wanted the gain from running smack, but none of the pain. The Hotel et des Palmes meeting put into place networks that kept the American mob relatively clean until it was time for actual street distribution. Since low-level soldiers, punks, and random hangers-on handled the retail level, the arrangement shielded the bosses. It was a deal that would be up for a rubber-stamp approval a month later at Apalachin.

Another presummit summit convened closer to home, at a similar luxe venue, Richard Boiardo's mansion in Livingston, New Jersey. Boiardo, the Mafia boss of Newark, was one of those crazy-mean berserkers who stand out even in a whole crew of stone-cold gangsters. As a twenty-year-old milk-man he turned his dairy route into a bookmaking sideline, and during Pro-hibition battled Jewish mobster Abner Zwillman for control of the northern New Jersey rackets.

Later Boiardo and Zwillman kissed and made up, becoming partners. Still later, Boiardo allied himself with Genovese to become one of Vito's mainstays in Jersey. From that point forward, Richard Boiardo owned New-ark. He earned his nickname "The Boot" for his love of stomping his ene-mies, pioneering the practice of "curbing"—propping a proned-out victim's head against a curb, then bringing his foot down hard enough to bust jaw, face, skull.

Wiretaps caught some of the casual sadism of the family. Boiardo's son Tony reminisced about a murder. "How about the time we hit the little Jew?"

"As little as they are, they struggle," a philosophical associate chimed in.

"The Boot hit him with a hammer," Tony Boiardo continued. "The guy goes down and he comes up. So I got a crowbar this big [and gave him] eight shots in the head. What do you think he finally did to me? He spit at me."

Equally fond were the memories of immolating a victim locked in the trunk of a car. "He must have burned like a bastard," a wiretapped voice recalled.*

Richard Boiardo's fearsome reputation and iron grip on Newark paid off rich dividends. He erected a bizarre, inordinately expensive mansion in the Wachtung foothills of Essex County, a massive confection made of imported Italian brick and stone, with gargoyles and spindly ornamental chimney stacks protruding from the roofline. The garden featured Roman-themed statuary and an equestrian rendition of Boiardo himself, done up in marble. *Life* magazine, in a double-truck spread on the mobster, labeled the style of the place "Transylvanian traditional."

---

* David Chase, creator of *The Sopranos,* modeled the HBO mob show partly upon the Boiardo crew. Chase heard tales about "Richie the Boot" from relatives in Newark's North Ward, where a cousin of his had "fuzzy connections to a prominent mob family in Livingston." Chase said about the Boiardos: "Ninety percent of [*The Sopranos*] is made up, [but] it's pat-terned after this [family]."

To Boiardo's Dracula mansion came the blood-suckers of the Genovese family at noon on Sunday, November 10, 1957. The summit in Apalachin loomed four days in the future. Vito saw the need to get his ducks in a row. Some of the topics chewed over late into the night: justifying Anastasia's murder, Carlo Gambino's elevation to the spot left vacant by Albert's demise, and smoothing out mob membership rules. The meeting broke up at five the following morning.

Together, Hotel et des Palmes and the Boiardo meet set the stage for Apalachin.

Midday on Wednesday, November 13, 1957, Ed Croswell and his partner Vince Vasisko stopped at the Parkway Motel in Vestal, New York, just west of Binghamton.

The Susquehanna River, Route 17, and the Erie Railroad all run parallel there, crowded in an east-west line along the bottom of the river valley. The single-story, white-brick motel sat on a small rise to the south of Route 17. Two miles to the west, convenient to the motel, lay the Tri-Cities Airport.

Croswell and Vasisko, both in mufti, were on the job, pursuing one of their myriad mundane investigative duties, following up on a fraudulent check charge. While speaking to Helen Schroeder, motel proprietor Warren Schroeder's wife, Croswell noticed a Cadillac limousine pull up outside.

When he saw twenty-one-year-old Joseph Barbara Jr., get out of the big land boat, Croswell reacted quickly. He pulled Vasisko into the office of the motel, out of sight but near the reception desk. The five-eleven, 235-pound Joe Junior was the image of his father, and Croswell recognized him from his extended surveillance on Barbara Senior—a period of intermittent but careful observation, which by that time had stretched to over a decade.

Croswell recognized Joe Junior, but Joe Junior failed to notice the investigator. Barbara appeared puffed-up, on important business. Mobsters often boast of their ability to smell cop, but the two men in suit jackets standing five feet away from Junior in the motel's office raised no hackles, set off no alarms. Croswell listened as the mobster's son approached Mrs. Schroeder at the front desk.

"We want three double rooms for two nights," Joe Junior said. "The best you got. I'll take the keys with me now because the people might be late coming in."

He instructed Mrs. Schroeder to charge the rooms to his dad's beverage company, Canada Dry Bottling Company of nearby Endicott. She produced the keys and asked whether Barbara Junior might register the names now to avoid delay when they arrived.

"No," Joe Jr. said. "I don't know exactly who'll they'll be. We're having a convention of Canada Dry men. We'll fix everything tomorrow."

Then he left, driving off in the big Caddie.

Given what Croswell knew about Barbara from keeping tabs on the man all those years, something about that "convention of Canada Dry men" prompted him to check on the truth of it. The two staties drove across the river to Endicott, cruising slowly past Barbara's business, the Canada Dry Bottling Company. All was quiet, the parking lot and vehicle sheds deserted.

"Wouldn't you think," Croswell said, "that if they were having a convention, there'd be a little activity?"

They took Route 17 out to Apalachin, turned off the highway through town, and climbed into the foothills on McFall Road. The stone ranch house had two sedans and a coupe parked outside it. Croswell recognized a Pontiac with New York State plates, 2W1645, as belonging to Pasquale "Patsy" Turrigiano, an Endicott grocer previously convicted of running an illegal still.

He jotted down that plate number and the numbers of the other two cars, HH4821 on a Cadillac from New Jersey and 62JL on a gaudy, coral-pink Lincoln coupe from New York. That low number on the plate struck him as noteworthy, as it usually indicated a person with power or connections.

Croswell still didn't know what he had. From Turrigiano's presence, he surmised the gathering might have something to do with Barbara's penchant for illegally producing hooch. Mobsters who had cut their teeth in the corn-sugar days of Prohibition were still at it in the fifties. It's what they knew. It's what Joe Barbara knew.

So when Croswell called in backup, he turned not to his fellow staties but to personnel from the Alcohol Tax Unit of the U.S. Treasury, summoning two agents in Binghamton he had worked with previously, Arthur Ruston and Kenneth Brown. The law enforcement personnel monitoring the doings at Joe Barbara's would now number four.

Croswell and Vasisko returned to the Parkway Motel, where they spotted another big limo, a Cadillac with Ohio plates, license number HM373. Croswell instructed proprietor Warren Schroeder to make sure the guests who showed up to take the rooms Joe Junior reserved all signed registration cards. But Schroeder had already made the request and been rebuffed.

"Joe will take care of it tomorrow," one of the guests told the manager, evidently referring to Joe, Sr.

Croswell and Vasisko again left the motel, but returned after midnight to see one of the cars from McFall Road, the Lincoln coupe with the low-numbered license plate, parked outside a room rented to the Barbaras. By that time, the teletype at the Troop C State Police substation at Vestal had given up names to match the plates. The pink Lincoln was registered to one James LaDuca, and the Cadillac from Ohio was the property of Buckeye Cigarette Service of Cleveland.

LaDuca proved to be the son-in-law of Buffalo mob boss Steven Magaddino. Buckeye Cigarette Service was a front company controlled by John Scalish, head of the Cleveland mob.

Croswell and Vasisko staked out the Parkway Motel for another two hours that night, leaving only at 2:30 a.m. after witnessing no activity. When they returned late the next morning, November 14, the Scalish Caddie remained parked but the LaDuca Lincoln was gone.

The state police detectives retraced their route from the previous day, passing the Barbara bottling plant to again find it deserted. They met up with Ruston and Brown, the revenue agents, and the four of them stopped for a late breakfast. Then they all headed up to Apalachin, Vasisko driving the unmarked state police Ford.

Croswell and company arrived at McFall Road a little after 12:30 p.m. There were many more cars than were present the previous evening, parked along the road, left at the rear of the main house, crowding the area around the compound's garage, over a dozen that Croswell could see. The sheer number of vehicles gathered at Barbara's compound forced Croswell to discard his theory regarding a possible illegal still. Something else entirely had to be going on.

It was a "we're going to need a bigger boat" moment. Two state police detectives and a couple of revenue agents weren't going to cut it. Croswell returned to his car and contacted the Troop C barracks in Vestal for another state trooper, Sergeant Walter Kennedy, to meet him in Apalachin. Then he reached out to Inspector Robert E. Denman in Sidney, New York, at Troop C's headquarters.

The call went out to other State Police substations. Traffic roadblock on McFall Road, Apalachin: assistance from all uniformed troopers in the area requested.

8

The Mob Meets

THE MOBSTERS GATHERED that day at Apalachin journeyed from all over the country to wind up at Joe Barbara's hilltop estate.

Two men, a mob attorney and a retired athletic club owner in Los Angeles, made their way east from California during the second full week of November that year, arriving in New York City on the 12th.

The lawyer, Frank DeSimone, forty-eight, had just inherited leadership of the Los Angeles crime family formerly headed by Jack Dragna. When Dragna died (in his sleep, at a comfortable old age of sixty-five), the L.A. organization decided to embrace a characteristically American method of choosing a new boss. They voted on it.

DeSimone masqueraded as a well-respected criminal lawyer who just happened to represent a lot of mob guys. Bart Sheela, a San Diego prosecutor who went up against him in court, said, "It was DeSimone's job to see to it when a Mafia figure was on trial that there was no spilling over, nothing getting out that would embarrass the mob."

After Dragna died, DeSimone conducted an aggressive but necessarily *sub rosa* campaign for the top spot. A mouthpiece trying to move into a position of leadership—not unheard of, but not common, either.

DeSimone served as a model for Tom Hagen, the lawyer-*consigliere* in Mario Puzo's *Godfather* saga. Born in what was back then the egregiously mobbed-up city of Pueblo, Colorado, DeSimone displayed none of Robert Duvall's serious cool. He won the vote, but the mob-attorney-turned-boss had a bad gut. He chewed antacid tablets obsessively.

His reign over the L.A. crime family lasted for over a decade, but one of his first acts as boss turned out to be easily his worst. DeSimone decided to heed the call for a mob meeting in New York state, introduce himself to the boys, press some flesh, get the East Coast imprimatur for his new status.

Simone Scozzari accompanied him on the trip, the manager (and operator of the cigar stand) at the Venetian Athletic Club in Los Angeles. The two were something of an odd couple, the suave, lawyerly DeSimone paired up with the older, heavily accented Scozzari, bespectacled, meek-looking, shambling along in a cheap suit, resembling a pie-hatted character actor in an Andy Hardy movie.

But the fifty-seven-year-old Scozzari could boast one crucial attribute that had him all over DeSimone. Rather than in some shitty Colorado steel town, he was born in Palermo, near Lercara Friddi, Lucky Luciano's home turf. As such, he functioned not only as underboss, bookmaker, and racketeer in the L.A. family's criminal enterprises, but also as a conduit to Luciano. He would be Charlie Lucky's eyes and ears during the East Coast sojourn and at Apalachin.

In New York, the two L.A. boys rendezvoused with DeSimone's cousin, the Louisiana-born, Texas-based dope dealer Joe Civello, himself recently ascended to the top leadership post in the old Piranio crime family of Dallas. Given mob geography, which held that Dallas existed as a suburb of New Orleans, Civello acted as boss Carlos Marcello's blade runner, underboss, and summit representative. Like DeSimone, Civello wanted to meet-and-greet the East Coast Mafia hierarchy, establishing himself as the newly fledged head of a family.

There to show the three westerners a good time in New York City was Russell Bufalino, a Scranton racketeer and a sort of unofficial cohost of the summit. Bufalino maintained his cover as an aboveboard businessman in the heavily mobbed-up area of northeastern Pennsylvania around Scranton. In reality, he was a creature of Steven Magaddino's making and a good friend of Joe Barbara. He worked for Barbara at his bottling plant in the forties, and had been to the Barbara property, just a short hop across the border of New York from Scranton, many times.

An affable columnist in a Scranton newspaper gave a portrait of Bufalino, the country squire whom he knew not as Russell, nor by his given name of Rosario, but as "Ross."

He had a brace of the finest mounts which he housed in the luxurious stables on the Barbara estate, and as we cantered the nearby South Mountain we almost always encountered the properly attired and well-seated Bufalino astride one of his thoroughbreds. Always he was urbane and suave, and if he joined us for a while, as he departed he never failed to courteously say, "Thank you for the nice ride." There was never a trace of hoodlumism.

This was the local model citizen who met the three out-of-town mobsters on November 13 at the Hotel New Yorker in the City. Bufalino drove DeSimone, Scozzari, and Civello to his home turf, putting them up overnight at the Casey Hotel in Scranton. The next morning, he shuttled the three north the sixty miles to Apalachin, driving the 1957 Chrysler Imperial that sparked Ed Croswell's interest parked alongside McFall Road. The car was registered not to Bufalino but to an associate, William Medico. They arrived at Joe Barbara's estate at 11:30 a.m.

Civello from Dallas. DeSimone and Scozzari from Los Angeles. The locally based greeter and facilitator, Russell Bufalino. This single carload of new guests for the Apalachin summit represents only one thread in a whole skein of journeys and arrivals, a coming together of mobsters from all over the country (and, a few of them, from abroad as well).

Dozens were summoned, and a hundred came, by planes, trains, and automobiles, as the old John Candy movie would have it. They hailed from thirteen states as well as Cuba and Sicily, and claimed membership in two dozen organized crime families. Almost half were related to others by blood or marriage, half were native born, half born in Italy, primarily Sicily.

Most of the New York bosses traveled by car, always in vehicles that were registered to others, as was the mob way—better deniability, more opportunities to squirm away from traffic stops. Some came with associates, some arrived alone along with their respective drivers.

- Steven Magaddino drove down from his base in Niagara Falls with son-in-law James LaDuca in the latter's snappy 1957 coral pink Lincoln. The summit had a whole hierarchy of hosts, with the actual owner of the estate, Joe Barbara, occupying the lower rung, and local boss Russell Bufalino, Brooklyn overlord Joe Bonanno, and Magaddino himself making up the rest of the hospitality pecking order.
- Family boss Joe Profaci, the Brooklyn olive oil king, an irascible man who tended to keep his own counsel, drove up with his long-suffering brother-in-law, Joseph Magliocco. Profaci owned a big hunting lodge on a 328-acre estate in New Jersey that used to belong to Theodore Roosevelt and would have been perfect for the meeting,

but the crime lord neglected to offer its use. The notoriously tight-fisted Profaci was the only Mafia boss who insisted on charging his soldiers monthly dues—$25 on the barrelhead—for the privilege of membership in the family. Small, plump, gray-haired, conservative in dress, and conspicuously religious, he could not have been an easy man to work under, perhaps the least popular leader among the five New York families. But government agents loved him, since they knew they could always easily pick up his trail at St. Bernadette's Catholic Church in Brooklyn, where he was a devoted parishioner.

- Joe Bonanno—Magaddino's cousin and, like Profaci, the boss of one of New York City's five Mafia families—hit Apalachin fresh from his participation, in September 1957, at the mob summit in Palermo, Sicily. On the evening of November 13, Bonanno flew to Bingham-ton's Tri-Cities Airport on Mohawk Airlines Flight 211 with his uncle, John Bonventre, arriving at 10:59 p.m. The trip represented a return engagement to the Southern Tier for Bonventre, who had been a passenger in the infamous Carmine Galante "speeding ticket of the decade" traffic stop. Bonanno would later claim not to have been in attendance at Apalachin at all, despite his being nabbed in a cornfield near the Barbara estate, taken to the Vestal state police substation, and positively ID'd there. His revisionist denial would earn him the sneering title, in the press, of "The Man Who Wasn't There," off the William Hughes Mearns poem: *Yesterday upon the stair/I met a man who wasn't there/He wasn't there again today/Oh, how I wish he'd go away.*"

- Another boss of one of the five families was indeed a man who wasn't there. Tommy Lucchese headed toward Apalachin at mid-day on November 14, accompanied by his driver Aniello Migliore and associate Steven LaSalle. The trio had the good luck to run late. They detected the heavy police presence long before they arrived at Joe Barbara's and subsequently tucked tail back to New York City.

- Carlo Gambino, fifty-three, heir-apparent to the Anastasia empire, arrived in Binghamton the day before the summit in a borrowed car with three other mobsters: his brother-in-law (and future mob boss) Paul Castellano, Brooklyn restaurateur Armand Rava, and Vito Genovese's right-hand man, Mike Miranda. ("You want to know who really rules New York?" Genovese asked a reporter on a visit to Italy in 1933. "It's four people: me, Lucky Luciano, Mike Miranda, and Dutch Schultz.")

- Vito himself boarded a Mohawk Airlines commuter flight and was picked up at the Tri-Cities Airport outside of Endicott by Barbara's deluxe seven-passenger Cadillac limousine, in which he rode to the host's estate.

The bosses who were non–New Yorkers, the out-of-staters, were more likely to travel by air to the summit, most of them leaving from the Newark airport on commuter flights to Binghamton.

- Tampa-Havana boss Santo Trafficante Jr. flew to Binghamton from Newark under the alias "B. Klein." He had hurriedly departed from New York City after meeting with Albert Anastasia only hours before the Brooklyn mobster's death, but resurfaced in time for the Apalachin summit, traveling from Havana to New York via his home base of Tampa.
- Sam Giancana, recently elevated to the head of the single most powerful criminal organization in the country, Chicago's Outfit, also flew to Binghamton. Giancana showed up at the summit, he later stated, "as a favor to Lansky and Costello," top mobsters who did not deign to attend. "They didn't go because they had a pretty good idea what pitch Genovese was going to make," Giancana stated. "But somebody had to be there."
- Colorado's James Colletti, operating out of the notoriously corrupt steeltown of Pueblo, suffered the indignity of driving the oldest model-year car of all the bosses at Apalachin, a 1954 Cadillac. Colletti himself did not drive the Caddie crosscountry, however, but flew to Binghamton, having had his car delivered to New York by an underling. Nicknamed "Black Jim" to differentiate him from an earlier Colorado mob boss named James Colletti, he partnered with Joe Bonanno in a Pueblo cheese factory that was a front for a narcotics trafficking operation.
- Frank Zito, based in Springfield, Illinois, the Chicago Outfit's man in the central and southern parts of the state, flew on a Mohawk commuter flight from Newark to Binghamton with Jersey motel owner Anthony Riela. Zito was fresh off being questioned in a local murder back in Springfield, the victim being a rival slot-machine

operator missing for two weeks until the man's pet collie brought his decomposed skull back home.

- Not a mob boss but a relative of one, Joe Marcello journeyed up from New Orleans as an envoy of his brother, Carlos Marcello, the "Mafia Kingfish," who ran Frank Costello's slot machines in Louisiana, handled smuggling routes from Cuba, and generally ran the rackets in the Big Easy. Together, his brother Joe and his Dallas associate Civello represented Marcello at the summit.
- John Scalish, who had been boss of the Cleveland Mafia since 1944, drove from Ohio with John Anthony DeMarco of Shaker Heights, a longtime associate and second in command in the Cleveland crime family. The tight-lipped Scalish would later distinguish himself by refusing to divulge his wife's maiden name before a Senate rackets committee, citing his Fifth Amendment rights, which prompted one senator-panelist to ask, "Are you ashamed of your own wife?"
- John LaRocca of Pittsburgh, who registered at Binghamton's Arlington Hotel as a representative of Coin Machine Distribution Company, drove to Apalachin. With him was the mobster who would take over as his eventual heir as Pittsburgh's mob boss—Michael James Genovese, Vito Genovese's cousin.

Many of the bosses who attended the summit were fairly newly minted: DeSimone, Civello, Gambino, Giancana, LaRocca. As a snake sloughs off its skin, the Mafia underwent periods of change and regeneration, and the late 1950s represented one of those times, which made the idea of a summit all the more compelling. Part of what went on at Apalachin resembled a trade conference of some automotive reps at a midlevel hotel in Akron: "Hi, I'm Frank, the new district rep for Los Angeles—good to meet you!"

Bosses, soldiers, and several important lieutenants. Gerardo Catena—the right-hand man of Joe Adonis before Joe's deportation, now one of Vito's main guys in New Jersey, a virtual Kefauver poster boy (he was mentioned sixty-six times in the committee's final report)—graced the summit with his presence. Carmine Galante showed also, risking another appearance in the neighborhood of that pesky traffic arrest that further cemented Ed Croswell's interest in the activities of Joe Barbara.

The bosses and their lieutenants came to conduct business, but there were plenty of midlevel and low-level soldiers, torpedoes and flunkies in attendance, too. Frank Majuri, forty-eight, a small-time bookmaker in the New Jersey DeCavalcante crime family, violated the terms of his probation to come up from Elizabeth. A Buffalo club owner named Roy Carlisi got picked up by the Cleveland boys, Scalish and DeMarco, and came to Barbara's place with them. Another Buffalo resident, Sam LaGattuta—identified as a "self-employed painter"—traveled to the meeting with four Utica mobsters.

The out-of-state guests had a convenient, if a little shabby, mob-owned stopover. Anthony Peter Riela managed a hot-sheet hostel near the Newark Airport that had been cited many times for vice-related charges, including a November 1955 charge of "maintaining a nuisance and permitting prostitution on premises."

To the louche digs of Riela's Airport Motel, Port Newark, New Jersey came a number of mafiosi from around the country to spend a few nights midweek in the days before the summit. The short, stocky Riela hosted James Colletti of Colorado, jukebox kingpin Joe Zito of Springfield, Illinois, and a dozen other summit participants, taking a pause prior to their commuter flight to Apalachin. When they flew north, innkeeper Riela tagged along.

A number of mob figures from nearby areas arrived: the Valenti brothers, Frank and Stanley, from Rochester, and the Falcone brothers, Salvatore and Joseph, from Utica. The Pittston-Scranton-Wilkes-Barre nexus sent several favorite sons. Locals, too—Joe Barbara's friends and subordinates from the nearby Triple Cities of Binghamton, Endicott and Johnson City: Anthony "Guv" Guarnieri, Patsy Turrigiano, and Emanuel Zicari.

The summit guest list bulged and burgeoned to the degree that Joe Barbara had to put his foot down: men only. Leave your wives, girlfriends, and dates at home. If Barbara started allowing guests to bring guests, the thing would spin out of control. He had a large estate, but it wasn't quite a full-blown resort.

Men only, and also only Italian men of a certain vintage. The average age was fifty-three years. *Paesanos, compares,* friends of ours. One exception was a luckless fellow with the perfect name of Melvin J. Blossom, an E-J worker moonlighting as caretaker to the Barbara estate, with perhaps an Irish or Scottish background, he didn't really know, also the rare person present that rainy November day without an arrest record.

So it was that after all the contracting and retracting and pulling in of tentacles, after the trains, planes, and automobiles deposited the most powerful collection of American mobsters ever assembled in one place, out of all the people gathered at the compound during the summit, only the help were not Italian, and only two—Josephine Barbara and her housekeeper, Marguerite Russell—were women.

At a little before noon that Thursday, the drizzle stopped, but the skies still did not clear. Almost all of the summit participants had already arrived. For a brief half hour the gathering stood poised before disaster. At first no one noticed the plainclothes lawmen nosing around the property, a short distance down McFall Road.

Then a fish deliveryman who had just left the compound turned around and came back. The bosses, sitting in the big pine-paneled living room of the main house, and the two women in the kitchen, could hear the fishmonger outside. He called out to the boys standing near the big stone barbecue and the ones sitting in the screened-in summer house.

"Roadblock," Bartolo Guccia said.

9

Croswell Makes His Move

ED CROSWELL WAITED as the big Chrysler Imperial nosed toward where he stood in the middle of McFall Road, just at the property line of the Barbara estate. One thirty in the afternoon that Thursday, still overcast, still drizzly.

A few minutes earlier, Croswell had done a sly thing. He allowed the first car that left the estate, a Lincoln with two men inside, to pass by without stopping. There was a method to this. He was well aware that the men gathered at Joe Barbara's were watching him watch them. They wanted to see what he would do.

So Croswell let that first car by, thinking it might lull those at the estate into a false sense of confidence, that they could leave the estate without being stopped. He didn't neglect to radio the passing Lincoln's license plate number, to make sure it would get picked up farther down the road.*

The ruse worked. As soon as the mobsters saw the first car pass through, a general exodus began. Big limos began to pull out of the lot next to the garage, one after another, more and more cars, emerging from the parking area in front of the garage and moving slowly, as though in a funeral cortege.

Croswell had a quick, worried thought: *There are too many of them.* He had sent Vasisko down the hill to organize additional roadblocks. He was alone with the revenuers, Art Ruston and Ken Brown.

When the Chrysler Imperial pulled up, Croswell walked around to the

---

* The two men in the first car were Endicott local Emanuel Zicari and a labor official named Dominick Alaimo, from nearby Pittston, PA. They were stopped by State Police on Route 17, three miles east of Apalachin.

passenger side. He didn't immediately recognize the fleshy, thick-lidded man wearing yellow-tinted eyeglasses as Vito Genovese. In the driver's seat sat Russell Bufalino, the Scranton-based racketeer who helped host the gathering at Joe Barbara's, while in the car's cavernous back were three others, all from New Jersey: Philly car dealer-cum-mob boss Joe Ida, Camden gangster Dominick Oliveto, and Vito's Jersey underboss, Gerardo Catena.

"You've all been at Mister Barbara's?" Croswell asked. "What were you doing there?"

Genovese pulled a long face. "He is very sick, the poor man. We just came to wish him a speedy recovery."

The mob boss paused, and then said to Croswell, almost gently: "But I don't have to answer these questions, do I?"

Croswell didn't reply. He requested IDs, which the mobsters readily gave up. They fished their driver's licenses from their shirt pockets, Croswell noticed, as if they had prepared beforehand to meet police. Asked if he had an arrest record, Vito refused to say. Croswell requested a look into the Chrysler's trunk.

"I'm just driving them to the airport," Bufalino offered.

The Cadillac that idled a few feet behind them showed itself packed with passengers, too, blank-eyed faces staring stonily ahead through the rain-spattered windshield. In back of it, more cars pulled up with more mobsters.

A single state cop and a couple federal tax agents against how many? Dozens. Croswell felt the prickly awareness of being outnumbered. A scene like this could get ugly real quick. It was important not to let them see him sweat.

As Croswell went around to get at the trunk of the Imperial, Ruston assumed his post next to Vito. Still keeping the tone light, the mob boss said, "I'll only answer questions about how tall I am."

"Well, how tall are you?" Ruston asked, willing to play the straight man.

"Five-eight," Vito said. This was a lie. He was five-seven, maybe, and only if he were standing atop his money roll. But he hewed to the principle of never, ever telling the truth to police, about anything, at any time, even about an innocuous question of height. Vito was of the Frank DeSimone school, the Los Angeles mob leader who once took the Fifth when asked the name of the current president of the United States.

Croswell slammed shut the trunk and returned to the front passenger window.

"Go about your business," he said.

Croswell decided to let the cars through. There were a lot of them now, a dozen, backed up toward the house, too many for him to process. He would allow those gathered at Barbara's to leave, to be picked up by State Police at roadblocks lower down the hill, at access points to Route 17.

The stopping of the Imperial had triggered another kind of exodus, a flight on foot across the fields surrounding the estate. Croswell watched the men leave from the big stone house, not running, but tromping along single file, slump shouldered, resembling a retreating army troop, heading, most of them, southeast. He worried about all the "George Rafts" disappearing into the thick deciduous woods blanketing the flank of South Mountain, and hoped the dragnet would be tight enough to pick them up, too.

A dairyman named Ray Martin worked outside on his farm that rainy Thursday, mucking out the yard behind his barn. The farmer loved his place, hidden, as it was, in the hills above Apalachin. Few people ever came there unless it was the tanker come to collect his milk. Martin's farm was secluded, and that was exactly the way its owner liked it.

Suddenly, out of the woods to the west, two immaculately dressed, middle-aged men fought their way out of the underbrush and practically tumbled into Ray Martin's lap.

"That was something I didn't see every day," Martin said later. "It scared me."

The two rushed up to him, breathless.

"Which way to Pennsylvania?" one of the men asked. The other requested a ride to the nearest train station. They were agitated, confused. Their good, citified clothes had become muddy and wet from the woods.

Perhaps the strangers meant Pennsylvania Avenue, a mile south, or maybe Pennsylvania itself. The state line was indeed only less than five miles away, but Martin couldn't help them. In fact, he was so stunned he couldn't get his mouth to work. For a long beat he just stood and stared.

The men didn't seem inclined to wait around for the laconic farmer to collect his wits and speak. As quickly as they came, they vanished down the dirt road to the farm, heading north toward town. Afterward, Martin recalled carefully watching them go, fixing them in his mind so he could be sure they had actually been there at all.

"I didn't want to think my mind was playing tricks," he said.

The two men were Frank Majuri and Louis Larasso, both hailing from New Jersey, both union reps there. Majuri, listed as vice president in Labor

Local 364, Elizabeth, had assorted robbery, moonshining, and bookmaking raps on his record, while Larasso held a trustee post in a New Jersey Laborers and Hod Carriers union.

Small-time, midlevel Mafia soldiers. After a July 1956 bookmaking conviction and a *non vult* plea, Majuri was under a probation order in New Jersey that banned him from leaving the state without permission from the government. A free-floating fact that came to light later indicated he might be more connected than was first assumed. When L.A. lawmen poked through Jack Dragna's notebooks after they arrested the crime boss in 1950, Frank Majuri's name had turned up.

Majuri and Larasso were at the big barbecue at Joe Barbara's when they joined the mass exodus into the woods surrounding the estate.

The magic word "roadblock" pronounced by Bartolo Guccia triggered the flight response in almost all the mobsters attending the summit, but only about a quarter of them took off on foot.

To cite a contemporary account out of the *Newark Star-Ledger*: "They fled like ballet belles in pursuit of the faun." A more sober account comes from the revenue agent, Ken Brown, who said he saw "eight or ten men walking single file" from the rear of the estate toward the woods.

Croswell ordered a newly arrived trooper, Frederick Tiffany, to fire his .45-caliber service revolver into the air as a warning to the fleeing mobsters. Tiffany did so, becoming the sole source of gunfire on a day fraught with tension but featuring no other outright gunplay.

Joe the Barber's fifty-eight acres sprawled onto the north-side slopes of South Mountain—only a hill, really, rising twelve hundred feet above the Susquehanna River—and he had carefully groomed the forests of ash, beech, oak, and pine with a series of rough, single-track riding trails. For anyone not properly shod with heavy boots ("I knew they were hoodlums," Ed Croswell said, "because of all the polished pointed-toe shoes"), Thursday would prove a miserable day to go stumbling around in the woods.

All the bridle trails looped back to the house, so in order to get anywhere, bushwhacking was the only option. The rains rendered the thick carpets of autumn leaves wet and slippery, concealing rocks and roots that were perfect for tripping over. Apalachin Creek cut off the most obvious escape route, east to Pennsylvania Avenue. Likewise, barbed-wire fences sliced through the property to the west, corralling the cows on Martin's farm, but making a breakout in that direction problematic.

The two city boys from Jersey did well enough at first. Though they picked up plentiful burrs and sticktights on their overcoats, they at least made it through the woods to what passed for civilization. After leaving the farm, walking northward on the dirt road, Majuri and Larasso encountered another local, one not so tongue-tied as farmer Martin. Glen Craig lived in a small trailer home.

"We came up from New Jersey, out here looking for real estate," Majuri told him. "What would you take for your trailer?" They wanted a vacation place, he explained, for hunting and fishing.

Craig thought there was something wrong with the two. They didn't seem serious. They were jumpy, constantly on the lookout. Craig didn't know what to make of them. "How about we offer you eight thousand dollars, but what if you say you want eight-thousand-five?" Majuri told him.

What was that supposed to mean? Majuri immediately switched tracks, telling Craig they'd pay him a sawbuck to take them into Binghamton. He flashed a big enough money roll that Craig immediately agreed. But the guy kept on repeating the bit about the funny real estate deal. Climbing into Craig's pickup truck, Majuri again said, "We offered eight, but you wanted eight-five, okay?"

At the bottom of McFadden Road, the situation became a little clearer. Trooper Thomas Sackel waited there, loaded them all into his black-and-white, and took them to the Vestal State Police substation.

It would take a full eight hours, until well past dark, for the State Police to round up all the mobsters who had fled into the forest. The haul represented one sorry-ass group of city boys. "There are no sidewalks in the woods," Croswell observed drily.

The smart money lay on those patient guests at Joe Barbara's who simply stayed put in the main house, didn't run, but waited it out. These included Sam Giancana, Tony Accardo, Carmine Galante, Steven Magaddino, Joe Marcello—names that never numbered on the lists of the sixty mobsters swept up in Croswell's net. They somehow understood the most difficult to learn of all tactical lessons, that at times the best course of action is inaction.

But the atmosphere remained fraught. They stayed put, yes, but the wait for the police pounding on the front door was excruciating. Likewise, the ignorance of what was going on outside. Giancana and company remained blind. In any battle, lack of intel is the most crippling state of affairs. They simply had to sit their asses down in Joe Barbara's cushy living room. Hanging around for what? For the hammer to fall? Or for their sweet release?

And what had happened to Vito, the one who had summoned them to Apalachin in the first place? He had left the house in Bufalino's Chrysler and then been stopped by the staties. But judging from the far-off glimpse that could be had from the kitchen windows, he and his fellow passengers in the car had been allowed to drive on.

The roadblocks, the sweep, the interrogations, the humiliations at the hands of the police—none of that could be known for certain by the ones left behind. They could only imagine, and what the human imagination comes up with is almost always pretty woeful. By two o'clock, it had become apparent that the State Police had no warrants to enter the private premises of the compound. The ones who had waited it out were, for the time being, safe.

A little after two p.m., Joe Barbara Jr. returned home from the bottling factory in Endicott, bringing news from the outside world. To get to the house he drove past two roadblocks, including one staffed by Croswell, Ruston, and state-police reinforcements.

His old man didn't look too good. "Everything is okay," Joe Sr. told him. Everything is okay? Really? Pay no attention to those men in the State Police uniforms lining the drive. Go back to the plant. Which is what Joe Jr. tried to do.

But while visitors were allowed to enter the Barbara estate, they weren't free to leave. Croswell and company detained Joe Jr. as soon as he hit the roadblock at the bottom of the hill.

The pasty, sweaty complexion of the summit host that afternoon was soon explained. Joe Barbara was dismayed at how disastrously his party had been crashed. But something else was going on, something not emotional but physical. His heart had been killing him all year, first from a major coronary in January, followed by other incidents, painful after-tremors following the big earthquake. The walls of the man's ventricles were paper thin, flabby, weak, his arteries clogged by waxy fat deposits from too much good living.

Minutes after his son left the house that afternoon of the summit, Joe Barbara had another heart attack.

No man picked up in the aftermath of Apalachin better symbolized the mob's infiltration into the mainstream world than a Buffalo businessman named John C. Montana. Well known in his hometown as owner of a taxi company and a liquor dealership, a pillar of the community who volunteered on the boards of multiple charity organizations, Montana's 1956 Buffalo

"Man of the Year" award, "for outstanding contribution to the civic advancement of the city," had been extended to him by the Erie Club, a police beneficence organization devoted to children and widows of patrolmen.

He had been made rich by his connections. His livery company, with revenues in excess of $1 million annually, had the taxi monopoly at the Buffalo airport. A liquor distributorship he owned claimed assets of $300,000 when it was incorporated in 1949, with a Republican state congressman serving as its stockholder-director. Montana had failed twice in his attempt to get a liquor license because of felons among the company officers, but refiled and was successful courtesy of his lawyer, Republican majority leader Walter J. Mahoney.

For a guy who started out his working life as a kid messenger in a candy factory, Montana's curriculum vitae made him out to be an inveterate overachiever. Director of the local minor league baseball franchise. Owner of Montana Race Horse Stables. Honorary head of the local chapter of the Humane Society. Active in Community Chest and Red Cross fund drives. Republican representative to the 1938 state constitutional convention. Two-time Buffalo councilman-at-large.

"I'm a joiner," he explained later, when his extra-legal activities came to light.*

The civic paragon drove down from Buffalo to Apalachin in his new Cadillac, chauffeuring one of his Mafia masters, Nino Magaddino, brother to boss Steven Magaddino. Montana and Nino were two of the nymphs who fled the gathering by hauling ass into the woods.

When he was picked up by Agent Brown and Trooper Sackel, Montana presented one of the more memorable images of a memorable day. The sixty-four-year-old Montana had gotten himself embarrassingly hung up on one of Farmer Martin's cow fences, his expensive camelhair overcoat tangled and caught, the precious Montana family jewels dangling just inches above the barbed wire.

Agent Art Ruston collared Nino Magaddino, overweight and out of

---

* A complete list of Montana's memberships is exhausting even to read: Chamber of Commerce, Elks Club, Buffalo Athletic Club, Isaak Walton League, Erie Down Golf Club, Fred Grenier Republican Club, Simon Siderie Republican Club, Paul Revere Republican Club, Buffalo Society of the Natural Sciences, Transit Valley Country Club, Buffalo Hotelman's Association, National Association of Taxi Cab Owners (past president), Buffalo Passenger Assocation, Canadian Biltmore Club, Half Century Club, State Association of Taxi Cab Owners (past president), Buffalo Federation of Italian-American Societies (president for five years), and chairman of the Buffalo Zoning Board.

breath, as he fled across a cow field. "Why are you running?" Ruston asked.

"I just stopped to see Joe Barbara"—puff, puff, wheeze—"he was sick"—puff, puff, wheeze—"and Montana's car broke down."

A few mobsters actually managed to make it out of the woods and avoid police to escape. Giancana claimed he was one, but the account, recorded in a book by his brother, is not particularly credible. All indications are that he simply waited out the police presence in Barbara's living room.

One who did evade capture was able to do so because he had intimate knowledge of the landscape around the Barbara estate. Modesto "Murph" Loquasto, one of Bufalino's bodyguards, had ridden the trails many times. Loquasto hid in the woods, then made the twelve miles to the airport, took a plane to Buffalo, and returned by train to Pittston. But he was a rare exception. Taking to the woods proved mostly to be a dead end.

A basic but wide-ranging transformation occurred when Croswell and company busted up the summit. The facade crumbled. The mask got ripped away. The Man of the Year was revealed as a cat's paw of the mob. Joe Bonanno showed himself as a lying fool. Joe Profaci wasn't just the Olive Oil King of Brooklyn and a devout parishioner at St. Bernadette's, he was a vile racketeer who could cause immense misery and pain whenever he lifted his hand.

On and on the list went, the charade penetrated, the disguise exposed. Santo Trafficante and Carlo Gambino were nabbed in the woods near Apalachin Creek by Trooper Tiffany. John Bonventre was picked up by Sackel and Brown in the cornfield just down Rhodes Road from where Montana got hung up. Troopers Smith and Teneyck swept up Colorado's James Colletti on Little Meadows Road, west of the Barbara property.

Mike Miranda, Joe Ida, Natale Evola, Gerardo Catena, Paul Castellano—the haul from the woods and roads around Apalachin included, as British journalist Alistair Cooke once put it, "a chamber of commerce of crime." It took the combined labors of a dozen staties to round up all the mobsters who had fled on foot into the outback.

The rout was so general, so contagious, that an employee of Barbara's who resided in one of the cottages at the estate, laborer Norman Russell, got caught up in the panic, fleeing his own home. I don't care if I do live here, I'm getting the hell out.

Busting up the summit did more than turn over the mob's rock. The exposure also shone a bright light on regions heretofore left dark. Testimony comes from inside the Mafia as to just what a killing blow Apalachin turned out to be.

"It was horrendous," wrote Joe Bonanno in his autobiography, *Man of Honor*. "All those men caught in the same place, a ton of publicity, a public-relations coup for law enforcement, a field day for journalists."

"The lid had been blown off our world," wrote Bill Bonanno, Joe's son, "and there was no way to put it back." The year "1957" was forever afterward burned into the Mafia's hide like a brand.

But it's hapless John C. Montana, no one's idea of a mob boss but rather an alabaster citizen, who somehow stands out from all the other trout. Not only for his barbed-wire balancing act, but for the elaborate facade he had been able to maintain over the years.

A troubling shadow passed behind the eyes of the American public when they heard about that one. If a man such as John Montana showed up corrupt and connected, who is to say that any city councilman—or alderman, Rotary chairman, legislator, church deacon, civic booster, next-door neighbor, anybody at all—wasn't also suspect?

The mobsters rounded up at Apalachin were ferried in loads of five or six to the State Police substation on Route 17 in Vestal, ten miles away, on the western outskirts of Binghamton. A few of them were taken in their own cars, a trooper riding along to make sure they got there. The small lobby of the substation soon got extremely crowded. The interior atmosphere became close. A faint smell of smoke hung in the air, wafting from the clothes of the detainees who had been standing around Joe Barbara's barbecue pit.

The exact number held by State Police that day was always in question. The *New York Times* reported sixty-five, other newspapers had fifty-eight or sixty-two. The confusion stemmed from those taken at Barbara's estate and additional detainees from traffic stops on roads and highways around Binghamton. These included Kansas City mob boss Nick Civella and his driver, Joseph Filardo, who were ID'd by cab companies but never officially detained.

The correct tally, according to both Croswell and Sergeant Joe Benenati, the two officers in command at Vestal, was an even sixty.

Technically, no one had yet been arrested. The summit mobsters were, to split a legal hair or two, detained. The law is an odd combination of vague and firm in regard to how long a suspect may be held by police without an

arrest, meaning without charges being filed. There is no proscribed number of hours, and the rules vary from jurisdiction to jurisdiction. The period is not indefinite, and is held to last only as long as it "reasonably takes
police to conduct the investigation."

Twenty-four hours has been widely used as a rule of thumb, but New
York had a twelve-hour deadline, state law requiring arraignment within
that time. The clock began ticking at around two p.m. on Thursday afternoon.

Those detained were processed by Croswell, Benenati, and other State
Police personnel. They were identified, questioned, and searched. "What
were you doing at Barbara's?" the staties asked the mobsters. Visiting a sick
friend, most of them said. Poor Joe had a heart attack recently. We all
wanted to wish him well. Nothing was planned. It was just a coincidence,
everybody showing up at the same time.

A lame story, but one the assembled Mafia members stubbornly stuck
to, no matter how much the police tried to shake it. Croswell and company
kept looking for something, anything that would allow them to make arrests. But they found no guns, no drugs, no contraband.

The Mafia, it turned out, had learned from its mistakes in the past.
When the December 26, 1928 meeting at a Cleveland hotel got busted, thirteen guns turned up, and a dozen mobsters were charged with illegal weapons possession. (Some of those detained at Apalachin had been among
those rousted in Cleveland almost three decades before, including Bonanno,
Profaci, and Profaci's driver, Magliocco.)

This time around, no one came heavy. Police confiscated not a single
weapon during their search of cars and persons at Apalachin.

Nevertheless, when one after another the mobsters turned out their
pockets at Vestal, a lot of interesting stuff materialized.

Money, for one thing, in cash and in great abundance. A lot of rubber
bands wrapped around a lot of fat rolls of greenbacks. The sixty detainees
possessed between them over three hundred thousand dollars. The record
was held by Scozzari, the L.A. import who held Italian citizenship and was
tied to Charles Luciano. His pockets yielded a grand total of $10,000, al-
though not all of it in cash. John Ormento, the East Harlem narcotics king,
ponied up $1,641, while union rep and bookie Frank Majuri had $450.

A few other noteworthy tidbits. Joseph Profaci's wallet contained the
business card of Larry Gallo, one of the Anastasia shooters. No one was
able to make the connection right then. That would come later. New Jersey
gambling boss Gerardo Catena and others carried tote slips scrawled with

numbers. Several of the detainees had business cards from the Airport Motel in Newark. Utica boss Joe Falcone kept a single battered playing card, an ace of spades, secreted in his otherwise empty wallet, which he had carefully cleaned out before having to face police.

Nothing illegal, nothing actionable. It wasn't a crime to carry large amounts of cash. As the afternoon wore on, it became clear that some sort of decision had to be made. This was America, and not wartime America, either. Soon enough, lawyers would come pouring through the doors of the substation, writs in hand.

Troopers worked the phones, racing against time to try to discover if any of the detainees had warrants outstanding. Arrests, violations, skipped paroles, anything, even a traffic charge would do. But in those days no central felony clearinghouse existed, no easily consulted computer database. Records had to be laboriously checked by hand. It took days, weeks. The substation's teletype chugged away, but nothing of use came out of it.

Croswell called up the FBI field office in Albany. Might the Bureau be interested in the largest collection of wise guys ever assembled in one place, currently under State Police guard in Vestal? No, he was told, the FBI was not interested.

And it wasn't just the FBI. The administration of the New York State Police also showed itself to be studiously oblivious to what Croswell had on his hands, even right after the raid. The higher-ups communicated a dispiriting message: Sergeant Croswell, you are on your own.

Hurried conferences in the Vestal back offices. Discussions about what charges they might possibly have to hold the men. Vagrancy, the desperate cop's time-honored fallback, was clearly out—not only because of all the money rolls, but because Broome County did not, in fact, have a vagrancy statute. Across the line in Tioga County, where the Barbara estate was actually located, a law was on the books, but that struck Croswell as grasping at straws.

Some talk centered around Section 722 of the state criminal code, which made it a crime for those of "evil reputation" to "consort with thieves and criminals," and held that such consorting itself represented prima facie evidence of a crime.

The afternoon wore on, the dark descending on the hills of the Susquehanna River valley. Croswell felt himself under a great deal of pressure. The switchboard at the substation lit up as calls began to come in, not only from the press but from law enforcement in other jurisdictions, interested in this or that big fish netted at the summit.

Ultimately, Croswell decided there was nothing for it. The ad hoc operation would simply have to be a catch-and-release-style sting. The police could file no charges because the men gathered at Joe Barbara's had not committed any crime. Some dismay and a little anger set in among the assembled troopers when the realization set in that those detained simply had to be processed and let go.

10

The Big Roundup

SITTING IN THE BACKSEAT of a police car at the roadblock, Man of the Year John C. Montana displayed himself as a contrite man. But it was difficult to discern if he was sad to be a front man for the mob or just sad to get caught at it.

"I'm very embarrassed at being here," he said when Croswell approached him. He told the first of many lies, maintaining that he "was not invited to the party."

He knew important people, Montana told his interrogator. He began dropping names. Richard Nixon, he said, then vice president, was "a personal friend." Governor W. Averell Harriman had him and his wife to dinner at the governor's mansion in Albany. He mentioned a State Police captain in the Batavia barracks near Buffalo, suggesting that Croswell contact him "to see what kind of man I am."

Ed Croswell already had a pretty good idea what kind of man John C. Montana was, simply by the company he kept, surmising that the slim, gray-haired gent before him, dressed in a conservative double-breasted suit, was in fact one mobbed-up son of a bitch. But Montana continued to whine, almost weeping.

"Please, just let me go up and get my car and get out of here. I might be able to do something for you." A bribe offer? Montana let the hint drop and babbled on. Again, more names dropped—judges, federal and state officials. Yes, he had lot of friends in high places, but when Croswell asked, Montana denied knowing either Vito Genovese or the recently deceased Albert Anastasia.

"We found you hung up on a wire fence," Croswell said. "Why did you run?"

"I was anxious to take myself away from trouble," Montana said.

He explained his presence at the summit this way. He was driving from Buffalo to Pittston on business when his brakes started to feel mushy and his windshield wipers quit. He was ten miles from the Barbara house. Montana thought Joe Barbara, whom he said he knew as a local businessman, might be able to hook him up with a mechanic.

When he arrived at the house, he saw "thirty or forty" men gathered around the barbecue pit between the summer house and the garage. He paid them no mind, Montana told Croswell, instead heading directly into the main house.

"I had an awful chill," Montana said. "I asked Mrs. Barbara to fix a cup of tea for me."

The Man of the Year maintained he spoke to the host only briefly, just to ask after his health. He said that Joe Barbara was busy, "in and out like a fly." Joe wanted to know if Montana, who ran a liquor franchise in Buffalo, could help him unload $10,000 worth of beer cluttering up his warehouse.

That was it, that was all. Montana didn't know anything about anybody else at the house that day. Him showing up there was just a coincidence. Just one of those strange mishaps that occur in life.

Ed Croswell was well familiar with the perennial plight of the cop, which involved a lot of sitting around listening to people lie to him all day. Still, the bald-faced nature of this particular tall tale shaded toward the outlandish.

For starters, Croswell the car man knew the odds were remote that a brand-new Caddie would develop brake and wiper trouble on the same trip. In the 1950s, luxury vehicles were built like tanks. That's exactly what customers paid for, not to have car trouble every time you pulled it out of the garage.

For another thing, Croswell had been hearing variations on the same story from everybody he questioned. To a man, no one had planned to be at Joe Barbara's manor house. They just . . . fell by. No invitations, no nothing, just an altruistic need seizing everyone at once, an urge to see their old friend Joe, sick with heart disease.

Two possibilities: the laws of chance and the rules governing randomness in the universe had somehow been suspended that day, or the mobsters had all agreed to tell the same lie. Croswell didn't have much difficulty choosing which possibility was more likely.

In police custody at Vestal, most of the summit participants put up more stonier fronts than the sniveling Montana. "What were all those people doing at your father's house?" Croswell asked Joe Barbara Jr.

"I'm not going to answer your questions," Junior said. And he didn't.

The Vestal barracks represented a second home for Croswell. He spent a lot of time there in the wee hours, sleeping in a bare-cell style of accommodation, watching the moonrise over Bunn Hill.

Now he glanced around the substation lobby, his turf, his house, two rooms in front and two in back connected by a hallway, fifteen-hundred square feet now crowded with five dozen sullen, disheveled detainees. They were gunless and guarded by a score of New York state troopers, who forced the mobsters to sit on the floor, hands kept painfully propped on their heads for hours, waiting their turn at processing. Some of them were mudcaked from romps in the woods. All were pretty well emasculated.

"We gave them a rough time at the station house," Croswell said. "But we couldn't even make them commit disorderly conduct down there."

Still, a touch of menace hung in the air. The detainees were surly, although they stayed disciplined, just on the safe side of the line. No one loud, no one disruptive.

The processing of the Apalachin participants took awhile. Croswell insisted on talking to each man. Between interrogations, fielding calls from other police, and talking to newspaper reporters, Croswell had gone a little raw in the throat. Still he stayed at it. Afternoon turned to evening, and yes, a thin last-quarter moon did indeed rise just before midnight, but no one saw it, because the night remained overcast. The sorting out of all the mobsters wore on.

Simone Scozzari had the biggest bankroll, if you counted the $8,455 cashier's check he had. "Would you mind telling me what you were doing at Mister Barbara's?" Croswell asked him.

"Not at all," the gnome-like Sicilian said. "I knew poor Joe was sick and I decided to come up and visit him."

"What, all the way from Sicily?"

"No, no," Scozzari said. "Just from Los Angeles. That's where I've been recently." He hadn't come five thousand miles, in other words, to wish poor Joe well. Just two thousand.

Croswell pushed a little more. "But what were all of these people doing there?"

"I guess we just happened to have the same idea at the same time."

Same old, same old. The sergeant let the little man with the big cashier's check go.

It neared two a.m. on Friday when Croswell got around to the last of the detainees, Steven Magaddino's son-in-law, Frank LaDuca. After being picked up in a car with Cleveland boss John Scalish, LaDuca had waited as five dozen others went through the wringer and walked out the door.

Secretary-treasurer of the Hotel and Restaurant Workers Union, Local 66 in Buffalo, with a clean record apart from a couple traffic citations, LaDuca started out as a driver with Montana's taxi company. Croswell knew the man carried some sort of weight in the Mafia hierarchy, since he had found LaDuca's business card on Joe Bonanno when the Brooklyn mob boss had been searched earlier.

As befitting someone who drove a coral pink Lincoln, LaDuca normally played the friendly hail-fellow-well-met. He liked to joke with cops. Later in his checkered racketeering career, he told federal agents a story about going to *The Godfather* movie. The ticket cashier told him the theater was sold out. "You've got to let me in," LaDuca pleaded. "This movie is about my family."

The mobster hadn't been that jolly that evening at Vestal. He wasn't at the summit, he said, didn't know anybody there, would never know anything about anything. Croswell asked where LaDuca's own car was, seeing how he had been nabbed in one bearing Ohio plates. LaDuca said his was parked in his driveway in Lewiston.

"What if I told you we saw yours yesterday at a motel here in Binghamton?" Croswell asked.

LaDuca barely hesitated. "Then it must have been stolen, because I know for a fact I left it in my driveway at home."

Croswell had also seen LaDuca's hard-to-miss Lincoln at the Barbara's estate when he performed a drive-by the evening before the summit. But it hadn't been picked up in the sweep and was nowhere to be found. Croswell wondered where the car could be hidden.

From receipts carelessly discarded in the wastebasket at LaDuca's room at the Parkway Motel, he could trace the mobster's progress for the past week. From November 7–11, he had been registered at New York's Lexington Hotel. While there, he telephoned Utica Mafia boss Joseph Falcone four times. Then he registered at the Utica Hotel on Tuesday, November 12, before winding up at the Parkway in Vestal on Wednesday night before the summit.

I know all about you, Croswell thought, questioning LaDuca. *But you don't know anything about me.* He resolved to track down the coral pink Lincoln. It had to be somewhere in the area. There were only a few possibilities.

LaDuca went out the door of the Vestal station at two a.m. on Friday, November 15. A little over twelve hours had passed since Croswell first confronted Vito Genovese in the big Imperial on McFall Road.

But the fun, if it could be called that, was only just beginning. Croswell would be up and hard at it straight through until Saturday evening, a sixty-hour stretch without sleep. He would repeat his story of busting up the summit dozens of times, with countless more recitations to come. To the public at large, he would become the face of Apalachin.

Around the State Police barracks, they used to call Ed Croswell the "tall ghost" for his stature and taciturn presence. As of two a.m. Friday, he might have been finished, for the time being, with the gangsters themselves. But the weight of the world would soon bear down on him, everyone wanting a piece—lawyers and lawmakers and journalists and critics. The tall ghost would turn even more ghostly, holding up gamely but suffering under the stress, his gut twisting into knots.

Would it be worth it? Would he have driven up McFall Road that Thursday noon if he had known what he was getting into?

Though he didn't realize it yet, in the days ahead a vicious campaign of second-guessing lay in wait for Croswell. He would be attacked for his actions at Apalachin, slammed in the press and, eventually, by the courts. And he would come to say about the reality of being a cop: "It's a good life, but it's a lonely one."

The sleepy little hamlet of Apalachin suddenly found itself overrun with outsiders. Teacher Edith Meyerman met up with several "well-dressed" men at the door of the local school as she headed into the principal's office to check for mail.

"Could we use a telephone to call a taxi?" one of the men asked. Principal Morris Cope thought the strangers were somehow connected to a construction project going on nearby, so he allowed them the use of the school's phone. The local switchboard operator had meanwhile gotten swamped with requests and reports about all the activity in the area, the big cars, the police roadblocks.

Ed Croswell wasn't the only person using field glasses that bleak November afternoon. At her simple clapboard home in the village, where

McFall intersected East River Road, Mrs. Joseph Valentino heard the ruckus outside her front door and got out the binoculars. She had a ringside seat for the action and held it for hours, watching the police set up a roadblock at the bottom of the hill. Her neighbor, Mrs. George Aikens, watched with her.

"We first became aware that something was happening when we saw a black car park nearby and back up into the field," Valentino said. "That was the police roadblock." This was the second barrier, manned by Vasisko and his cohorts and put in place around two, after Croswell pulled back down McFall Road.

"Then three cars coming down the road were halted by the plainclothesmen in the parked car," Valentino said. "They pulled the first car over and hauled out six men. One of them got away and ran into the second car, and the second and third cars wheeled around and went back up the hill."

It didn't matter who ran or what car wheeled around. The State Police had the Barbara estate effectively bottled up.

"The police took the men out of their big fancy cars and took them away a few at a time," Aikens said. "It kept going on all day."

The faint sneer of "big fancy cars" typified the local attitude toward the intruder in their midst, the wealthy owner of the sprawling estate tucked away on a hill overlooking town. "Swarthy" was another tribal marker, cropping up again and again in the descriptions of the summit participants.

"We've seen lots of big cars shoot by on weekends, driven by dark, swarthy, husky cigar-smoking men, real gangster types," Valentino said. So enthralled were she and Mrs. Aikens by the nearby police action, they said, that they both entirely failed to get dinner on the table for their husbands that evening.

The village of Apalachin was just the kind of small-town place where wives and mothers served home-cooked meals every night. First settled in 1786, it began as a farming center on the banks of the Susquehanna. By 1957 the little town had evolved into something else, a bedroom community for Binghamton, fifteen miles to the east, and Owego, which had a big IBM plant, ten miles across the Susquehanna to the west.

First reports in the big city press delighted in giving the Apalachin population as 277, a number that mystified the residents. Their town, they knew, was much bigger than that. "We have sixteen-hundred voters in Apalachin, and 650 pupils in the new Apalachin Elementary School," wrote steamed-up local Pansy Kues in a letter to the editor.

The different numbers could be explained by comparing village and township populations, but the tiny-hamlet tag that out-of-town reporters hung on Apalachin stuck. The village boasted a library and a grange, though the Apalachin Grand Union grocery store had burned down four days before the summit. The village remained too small for a mayor, too small for an airport, and possessed exactly one traffic light, which didn't change but blinked.

And about that name, which had gotten to be, in 1957, the most mispronounced word in the country. Despite the similarities in spelling, and despite its location at the edge of the Catskills, Apalachin was not called after the Appalachian Mountains, which were named for a tribe of Florida natives. When they incorporated the township in 1846, the founders settled on "Apalacon," from the Algonquin name for the stream that cut through the area, "Appelacunck," meaning "from where the messenger comes."

Locally, the name of the village was pronounced "app-uh-LAKE-kin." But on national radio news and the then-nascent television networks, the name of the village was slaughtered with regularity. The hard "ch" used by the locals rarely got voiced, and the accented emphasis tended to wander over the syllables like someone lost in the woods. Technically speaking, the mispronouncers mistook a voiceless velar plosive for a voiceless palato-alveolar affricate. Most people just gave up and said it the same way as the mountain chain.

With a mixture of excitement and dismay, locals watched as the news story blew up big, spreading across the country and around the world. The French, especially, were always in a mood for a good dose of American noir. *Paris Match* ran a story headlined LE PICNIC DES GANGSTERS. Hy Singer, a local Apalachin pharmacist on a European vacation, was startled while in Paris to see news reports mentioning his tiny hometown. *Oui*, Mafia!

Apalachin sent the message out all over the globe, that the American Mafia was a real and potent force in organized crime. From where the messenger comes, indeed. The locals wanted to know, just as everyone else did around the world, what really happened at that house up on the hill.

Two hundred twenty miles to the south of Apalachin, in Washington, D.C., a sleeping giant would finally stir after some twenty-five years of dormancy. Because of what happened in a tiny hamlet in rural New York, the federal government would at last wake up to mount a concerted campaign against organized crime.

Two prominent figures in that fight would appear. But only one of them would prove to be any kind of effective ally for Ed Croswell.

PART II
Bobby and J. Edgar

11

The Rackets Committee Convenes

ON NOVEMBER 13, 1957, the day before the Apalachin summit, Senator John F. Kennedy's younger brother Robert led a very different sort of gathering, though one that devoted itself to some of the same concerns as the meeting in upstate New York. He attended a hearing held in a caucus room of the Old Senate Office Building on Constitution Avenue, just north of the Capitol in Washington, D.C.

Bobby filled the chief counsel post for a Senate subcommittee on which Jack Kennedy had a seat. JFK, as the freshman senator from Massachusetts, joined such eminences as Sam Ervin (future Watergate star), Barry Goldwater (future presidential candidate) and Frank Church (future early opponent of the Vietnam War).*

Created in January of that year by the Eighty-Fifth Congress, the panel was formerly called the Select Committee on Improper Activities in the Labor or Management Field of the Permanent Subcommittee on Investigations of the U.S. Senate Committee on Government Operations, but was more often referred to by the less unwieldy name of the Rackets Committee or, alternatively, the McClellan Committee, after its chairman, the senior senator from Arkansas, John Little McClellan.

The committee was largely Bobby's baby. He convinced McClellan, a hard-bitten Baptist who came to see the younger Kennedy almost as a son, that it would be a good idea to go after labor racketeers. Jack Kennedy and, more to the point, father Joe Kennedy were not so sure. Unions formed the

---

* Senator Joseph McCarthy was one of the original members of the subcommittee, but he died in May 1957.

bedrock of the Democratic base. The headstrong Bobby mucking around in the odiferous world of kickbacks, paper unions, and pension funds could conceivably bring family skeletons out of the closet. Joe described the idea of targeting the mob as "madness."

In the end, Jack accepted a seat on the panel to prevent the next-in-line senator from taking it, conservative firebrand Strom Thurmond. Bobby wrote later that his brother only "reluctantly" served, while Jack said simply, "Bobby wanted me on that committee."

The handsome, toothy older Kennedy often appeared bored and restless at the McClellan Committee hearings. He already felt afflicted by symptoms of Addison's disease that would become more and more pronounced as time went on, and which made it difficult for him to sit for long periods—a difficulty exacerbated by a back ailment incurred during his military service. JFK often skipped the proceedings altogether, and was in fact absent from the hearing of November 13.

If Jack's commitment to the committee wavered, he could depend on Bobby, his own personal attack dog, to monitor the hearings and keep them honest. That day in November 1957, RFK was still a week shy of his thirty-second birthday. Tentative in manner and maddeningly halting in his speech, he surely lacked the legal résumé for the position. A counsel on a congressional committee often acts as lead questioner, chief strategist, and primary beast of burden, a point-man while the legislators sit back and content themselves with occasional grandstanding.

Later, at a 1961 news conference when Jack announced the nomination of his brother as attorney general, he joked about Bobby's greenness: "I can't see that it's wrong to give him a little legal experience before he goes out to practice law."* The press corps, at least, laughed, but Bobby was incensed. He confronted his brother, furious, his "fists clenched," according to observers.

"You shouldn't have said that about me," he said.

"Bobby, you don't understand," Jack said. "You've got to make fun of yourself in politics."

"You weren't making fun of yourself," Bobby said. "You were making fun of me."

Bobby's inexperience didn't matter—he was a Kennedy, and that was enough. All his myriad insecurities stayed within the family. With outsiders, he could fake a frosty, obdurate confidence if he needed to.

---

* Others remember the comment being made at a dinner the day after the inaugural. Either way, the quip was widely reported in the media.

In Washington as in Apalachin, November 13, 1957 was a drizzly morning. Federal Bureau of Narcotics (FBN) agent Joseph Amato appeared as a witness before the committee, providing the senators with insights from his area of expertise: the Mafia. The McClellan Committee might possess a puffed-up official title that referred to labor and management, but the improper activities it zeroed in upon were those of organized crime. Bobby was sniffing that day at the spoor of the mob.

Amato counted himself a charter member of the so-called "Italian Squad" of the FBN, a gang of four that since 1946 had operated out of the agency's New York office, all of them devoted to bringing down the Mafia, and all of them Italian-Americans themselves. Under the leadership of the legendary narc, Charles Siragusa, the agents of the Italian squad had recently expanded their activities into international territory, tracing the French Connection's heroin pipeline into the United States.

Bobby wanted to know about dope. In questioning before the committee, he fussed with Amato over the street worth of a pound of heroin, wanted to know what a "deck" of heroin was (it's a packet or bag), plumbed the FBN's agent knowledge of the activities of Vincent J. Squillante.

Squillante, a.k.a. "Jimmy Jerome," was the shooter who had, five months before at Albert Anastasia's command, put two into the head of Frank Scalise—one of the murders that precipitated the Apalachin summit. He also had sat a barber chair away when Albert got his.

FBN agent Amato was not yet aware of Squillante's connection to either killing, nor of his later hit on Scalice's brother, Joe. But Amato could, and did, regale Bobby and the committee with the man's activities as "a major source of supply for narcotics, as well as being a prominent racketeer" involved in "policy and dock rackets."

Then Bobby posed the $64,000 question, one that could still naturally be posed that Wednesday, but which would be definitively answered, once and for all, by the events of the next day. It is a query that in hindsight seemed quaint and naïve, though it perfectly indicates the tenor of the pre-Apalachin attitudes toward the mob.

"Is there any organization such as the Mafia," Bobby asked agent Amato, "or is that just the name given to the hierarchy in the Italian underworld?"

"That is a big question to answer," responded Amato. "But we believe that there does exist today in the United States a society, loosely organized, for the specific purpose of smuggling narcotics and committing other crimes in the United States."

Did the Mafia exist in America as a nation-wide criminal enterprise? Proving the truth of that premise, and attacking organized crime in all its hydra-like incarnations, would become a singular, defining quest in Robert Kennedy's life. It formed one of the crowning achievements during his tenure as United States Attorney General. While his racket-busting activities did not begin with the Apalachin summit, they gained tremendous energy and focus from it, rising, eventually, to the level of an obsession.

"RFK didn't really become engaged in the organized crime issue until Apalachin," recalled FBN agent Marty Pera, like Amato, a member of the Bureau's Italian Squad. As author Peter Maas wrote of Bobby: "To him, [Apalachin] was prima facie evidence that there was a Mafia. He took it seriously." The summit pushed Kennedy's understanding of the problem beyond labor racketeering to the existence of an "invisible government" fed by gambling profits, political corruption, and narcotics.

What's remembered today of Bobby's push against organized crime is the "Get Hoffa" squad at the Kennedy Justice Department. The dramatic, marathon face-off with Teamsters president Jimmy Hoffa during the rackets committee hearings transfixed the nation. Again and again, Kennedy summoned Hoffa for questioning, and the two men tangled verbally with each other. One commentator characterized Kennedy's targeting of Hoffa as an "Ahab-like pursuit."

Bobby viewed the union leader as an evil, crooked force in American labor. But Hoffa has to be seen within Kennedy's larger concern with the corrupting influence of organized crime as a whole.

Robert Kennedy had a strong obsessive streak. His life represented a series of over-the-top passions, most of them well recognized, beginning with his family, with sailing and football in childhood and college, moving on through anticommunism and, finally, in the period before his death, social justice.

Bobby's six-year-long antimob offensive, first with the McClellan Committee and later as attorney general, epitomizes that dogged, obsessive personality. He threw everything into it. Beginning in November 1957, during the days following the bust-up of the Mafia summit at Joe Barbara's, Kennedy's fixation would grow and mature. The obsession continued for a full six years to the month, coming to an abrupt halt only in November 1963, as a collateral casualty of Dallas.

With his brother's death, Bobby's trajectory came crashing down to earth. RFK "appeared to lose all interest in the underworld on November 22, 1963," writes one biographer. The crash was abrupt, total. Bobby suddenly realized his crusade against organized crime possessed a dark side. Inevitably, the mob had exacted its revenge.

Later on in life, in the short five years between his brother's assassination and his own, Robert Kennedy would come to believe that his aggressive campaign against organized crime led directly to the president's murder.

U.S. district attorney for Manhattan Robert Morgenthau was with Robert Kennedy when the call came in from J. Edgar Hoover informing him of Jack's assassination. They had been discussing antimob strategies, with Bobby in full obsessive mode, the high gear he had been locked into ever since Apalachin. "I saw him often after that," Morgenthau recalled, "but he never mentioned organized crime to me again."

As was the case with many of the Kennedy family's idealistic initiatives, Robert Kennedy's development as a mob nemesis began as a political consideration.

In 1956, Bobby and Jack had stood by helplessly as a flamboyant Mafia foe with a much higher profile than their own snatched a political plum from their grasp. Battling organized crime demonstrated itself to be a superb enhancer of political reputation. It would be a lesson both brothers took to heart.

Estes Kefauver embraced progressive views in the post–World War II American South, a fact that should have relegated him to political purgatory. But with the backing of the liberal *Nashville Tennessean* newspaper, Kefauver forged a career in Tennessee politics, defining himself in opposition to Democratic Party kingpin E. H. "Boss" Crump.

When Crump accused him of a raccoon-like deviousness in hiding his liberal bias, Kefauver adopted a coonskin cap as a campaign symbol. He won against the Boss Crump machine, first gaining a congressional seat and then, in 1948, election to the United States Senate.

His horn-rim glasses and insurance-salesman looks aside, "Keef" showed himself to be energetic, ambitious, and something of a grandstander—all components of a successful national politician. Lyndon Johnson, who knew a thing or two about pressing flesh, called him "the greatest campaigner of them all."

But to break out of his provincial limits, he needed a national issue. He backed many of the New Deal programs, including the controversial public works of the Tennessee Valley Authority. He fastened upon antitrust legislation and monopoly busting as a pet cause. Still, as the 1950s dawned,

Kefauver remained just another face in the jostling, preening, bloviating crowd of United States senators.

All that changed with the creation of the United States Senate Special Committee to Investigate Crime in Interstate Commerce, which came to be known as the Kefauver Committee after its chairman. Growing out of Kefauver's antitrust activities and interest in how businesses operated across state lines, the panel would bring organized crime into the center of the nation's consciousness.

Kefauver had the great good luck to convene his hearings in 1950, just as television became a commonplace phenomenon in American life. The resulting national exposure proved to be a politician's dream. Riding on the coattails of the country's fascination with crime and mobsters, Kefauver became an immediately recognizable figure, one of the first media-created political celebrities, an aw-shucks country boy from the foothills of the Smokies who kept a deodorized pet skunk named Shanghai as a pet.

These were the committee hearings that transformed mobster Frank Costello's appendages into the most famous hands in America, and they likewise made iconic the horn-rimmed visage of the junior senator from Tennessee. "Senator Legend" *Time* magazine dubbed him ("half-man, half-fiction"), after he trounced Harry Truman in the 1952 New Hampshire presidential primary. Truman had another nickname for him: "Cowfever."

Nineteen fifty-two was also the year that a young Massachusetts congressman moved up to join Kefauver in the senate. John F. Kennedy looked on jealously as Kefauver turned his high-profile crime hearings into a dark-horse run at the presidency. As things shook out, Truman decided not to run.* The Democratic Party establishment ignored Kefauver's primary victories and chose a presidential candidate it was more comfortable with, Adlai Stevenson. After all that, Dwight Eisenhower's Republican run rendered the whole Democratic primary process pretty much moot.

Four years later, it happened again. In August 1956, at the International Amphitheater on Chicago's South Side during a sweltering Democratic convention, Jack and Bobby Kennedy attempted to step into the role of political power players. Jack had something of a national reputation by then, as a fresh, appealing presence in the senate. He wasn't ready for a presidential candidacy quite yet, but during the convention he decided to make a

---

* The 22nd Amendment to the Constitution, ratified in 1951, precluded presidents from running for third terms, but contained a grandfather clause that would have technically allowed a Truman candidacy.

quixotic, last-minute run for the vice-presidential slot on the ticket, which once again featured Stevenson as the top pick.

Spearheading the push as his brother's chief strategist, Bobby made a hash of it, mounting, as one biographer put it, an "impromptu campaign for the number two spot [that] was done in by clumsy amateurism." Estes Kefauver took his place as the vice-presidential candidate in what turned out to be a losing ticket in the 1956 election. Voters returned Eisenhower to office, and the Kennedys retired from the field of battle, their first attempt at placing Jack in a national office a failure.

Among the lessons was this one: the fight against organized crime could pay tangible political dividends. Kefauver trumped Jack for the VP slot because of those high-profile mob hearings. There were other examples, a prime one being the racket-busting former New York district attorney Thomas Dewey, who climbed to a governorship and then almost became president, largely on the basis of his tough antimob reputation.

It didn't matter that it was probably television, rather than the issue of organized crime, that was the true engine for Kefauver's rise to prominence. Throughout their political careers, Bobby and Jack learned more from their relatively rare defeats than from their victories. Senator Legend rode an antimob hobby horse, so the Kennedys made sure they would climb aboard, also.

Bobby, at least, had some experience with anticrime work. Apalachin might have galvanized him as a foe of organized crime, but via an odd, twisted trail, the younger Kennedy had already developed a personal awareness of the mob's labor racketeering, narcotics smuggling, and other corrupt practices, independently of what the Kefauver debacle at the 1956 Chicago convention taught him.

The trail begins with RFK's position on Joe McCarthy's staff in the early 1950s.

At the dawn of the fifties it was anticommunism, not anticrime, that seemed to be the most effective vehicle for political opportunists. It might be difficult to recall, given the liberal icons they were to become, but the Kennedys always maintained close personal and political ties to Senator Joseph Mc-Carthy, the manic Red-baiter from Wisconsin.

Both Bobby and Jack were delighted to invite McCarthy into their orbit, and he visited the family's Hyannis Port compound (where the brothers pranked the nonswimmer by throwing him off the dock). McCarthy dated two of the Kennedy sisters, Pat and Jean, with the latter recalling that the crapulous anticommunist "kissed very hard." RFK arranged an invitation for McCarthy to speak to his law school at the University of Virginia.

In December 1952, McCarthy got a call from Joseph P. Kennedy, the patriarch of the family, asking the senator to give a job to his son Bobby. McCarthy complied by hiring the twenty-eight-year-old recent law school graduate as a lawyer for the Senate Permanent Subcommittee on Investigations, a panel that had become the chief vehicle for its chairman's demagogic assault on communist influence in government.

Bobby signed on in January 1953, working as McCarthy's aide. But he could not stomach the subcommittee's chief counsel—and head henchman for McCarthy's anti-Red campaign—the reptilian Roy Cohn. Joe Kennedy had asked for the chief counsel position for Bobby, but McCarthy went with Cohn instead. When Kennedy quit the subcommittee a short five months later, it was not out of any scruple over its scurrilous tactics, but simply because he could not work under Cohn.

The episode left Bobby bruised and out of work in the summer of 1953, a not-quite-innocent bystander as his former boss's witch hunt trashed reputation after reputation and smeared witness after subcommittee witness via insinuation, vague accusations, and guilt by association.

Still, Bobby refused to repudiate McCarthy. When he returned to the panel in the summer of 1954, it was to secure a ringside seat (as chief counsel for the minority Democrats) when Fightin' Joe went down in flames. During this period, Cohn and Kennedy once actually came to blows in the Senate hearing room.

Cohn elbowed his rival out of any substantive role of the committee, shunting him into what Bobby considered a dead-end job investigating communist influence in European shipyards. Lowly and unlikely as the position was, this was the work that would first set Robert Kennedy on the trail of organized crime.

Crews off-loading Marshall Plan supplies, Bobby discovered, were caught in a deadly postwar battle between left-wing labor organizers on the one hand, and corrupt mob-controlled unions on the other. He found evidence of British longshoremen illegally off-loading goods from communist North Korea.

Bobby's work on the McCarthy subcommittee yielded a worthy new enemy for him to focus upon—not communism but organized crime, especially its involvement in labor racketeering. Toiling in obscurity, far from the limelight of the infamous Army-McCarthy hearings, Bobby stumbled upon corruption in the purchase of military uniforms by the government. Albert Anastasia had taken the lead in the looting, with an assist by garment center racketeer John Dioguardi, a.k.a. Johnny Dio.

So it happened that his deep roots in McCarthy-style anticommunism brought Robert Kennedy into his campaign against the mob. Years later, in the wake of McCarthy's disgrace, he explained to writer Peter Maas his devotion to Red-baiting. "At the time, I thought there was a serious internal security threat to the United States, and that Joe McCarthy seemed to be the only one who was doing anything about it." Bobby paused and then made what, for an ordinary politician, would represent a rare admission. "I was wrong."

Once he found evidence of mob corruption, Bobby the young anticommunist turned racketbuster with a vengeance. For Kennedy, it was a moral campaign. Writes RFK biographer Evan Thomas: "Sin held a fascination for the prudish son who, unlike his brothers, had been abstemious enough to win his father's $1,000 reward for not drinking or smoking until age twenty-one."

Theodore Roosevelt's daughter, the longtime Washington doyenne Alice Roosevelt Longworth, said that Robert Kennedy's moral outrage gave him the makings of "a revolutionary priest." His mother Rose Kennedy had in fact held ambitions for her young son to take the vows.

A priest needs demons to battle. In the fight against organized crime, Bobby discovered a Manichean world, a white-hats versus black-hats realm that appealed to his innate sense of justice. Said one Justice Department official, "Kennedy's zeal to break up the syndicates was reminiscent of a sixteenth-century Jesuit on the hunt for heresy."

His new passion led him into some odd situations. Poking around in the activities of stateside crime families, Bobby met Joe Amato and the rest of the agents on the Federal Bureau of Narcotics's Italian Squad, working out of the bureau's New York office. In concert with a platoon of hard-nosed Irish cops from the intelligence division of the New York Police Department, the FBN agents hit the streets of Harlem, Brooklyn, and the Lower East Side, harassing addicts and busting dealers, arresting as many as ten per night.

During the long hot summers of 1955 and '56, Bobby Kennedy went along for the ride. The privileged kid with the Harvard education gloried in the gritty street mentality of the "flying squad" narcotics patrol. Skulls were cracked and faces bloodied, hookers frisked and junkies rousted. He witnessed firsthand the depredations that the mob's French Connection heroin—so lucrative for Vito Genovese, Joe Bonanno, and other Mafia dons—wreaked upon the streets of the city.

Writer Norman Mailer once labeled Robert Kennedy "the sheriff who could have been an outlaw," and during his flying squad nights on the streets of Manhattan, Bobby got to inhabit a bit of both roles. The Irish cops he so admired had outlaw ways, proving themselves unbothered by niceties such as the legal rights of their suspects. Their example might have been what Bobby followed later, in his days as attorney general, when he could be equally cavalier about due process and limits on search and seizure.

Historian Doris Kearns Goodwin, in her work on the roots of the Kennedy family, was perhaps the first to use Oedipal-flavored psychoanalytic theory to describe Bobby's attraction to the campaign against organized crime.

The idea suggests itself easily: Joe Kennedy, sometime bootlegger and certainly a man familiar with the murky world of gangland, could not personally serve as a focus for young Bobby's rage. Love and propinquity precluded that. But the boy could attack a target in lieu of his father—the gangsters, criminals, and racketeers with whom Joe had sometimes associated.

This turned out to be a viable psychological dynamic, since Bobby's activities as a racket-buster wound up indicting and convicting several of his father's old cronies and friends—for example, James M. Landis, a legal advisor of Joe's and special counsel to JFK, whom Bobby busted for tax evasion.

All the Kennedy children, but Robert most especially, hungered after their father's approval, at the same time bitterly resenting their need for it. Joe closely managed his son's lives, and paternal approbation was only occasionally forthcoming. After his stroke in 1961, Joe Kennedy could utter only a single word: "No."

There may have been other, less Freudian, explanations for Robert Kennedy's enthusiastic embrace of his crime-fighting role. As a middle child in a sprawling family, he often felt passed over. Joe Kennedy Jr. acted as the clan's favored son, and after he perished on a flying mission in World War II, Jack stepped into the role. Something basic and elemental fueled Bobby's righteous anger and his devotion to the underdog. During his school years, and all the way through his twenties, friends and acquaintances remarked upon his surliness, his short fuse, his volcanic outbursts.

In the mob, according to his biographer Evan Thomas, "Kennedy had at last found an enemy worthy of his passion." More than any other element in his professional career, more than his later devotion to civil rights and social justice, his opposition to organized crime during the late fifties and early sixties made Robert Kennedy into the man he would become.

Indeed, Bobby eventually conceived of the fight against organized crime in terms of social justice, favoring the weak and the poor in their battle against the strong. He based his poisonous hatred of Hoffa, for example, on the fact that the Teamster president swindled rank-and-file union members. He came to recognize Vito Genovese, Joe Bonanno, Carlo Gambino, and the rest of the mobsters gathered at Apalachin for what they were—not glamorous outlaws or Robin Hoods, but simply a gang of violent bullies. The lessons of the schoolyard and the intimate dynamics of his family taught him to hate bullies.

Given these interior reasons, in the aftermath of the Apalachin summit, Bobby Kennedy stepped into the battle against the mob with both fists flailing.

12

Hoover Denies the Mafia

AFTER THE APALACHIN SUMMIT story broke, Robert Kennedy, in his role as staff director and chief counsel on the McClellen Committee, left the Senate Office Building and headed ten blocks west on Constitution Avenue to the Department of Justice between Ninth and Tenth streets. He took the elevator to the director of the FBI's office on the fifth floor and requested all the information that the bureau had on the mobsters detained the previous Thursday at Joe Barbara's country house.

The initial haul at Apalachin amounted to sixty names. Ten more suspects had been added in the aftermath. Others in attendance slipped through the net, but Ed Croswell and his State Police cohorts had ID'd the ones they caught, and Kennedy sought information on those.

In that bureaucracy-busting way of his, Bobby personally went straight to the top, penetrating the inner-sanctum offices of the FBI director himself, J. Edgar Hoover. To his dismay, he found that the FBI "didn't know anything about organized crime, didn't know anything, really, about these people who were the major gangsters in the United States."

"After the meeting at Apalachin," Bobby recalled later, "which seventy people attended, I asked for files from them on each of the seventy, and [the FBI] didn't have any information, I think, on forty out of the seventy.* Not even the slightest piece of information." The FBI dossiers that did exist were paltry. The file on Frank Costello's shooting, for example, contained only newspaper clippings.

---

* The FBI, in an official revisionist history, disputes this, stating that the Bureau had files on fifty-three out of sixty.

But just across 10th Street from Justice, the Treasury Building housed another government entity, another federal law enforcement arm—Hoover's despised rival, the Federal Bureau of Narcotics. Kennedy found a very different story there. "They had something on every one of [the Apalachin mobsters]," he said.

Bobby was perhaps playing out a political charade in order to show up Hoover. From his work on McClellan's Rackets Committee, he already well understood the relative merits of the FBN and the FBI. "I knew from my experience with both of them that the Bureau of Narcotics had much more information—much more accurate information, much more thorough information, much more complete information—on organized crime in the United States than the FBI did."

The question of which government agency led the fight against organized crime mattered very much. The FBN had nowhere near the resources that the FBI did. Being limited in its mandate to drugs, the FBN could not act in instances of extortion, loan-sharking, gambling, or murder-for-hire. The extremely well-staffed FBI, on the other hand, acted as the premier investigative arm of the United States government.

In the immediate wake of the Apalachin summit, the mood was decidedly sour at the FBI headquarters—the holy sanctum always referred to, in the curious clipped anagram-speak of official bureau memoranda, as "SOG," for "seat of the government," a phrase lifted, in a typically grandiose Hooverian manner, from the U.S. Constitution.

On November 15, the Friday after Apalachin, Hoover himself "boiled through the building in a furious rage." Agents scattered, avoiding the boss, keeping their heads down, finding reasons to stay in the field.

Denial of responsibility, the time-honored first resort of the bureaucrat, resulted in a petty contretemps in the SOG offices that Friday. The Albany agent in charge produced a map that showed the town of Apalachin lay within the Buffalo FBI office's jurisdiction, while the Buffalo agent in charge counterclaimed with a map that proved the little town belonged to Albany. The quirks of mob geography and the primacy of Buffalo's chieftain Steven Magaddino should have meant the former to be true, but Albany took the fall.

The special agent in charge (SAC) at Albany proffered a lame excuse. The reason the mob convened in his bailiwick, he stated in a memo, was that he had successfully eliminated all vestiges of organized crime within the district, and therefore it represented a neutral meeting ground. An ingenious, if specious and quite untrue, line of argument.

J. Edgar Hoover's anger should have more correctly been directed not toward his field agents, but toward himself. He recognized Apalachin for what it was—the most serious challenge ever to his reputation as the nation's top law enforcement officer. Dozens of top Mafia leaders gathered from all over the country, and he and his vaunted bureau of mythic G-men were caught flat-footed. The fact called into question not only the air of omniscience that Hoover took pains to project, but more basically his competency.

Before Apalachin, before, say, 12:40 p.m. on November 14, 1957, there was no mob. No organized crime at all in America. Citizens believed this because the country's head copper told it to them again and again, obsessively, as he did almost everything, like a bulldog, the breed Hoover famously resembled. The director repeated the line so often that it became a sort of reality.

In those days, the director of the FBI acted as an unchallengeable oracle. His word was law. Out in the heartland, especially, Mr. and Mrs. Front Porch America believed in him unreservedly.

The accepted notion of no Mafia in America made it appear that Hoover was a genius and the FBI was doing its job. Believing any other way meant you were some sort of trouble-stirring rascal, a Red maybe, or at any rate an enemy of the Director and thus of all civilized humanity.

Which meant the mob threat went largely unchallenged in any focused, plenary way. The criminal conspiracy comprised mainly of Sicilian Mafia immigrants grew into a national cartel totally unhampered by the FBI. "Hoover's not a problem," one mob boss was caught saying on a phone wiretap. The brutal campaigns of extortion and violence, the beatings, the murders, the organized crime tax that all citizens paid whether they knew it or not, the corrupting influence of the mob, all proceeded unchecked by the nation's premier federal law enforcement bureau.

Recalled United States district attorney for New York Robert M. Morgenthau: "For pretty much close to twenty-five years, organized crime had a free run. I mean from the end of Prohibition down to 1960. And I think it kind of had woven into at least part of the fabric of society."

In Sicily, one of the nicknames for the police is *la sunnambula,* the sleepwalkers. Hoover fit the bill perfectly.

There were reasons for the FBI's stubborn refusal to face reality, and they all flowed from the dark currents of the director's personality. Hoover abhorred cooperation with other bureaucratic entities such as the INS, the FBN, and the IRS. Any comprehensive move against the mob required government-wide coordination. He also realized that the resulting legal cases would be complicated and might mess with the Bureau's vaunted 95 percent crime-case clearance rate.

But there lurked a more personal reason. At the Stork Club, and at the racetracks he habituated as well, Hoover swam in much the same waters as Frank Costello and other organized-crime figures. Washington political operative George E. Allen (he was an intimate of Truman and Eisenhower and director of the Reconstruction Finance Corporation) said he was present when Costello encountered Hoover at the Waldorf-Astoria barbershop.

The mobster attempted to open a conversation, but the FBI director refused. "You stay out of my bailiwick and I'll stay out of yours," Allen quoted Hoover as saying to Costello. Just a gruff rebuff, but it actually accurately portrayed reality. Hoover largely left the mob alone.

There have been darker hints, over the years, of a more scandalous reason Hoover laid off organized crime: he was being blackmailed over his supposed homosexuality. Meyer Lansky, so the story goes, possessed a photo or photos of J. Edgar Hoover orally pleasuring his longtime companion of the bosom, Clyde Tolson, the associate director of the FBI.

No such photos have ever surfaced, even decades after Hoover's death. It's unlikely they ever existed. Since the source for these allegations were the mobsters themselves, the story should be rejected until conclusively proven. Lansky, at least, demonstrated himself over and over quite eager to muddy the waters around his enemies with half-truths, outright lies, and indecent innuendos.

As Carl Sagan noted, "Extraordinary claims require extraordinary evidence." In this case, evidence, extraordinary or otherwise, is just not there.

Yet the fable of the blackmailed FBI director has assumed a curious life of its own. Something about Hoover's personality and character—his pompous self-righteousness, his arrogant hypocrisy, and especially his own habitual black-bag criminality—made the modern, post-Watergate public want to believe whatever lurid stories were told about him.

Anthony Summers' infamous portrait, in his book *Official and Confidential,* represents the prime example: a cross-dressing Hoover at a party, begging fellow revelers to call him "Mary." Summers' single source demonstrated herself to be unreliable and was once, in fact, convicted of perjury. His backup substantiation remained wholly dubious. But once again, the tale has taken on the weight of fact, to the degree the transvestite FBI director became a staple of casual talk-show references.

To understand the reasons for Hoover's recalcitrance in matters of organized crime, it's necessary to journey back to the 1920s, when the modern mob and the modern FBI were both born, almost at the same moment.

Like young Robert Kennedy three decades later, J. Edgar Hoover first came to law enforcement via the effort to control communist infiltration into labor unions. Hoover's Red-baiting roots influenced his whole career. Early on, he became what he would always remain, a hunter of political radicals. He missed Apalachin because he still had his eye on the communist menace.

John Edgar Hoover was in every sense a product of Washington, D.C., born there, on New Year's Day in 1895, and growing up in a house on Seward Square, in a middle-class neighborhood called Pipetown a few blocks from the Capitol. His father served as a government clerk and his mother descended from Swiss diplomats. Their son gloried in a stint as an ROTC-style cadet in high school, sang soprano in a church choir, and studied law at night while working at government jobs during the day.

What he learned on one of those jobs, at the Library of Congress, had a lasting impact on American society for the next half century. In his position as a lowly file clerk, the twenty-year-old Hoover became enamored of the card index, similar to the Dewey Decimal System, used to keep track of the Library's burgeoning collection of publications. The classification procedures appealed to Hoover's meticulous mind.

"I'm sure he would have been the chief librarian if he'd stayed with us," noted a fellow Library of Congress clerk. A road not taken, for Hoover and the country.

Upon graduating George Washington University with a law degree in 1917, the twenty-two-year-old faced a crisis. The United States Army hungered for likely young men, drafting them for lethal trench warfare in Europe. At the same time, Hoover's father lost his job as a government clerk, beginning a decline that would have him in and out of mental asylums, never to work again. John Edgar became the family's breadwinner, and a soldier's salary just wouldn't do.

Between combat death in Flanders and impoverishment in Washington, the bright young man chose a third path, securing himself, through family contacts, a reasonably well-paying, draft-deferred position in the U.S. Department of Justice. He started there in the midst of wartime hysteria, embracing a high pitch of official paranoia that Hoover never really lost. He worked as a special agent in the Justice Department's War Emergency Division's Alien Enemy Bureau.

Those two words, "alien enemy," fit Hoover's psyche like a glove, and would set the course for the rest of his career. After the war, he stayed at Justice, discovering one of his greatest mentors in the new U.S. attorney general, A. Mitchell Palmer. Anti-immigrant, anti-leftist feeling in the country remained at a fever levels, exacerbated by the events of the Russian revolution.

Palmer installed his protégé as the head of a new bureaucratic entity, the Radical Division, responsible for tracking internal threats from anarchists, Bolsheviks, and alien enemies of whatever socialist stripe. The threat was real enough. For Palmer, it was extremely personal. On June 2, 1919, an anarchist's bomb had torn off the front of his residence, nearly killing the attorney general, his wife, and daughter.*

Palmer and his young blade runner embarked upon a campaign of official terror against what they termed "subversives," a catch-all term that included labor activists and immigrants, anarchists and communists. Working energetically, Hoover brushed aside constitutional niceties such as due process and probable cause to engineer the infamous "Palmer Raids" of November 1919 and January 1920.

The actions represented the McCarthyism of its day, and as he would do three decades later with Senator Joe McCarthy, Hoover played the man behind the scenes, organizing, facilitating, developing intelligence information. The illegal roundups may have had Palmer's name on them, but they were Hoover's operations all the way.

Coming as they did in the same month, it is interesting to place these two historical dates side by side: January 2, 1920, when the largest and, from a civil rights point of view, most disastrous Palmer Raid rounded up an estimated five thousand suspected radicals, and January 16, 1920, the date that nationwide Prohibition began.

The latter could be said to be the birth date of the mob in America. There had been gangsters before, to be sure, and the Black Hand, the Mafia, and numerous other crime cartels existed well back into the nineteenth century. But Prohibition would allow the creation of organized crime as we know it, a criminal enterprise on a national scale. With the Volstead Act, the Mafia hit gold.

Meanwhile, what was the man who would become the nation's top

---

* In an odd bit of historical synchronicity, the bomb attack on Palmer's house that triggered the Red Scare raids would eventually be traced to the Galliani anarchist group in Massachusetts. Heading the group was Carlo Tresca, the same left-wing rabble rouser whose murder had helped put Ed Croswell on the path that led to Apalachin.

crime-fighter doing at that precise point in history? Coordinating mass extralegal attacks on enemies of the state, false and otherwise. Hoover lied brazenly about his tactics, cut Constitutional corners, and generally employed his organizational genius in ways that posed one of the greatest threats to civil rights that ever occurred in this country.

For both the mob and the Federal law enforcement battle against it, the year 1920 set the course for what was to come for the next half century. The nation's top cop would perennially have business elsewhere.

"Edgar began to see his anti-Red mission as more than a job," writes one biographer about the 1920s-era Hoover. "It was fast becoming his life's crusade."

Around the time when he discovered his new identity as a Red-baiter, Hoover changed his name. There was another John Hoover running around Washington, D.C., writing bad checks. In order to distinguish himself from this nefarious paper hanger, John Edgar Hoover initialized his first and brought his middle name up front. He was born again.

Young J. Edgar allowed himself to be thoroughly swept up in the excitement of his new radical-hunting assignment. Forget the Volstead Act, the Eighteenth Amendment, and the rise of organized crime. He was fresh out of law school and commanding a swarming army of federal agents. Acting as field marshal on the roundups themselves, the tightly wound twenty-four-year-old appeared to one observer to be "a slender bundle of high-charged electric wire."

Just as he would later do with McCarthy, when Palmer's reputation crumbled in a shift of public sentiment against the raids, Hoover effortlessly lied his way out of all responsibility, presenting himself as a mere Justice Department functionary. In a brilliant demonstration of bureaucratic shape-shifting, he managed to remain at Justice even when a dedicated civil libertarian, Columbia law school dean Harlan Fiske Stone, took over as U.S. attorney general in 1924.

"Edgar had discovered the art of making himself useful, and soon, indispensible—a talent he would practice more effectively than any single other American official of the twentieth century," writes Hoover biographer Kenneth Ackerman.

When Hoover first moved to Justice in the Alien Enemy Bureau, he brought the Library of Congress card index method along with him. Utilizing it, he instituted a classification system not for books but for people, taking the first steps in creating his infamous secret files on radicals, celebrities, politicians, adversaries—everyone, it seemed, except mobsters.

Soon enough, Dewey had gone Orwellian. The card index multiplied like a virus: 50,000 entries in the fall of 1919, after Hoover had been at Justice two months, 100,000 within a year, 200,000 by 1920 and 450,000 by 1921. The system represented a precomputer database compiled laboriously by hand. By the Director's death in 1972, he had personal cards on twenty-five million people.

Nested within the system was a sequestered cache of sensational material, dubbed "Official and Confidential," and one even more explosive, labeled "Personal and Confidential," both kept segregated in Hoover's private office. The filing system was self-cleansing, with sensitive material de-sourced and summarized, the original reports destroyed. It spawned more and more subsets: files on "black-bag" burglaries perpetrated by FBI agents, an "Obscene File" on particularly egregious sexual peccadilloes.

Hoover had evolved into "the most dangerous file clerk in America." The existence of these card index files became an open secret around Washington. Everyone knew the FBI director had them, but nobody knew exactly what they contained. Their existence played on human nature like a harp. Guilty imaginations ran wild. When you came down to it, was any person's conscience totally clean?

With their queasy mix of fact, unsubstantiated allegations, and outright lies, just the idea of those secret index cards was enough. Hoover's victims effectively blackmailed themselves. The files came to function in the same way as Foucault's internalized police, engendering a constant, behavior-checking fear, maintained not only by Hoover but by the individuals involved.

Chief among the behaviors they checked was opposition to J. Edgar Hoover, his associates and allies, or the sacred institution of the FBI. Any hint of challenge triggered an investigation, reports from the field, an index card entry in the dreaded files. Criminality wasn't the gauge. Political heterodoxy was, or something more petty, a brand of bureaucratic gamesmanship that became Hoover's specialty.

When Robert Kennedy wanted the facts in the wake of Apalachin, Hoover's vaunted index cards were an obvious place to look. But they failed Bobby, coming up totally empty, as he noted later, about half the time. That's because the files were not what they should have been, an accurate précis of criminal intelligence, the purpose they could have usefully served.

Rather, they represented a Rorschach for the dark recesses of the Director's mind. Welcome to J. Edgar Hoover's world, where human beings fell into two categories—those who could be exploited for gain, and those who were enemies. Card after card, file after file, dossier after dossier indicated more about Hoover's myopia and paranoia than any situation in the real world.

Thus, before the Apalachin summit changed everything, Supreme Court Justice Felix Frankfurter had a card, but not Brooklyn crime boss Joe Bonanno. Left-wing activist Carlo Tresca, but not the gangster who killed him, Carmine Galante. A fat file on Marilyn Monroe, but nothing on the homicidal mob madman, Larry Gallo.

The first entry of the FBI file on Vito Genovese, perhaps the most explosive and dangerous organized crime figure of the era, dates from January 1958, two months after Apalachin. Even then, the file itself is pathetic, dwelling on contacts with business people who resisted Genovese's attempts to move in on their firms, rehashing reports of the U.S. District Attorney's office, collecting secondhand accounts of the mobster's prison activities once he had been safely put away on narcotics charges in 1959. The file clearly portrays the FBI scrambling to play catch-up, once Genovese had been nailed in the roundup at Apalachin.

What was the proper purlieu of the Federal Bureau of Investigation? Reds? The mob? Both? The country long accepted what Hoover told it, that there was no such threat as organized crime. Communism—the Director always derisively called it "commonism"—served well as the country's perennial bogeyman. His countrymen lionized Hoover for his stalwart efforts against it.

"We are delighted that you have dealt so successfully with the Communist menace," Brooklyn Congressman John J. Rooney told Hoover at one of this annual appearances before the House Appropriations Subcommittee. "I do not know what we would have done in this country if it had not been for the FBI."

The timing of Rooney's pronouncement proved significant. The year was 1957, two weeks before the national leadership of the mob gathered at Joe Barbara's.

Apalachin caught the crusading hero lawman by surprise. He responded reflexively, by denigrating the event. If J. Edgar Hoover didn't know about it, it couldn't be that important. In FBI memoranda embedded in those voluminous card index files, agents attached a dismissive epithet whenever they felt the need to refer to the summit, terming it "the so-called crime meeting."

So-called. Two people who were calling it exactly that, in its immediate aftermath, were Edgar Croswell and Robert Kennedy.

13

The Mystery of Apalachin

THE MOST LASTING REPERCUSSIONS of the Apalachin summit were played out not in the courts, where legal cases against the participants came together only slowly and finally fizzled out, nor in the hearing rooms of government, as numerous as those hearings were, nor even in the streets, where the mobsters involved largely escaped retribution for their folly. While those venues were all inarguably important, the deepest wounds to the mob were inflicted by the press, which meted out punishment in the form of wide-ranging and often derisive exposure.

During those days in early November, Elvis Presley lit up the nation's movie screens with his hip-shaking turn in *Jailhouse Rock*. Weird tales came out of Wisconsin, where police investigated activites of the mad taxidermist Ed Gein. Russia's Sputnik II was in orbit, visible on clear nights in the sky above the Southern Tier. Prince Charles celebrated his ninth birthday.

The day after the Apalachin story broke, President Eisenhower took off with wife Mamie for Georgia, beginning a weeklong residence at Augusta National Golf Club. But November 15, 1957 was a very black Friday for the Mafia. If he wasn't too busy out on the links, Ike could have read all about it in the newspapers, the initial broadside in a sustained press bombardment that would stretch into weeks and months.

THE MOB MEETS ran the 72-point headline in the *New York Post* that day, and the other tabloids followed suit. The *Daily News* splashed the summit across the front page, SEIZE 62 MAFIA CHIEFTAINS IN UPSTATE RAID, and headlined the article inside with UPSTATE RAID COLLARS 62 MAFIA BIGSHOTS FROM COAST TO COAST. The *New York World-Telegram and Sun* had RAID BARES MAFIA CHIEFS, with a prominent subhead, HINT BLACK HAND, TEAMSTER TIE.

The *Chicago Daily News* went a little more wry, printing a page-one photo of the Barbara house matched with the caption, HEY, MA, THERE'S SOMEONE AT THE DOOR!

A few journalists demonstrated a clear-eyed grasp of the organized crime landscape, completely shrugging off J. Edgar Hoover's repeated, fiercely pronounced insistence that there was no such thing as the Mafia in the United States. To those reporters, the descriptive tag "Mafia" appeared as a casual, accepted truth. "Sixty-two top leaders of the dreaded Mafia, the ruling crime syndicate in the U.S. . . ." began Howard Wantuch and Sidney Kline's coverage in the New York *Daily News*. The story likened the fleeing mob bosses at Apalachin to "vermin scuttling out of burning woodwork."

Reporters and columnists most loved the image of mobsters getting lost in the woods. The whole saga of the summit got distilled into one indelible picture: city boys, tough guys, made men, slip-sliding in the country muck, tangled in barbed wire. Many of the accounts contrasted the flashy clothes of the mobsters with the woodsy South Mountain surroundings, as if their taste for two-toned Oxfords or camel-hair overcoats had somehow betrayed them. As the *Saturday Evening Post* had it, "The raid was the best visual aid in the history of criminology."

The city mouse–country mouse myth is virtually universal, with folktale expressions in almost every culture. Here was an example played out in contemporary rural New York. Irresistible. A journalist could pluck on that particular lute string without even being conscious of doing it. Who cared if only a bare quarter of the mobsters actually fled into the woods? What did it matter if the phrase "went scrambling pell mell" did not, in fact, accurately describe what happened? The story readily reduced down to that simple, indelible plotline. It's what everyone remembers.

Indelible, but perhaps not as simple as it appears at first glance. In the Mafia homeland of Sicily, the traditional response to trouble had always been to flee into the maquis, the thickly vegetated wild areas on the island that from antiquity provided an ideal refuge from authorities. Perhaps the summit participants who fled were only acting upon an atavistic impulse, like salmon heading upstream. The flight into the forest rested deep in the Mafia genes.

Inevitably but somewhat surprisingly, Sergeant Ed Croswell came in for some withering criticism in the press. The *New York World-Telegram and Sun* spearheaded a campaign against him, largely, it seemed, because it had been scooped by its main competition, the New York *Daily Mirror,* in the newspaper race to get the lowdown on the summit.

The *World-Telegram* blasted Croswell for not detaining the mobsters longer, for failing to arrest them, for letting them go at all. The paper incorrectly maintained that Croswell had not consulted with his superiors before freeing the detainees. It portrayed Governor Averell Harriman as "furious over the conduct of the raid."

Which was not at all the case. In response to the *World-Telegram,* Harriman went out of his way to praise the New York State Police in general and Croswell in particular. George M. Searle, deputy commissioner of the State Police, characterized the press backlash as mere second-guessing. "[Croswell] should be given a pat on the back, not a kick in the pants," Searle said. "We can all be Monday morning quarterbacks."

Croswell never responded to the attacks directly. He emphasized his long, lonely surveillance of the man at the center of the summit. "I have tried for years to draw public attention to the activities and associates of Joseph Barbara. I hope the community now realizes what a menace a man of this type can be, operating under the cloak of legitimate business."

The initial press reports had the who, what, where, and when of the incident pretty much down pat—mobsters, summit, Apalachin, November 14—but the journalists all obsessed over the "why" of the gathering.

Why were the mobsters there? What was the reason the top hierarchy of the Mafia assembled at Joe Barbara's? What were they up to? That "why?" reverberated throughout the media response. It would continue to throb in the follow-up coverage, the committee hearings, and the court proceedings that followed the exposure of the summit. The "mystery" of Apalachin had been born. In the aftermath, an immense amount of energy, verbiage, and theorizing would be put toward solving the puzzle that the summit presented to outsiders.

The press coverage indicated the degree that J. Edgar Hoover's cardinal truth, "there is no such entity as the Mafia," had worked its way into the national consciousness. Along with its front page headline, the *Post* published an article entitled "The Mafia: Folklore or Death Syndicate?": "Is there a Mafia here, cloaked in the tradition of silence and secrecy? The suspicions are fat and strong, available facts, sparse."

The next day, *The New York Herald Tribune* ran with "Mafia's Existence a Police Mystery: Some Call 'Black Hand' a Fancy, Others Say It Rules Underworld." Likewise, the Associated Press offered a feature a month after the event, headlined "Mafia: Myth or Menace?" The text, by AP writer Jack

Hand, posed what today seem naïve questions: "Is the Mafia ominously real? Or is it a storybook word to catch the headlines?"

The AP story reached back to the early years of the decade to quote Senator Estes Kefauver's definitive portrayal of the Mafia as "ominously real, a shadowy international organization that lurks behind much of America's organized criminal activity." Federal narcotics agent (and Robert Kennedy mentor) Joseph Amato weighed in on the street-level reality of the mob. But the article also cited an unnamed FBI source as saying the Mafia was nothing more than "a nice storybook phrase."

In Sicily, at least, where it had a long and storied history, the reality of the Mafia could not be questioned. The dramatist and Nobel laureate Luigi Pirandello once suggested that a Mafia enforcer would "strangle a child for three pennies." But the question Hoover and others consistently raised was whether the "Honored Society" of Italian mobsters transferred in any way to the United States. Again and again, that possibility was denied.

Difficult as it is to understand today, in 1957 there remained a mulish doubt in the minds of many people as to whether the American Mafia actually existed. Even after the Kefauver hearings and the Rackets Committee hearings (which were still going on), even after the blood in the streets during Prohibition, after the spectacular murders of Richard Lonergan and Albert Anastasia (to single out just two in a long, long list), after high-profile media events such as Louis Buchalter's surrender to Walter Winchell on his way to the chair in Sing Sing—even after all evidence to the contrary, the majority of the American public was still in denial.

At the helm of that denial, wrapped in the American flag, stood J. Edgar Hoover.

Louis B. Nichols, Hoover's official flack and the man responsible for diligently preserving the Director's sacrosanct image, gave an extraordinary interview in the immediate aftermath of Apalachin.

First he pronounced "strong doubts as to the Mafia's existence," citing the Director's view that "certainly nothing of any substance has ever been shown in this respect, nothing has even come close to doing so."

Nichols then admitted, "The FBI has never investigated the Mafia." He went on:

When reporters write newspaper stories about the Mafia in the United States, they're writing off the west wall—they want to make their stories sound good. Remember how some police reporters used to write around the Tongs clash in the Chinatowns of New York and

San Francisco? As for the claim that the Mafia has been taken over by the Siocillian Unione [sic], that's just added phraseology. The "boys" involved in these "parties" in the United States just drift together for a number of reasons, all pretty clear when you think things over. It's like a bunch of Dutchmen getting together, and while hoisting their glasses, exclaiming, "we together are sticking."

Here was Hoover's official mouthpiece, his number two, head of Crime Records, the Bureau's massive public relations apparatus, "laughingly" discounting the existence of the Mafia in an interview published one week after the bust-up of the summit. Even with the Director himself fuming and slamming doors around the SOG offices, the FBI battleship proved slow to change direction. The message remained stubbornly the same. As the headline of the article read: NO MAFIA AT BARBARA'S, NONE IN U.S., SAYS FBI.

Among the wordsmiths of the press, a nagging worry developed around just what terminology to employ when referring to the mob. Words were important to the hacks, who occupied themselves in dithering over "phraseology," as Nichols put it. The extended name game played out in newspapers across the country.

Just what do we call the criminal underground in America? The Mafia? That's strictly Sicilian, isn't it? The Organization? The Honored Society? The Combination? The Confederation? The Syndicate? How about Unione Sicilliano, the name of a long-established Italian fraternal organization, which insisted it was aboveboard and not engaged in illegal rackets, but nonetheless had been thoroughly subjugated by the mob? Or *Fratellanza*—the Brotherhood? There were regional slang phrases, also—the Outfit in Chicago, the Arm in Buffalo, the Office in Providence, Rhode Island. And there was always the Commission, the mob's ruling body.

Later on, in 1963, when mob insider Joe Valachi gave his testimony to the McClellan Committee, a new candidate emerged, "La Cosa Nostra." Never mind that the phrase was a grammatical tautology ("the our thing"?), a casual nonce formation dropped into conversation, not a universally used term at all. It allowed Hoover an opening. He had been denying the Mafia for years. But this new beast of which Valachi spoke, La Cosa Nostra, well, the FBI had been on top of that from the beginning.

Hoover's public relations apparatus, always vigilant and always effective, arranged for an article to appear in *Readers' Digest*. The Pleasantville, New York, magazine, a favorite of middle America, was such a pet publication that it amounted to an FBI house organ. The piped, revisionist article recounted the Bureau's long battle, not with the phantasm of the Mafia, which as the Director said didn't exist, but with the shadowy La Cosa Nostra crime syndicate that did.

For Hoover, as one commentator put it, "'Cosa Nostra' meant 'save face.'" In FBI memos, the mob became La Cosa Nostra, or, in Bureauspeak, LCN.

The truth on the street was that nobody formalized anything. No mobster in good standing gave a damn about which words to use. The name game was played only by journalists stuck behind typewriters in the press room. Alphonse Capone never allowed the word "Mafia" to pass his lips. What the mob called itself just wasn't a question that made sense out on the bricks.

The last word on the name game belongs to Robert Kennedy, who on the subject of the mob would tell his troops at the Justice Department: "Don't define it—do something about it."

The wordsmiths of the press demonstrated an additional worry: what to call the rounded-up mobsters. Many newspapers settled on "delegates," as if what went down at Joe Barbara's was some sort of political convention, or "guests," as though the mobsters were at a garden party. "Summiteers" had a Walt Disney, Mickey Mouse Club ring to it. "Attendees" was popular, and a few reporters tortured themselves into using "conferees." To the disgust of the locals, "Apalachinites" also came into play. "Steak-eaters" was jocular and poetic enough, but never gained wide currency.

Later on, during proceedings that saw the Apalachin mobsters hauled en masse before a judge, the name game played itself out with all judicial gravity. Defense lawyers objected both to "gathering" and "meeting" to describe the summit. Both words, argued the lawyers, implied forethought and premeditation, which the defense was not ready to concede. After a good deal of legalistic hemming and hawing—was it a parley? a conference?—the court settled upon the colorless and more nonjudgmental "incident."

The nervous uncertainty over terminology led directly to one of the central themes of the press coverage, that there existed some essential mystery or puzzle surrounding the summit. Associated Press reports habitually cited the "riddle" of what went on at Joe Barbara's.

Slow to kick over, the vast engines of government began to rumble into life, preparing to do their bureaucratic best to plumb the mystery, answer the riddle, and solve the Apalachin puzzle. The results would be spotty at best.

Whether in denial or not, Hoover recognized that the press furor surrounding the summit demanded some kind of action on his part. On Monday, November 18, 1957, he ordered the launch of a major antimob initiative. He directed his SACs, his "special agents in charge" of field offices, to develop target lists of top racketeers, especially in New York, Chicago, Buffalo, and other major cities from which the summit participants hailed.

Hoover's vaunted "Top Hoodlum Program" (or THP, in Bureau-ese) was much ballyhooed by the Bureau's ferocious public relations apparatus as an effective response to organized crime's recent high-profile activities. The word "Apalachin" was carefully avoided, as was, naturally, "Mafia."

Actually, THP simply extended several nascent moves by the Bureau rank and file to take on the mob, activities that flew in the face of the Director's denial of the Mafia's existence. In 1953, agents in the New York office, facing off with the Five Families on the front lines in a post-Kefauver era, requested permission to "open intelligence files on thirty top hoodlums in the city to get a general picture of their activities and to keep an eye out for violations of federal law," according to an internally produced FBI history.

In August 1953, the intelligence-gathering program went national. The Top Hoodlum initiative that Hoover announced in 1957 had already essentially been in place for over four years when the Apalachin summit happened. But the FBI was a top-down, not a grassroots bureaucracy. The push from the field offices had little support from Hoover or his SOG apparatchiks.

Even in 1957, the year of Apalachin, the preoccupations of the Bureau continued to be extremely lopsided. The New York field office had four hundred special agents assigned to Hoover's bête noir, subversives, and four to organized crime. THP assigned twenty-five more, but the ratio stayed uneven.

Hoover's Top Hoodlum initiative was a quota program, with each SAC directed to develop a list of target mobsters to identify, investigate, and surveil. "Surveil," in the Director's morally twisted universe, meant sending "black-bag" teams to break in at selected Mafia homes, businesses, and meeting places, in order to plant electronic bugs so that field agents could afterward monitor the proceedings. Eight hundred of the eavesdropping devices were deployed in this manner.

Warrantless and technically illegal, of course, and none of it would stand up in court, but Hoover wasn't a detective seeking evidence. He was a bureaucrat who wanted intel. Information was the coin of the realm in his world, and those bulging file cabinets with their Library of Congress reference system had always come through for him in the past.

The ostensible legal authority under which the FBI black-bag teams operated was the National Security Act of 1947, which allowed agents enormous leeway in eavesdropping and wiretapping political radicals—specifically, anyone who had even a passing acquaintance with the American Communist Party. Hoover had used this legal empowerment to snoop not only on fringe leftists, but also on movie stars, union officials, politicians, journalists, and most especially anyone who dared oppose the Director or criticize the Bureau.

Mobsters, on other hand, had never been singled out for targeting. But the legal provisions under which the black-bag teams operated proved to be highly elastic. The Mafia, it seemed, could be seen as a threat to national security. Therefore they warranted the electronic attentions of a concerted FBI tapping and bugging campaign. This was only a convenient fiction. The rationale would not have stood up to any serious legislative examination, but Congress had never been much in the mood to examine what Hoover did.

The truth was—though you couldn't prove it by Hoover—the mob had always been a much greater threat to at least the economic well-being of the nation, if not its security, than the Communist Party ever was. The Mafia represented a true infiltrating force, internationally integrated, pervasive, insidious, secret. The tale of the tape, when the two are set side by side, is instructive. The Mafia had 5,000 core members, the Communist Party 5,000 active ones. But the mob knocked down an estimated $7 billion annually in illicit revenue, while the Soviet-supported Communist Party yearly received a mere $150,000 in "Moscow gold."

With the wave of publicity after the bust-up of the summit, the Director had no time at all to bring the Bureau up to speed on the long-denied Mafia. But he readily grasped a convenient truth: he could utilize the same intel-gathering apparatus that the Bureau employed against political radicals to surveil the mob. The techniques, equipment, and experience were already in place, ready to be retrained and refocused.

Once Hoover unleashed his dogs, they went at it with ferocious energy. Black-bag teams fanned out across the country, breaking and entering hundreds of venues habituated by mobsters, passing through walls like ghosts, leaving behind hidden electronic gifts, spike mikes, wiretaps, and radio-operated recorders. They were the kind of gifts that kept on giving, yielding mountains of transcribed conversations.

In addition to bugs and taps, field agents copied documents, rooted through financial records, conducted extensive physical surveillance. This was the period when the FBI started showing up with cameras at mob funerals. Along with the private residences of the "top hoodlums," teams hit businesses and social venues, the homes of girlfriends and the offices of lawyers.

The flaw in Hoover's strategy—and it was a killing one—became clear only when mobsters were hauled into court. Under the "fruit of the poisonous tree" judicial principle, which excluded evidence obtained by such warrantless means as the FBI used extensively, cases collapsed as soon as any hint of the illegal surveillance activities came to light.

The black-bag teams went to elaborate ends to make sure this didn't happen. Two agents trailed the target to ensure against an unannounced return to the premises. While a pair of agents made the actual entry, three or four monitored the exterior of the targeted building. Even so, black-bag jobs had a way of going off the rails. An FBI team had to knock unconscious a local police officer who stumbled in on one of their break-ins. Another time, after an agent put his foot through a ceiling joist, the team had to quickly plaster over the hole he had made.

As he did habitually, Hoover fudged the rule of law in order to do what he wanted to do. He himself admitted the break-ins were "clearly illegal." Attorney General William P. Rogers, who took office a mere three weeks before Apalachin and was still getting his feet wet at Justice, did not immediately grasp the extent of the Top Hoodlum surveillance, primarily because Hoover kept him in the dark.

In order to do this, the Director relied specifically on an iffy interpretation of a secret May 20, 1954 directive by Rogers's predecessor, a highly malleable attorney general named Herbert Brownell Jr. The memo covered FBI activities against "espionage agents, possible saboteurs, and subversive persons." Even though Brownwell's directive clearly did not cover the Top Hoodlum black-bag jobs, Hoover acted as though it did. No one was around with enough power to correct him.

Much of the time, the Director simply resorted to an elaborate bureaucratic lie to hide his activities. Documentation for the jobs was labeled "Do Not File" and did not enter Hoover's elaborate Library of Congress–style records system. Instead, reports were routed to a top-secret cache within the Director's private office. The existence of the "Do Not File" files—an existential concept if there ever was one—thus could not be detected by any cursory search, and their destruction could likewise be accomplished without exposure or leaving behind telltale traces.

Nevertheless, and for all their elaborate precautions, the FBI teams saw their illicit surveillance activities poison case after case. "An FBI wiretap," writes one longtime Bureau watcher, "in effect immunized a crime leader from prosecution."

Coming, as it did, in the immediate aftermath of Apalachin, the onslaught of black-bag jobs targeting organized crime figures naturally turned up evidence of the summit, registering the shock wave that passed through the mob. It was as if the agents, listening in, were hearing the reverberating echoes of what happened on November 14.

In Chicago, for example, teams placed microphones in over a dozen venues, including a large "pineapple" mike in a downtown tailor shop and several bugs in a former speakeasy called the Armory Lodge, both frequented by Sam Giancana. The result was a flood of tape-recorded words, most of them couched in the Sicilian dialect. None of it was legally admissible or forensically suitable, but much of it was enlightening, representing a veritable crash course in Mafia 101. The Bureau, kept in the dark for so long, had a steep learning curve, but its agents caught up quickly.

Amid the jabbering of the boss and his henchmen came this gem, caught on a phone tap, providing Giancana's stinging postmortem of the meeting at Joe Barbara's. A contrite Steven Magaddino offers his regrets for the debacle that, after all, happened on his home turf.

> Giancana: I hope you're satisfied. Sixty-three of our top guys made by the cops.
> Magaddino: I got to admit you're right, Sam. It never would have happened in your place.
> Giancana: You're fucking right it wouldn't. This is the safest place in the world for a big meet. We got three towns just outside of Chicago with the police chiefs in our pocket. We got what none of you guys got. We got this territory locked up tight.

Hindsight, always 20/20.

The eavesdropped conversation, apart from indicating that Giancana had in fact been present at Apalachin but slipped through the police net, offered insight into the degree the Mafia had penetrated the mainstream political establishment. Mobsters were inveterate liars, and that boast about three dirty police chiefs could have been Giancana just gassing on. Still, there did seem to be a lot of John C. Montanas running around America, putting up careful facades that concealed corrupt cores.

Years of solitary police work by Sergeant Edgar Croswell culminated in his Nov. 14, 1957, face-off with dozens of high-ranking mobsters in Apalachin, New York. (Courtesy of Robert Croswell)

Sergeant Joe Benenati, later longtime sheriff of Chenango County, New York, participated in the bust-up of the mob meeting and conducted follow-up investigations. (*The Evening Sun*/Norwich, CT)

Croswell's partner, Trooper Vincent Vasisko, manned the roadblocks alongside him. (Courtesy of Delores Vasisko)

Vito Genovese aspired to "boss of bosses" status, and the gathering at Apalachin was to be his coronation. (NYC Municipal Archives)

Albert Anastasia's murder triggered the need for a meeting to determine succession questions and a parceling out of the spoils. (Bettmann/Corbis/ AP Images)

The press lampooned Joe Bonanno as "the man who wasn't there" for his bogus denial of being present at the summit. (AP/Wide World)

Tight-fisted "Olive Oil King" Joe Profaci served as one of the models for Vito Corleone in *The Godfather*, and was the first New York City mob boss to arrive at Apalachin. (Library of Congress)

Tommy Lucchese approached the meeting late, spotted state police roadblocks, and fled. (AP/Wide World)

Buffalo mob boss Steven Magaddino campaigned to hold the gathering in his territory and attended as host, but managed to elude state police dragnets. (Library of Congress)

Frontman to the mob in the Scranton, Pennsylvania, area, summit co-host Russell Bufalino often rode the extensive horse trails around the Apalachin estate. (AP/Wide World)

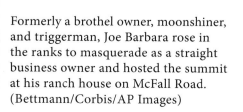

Formerly a brothel owner, moonshiner, and triggerman, Joe Barbara rose in the ranks to masquerade as a straight business owner and hosted the summit at his ranch house on McFall Road. (Bettmann/Corbis/AP Images)

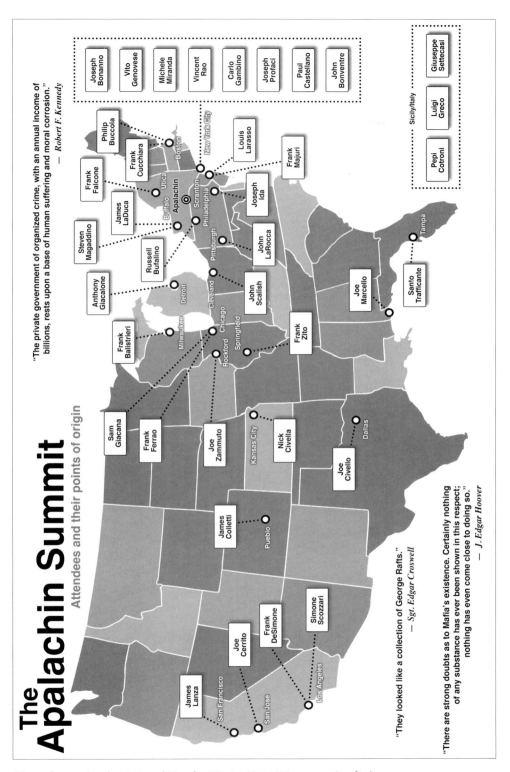

The
Apalachin Summit

Attendees and their points of origin

"The private government of organized crime, with an annual income of billions, rests upon a base of human suffering and moral corrosion."
— *Robert F. Kennedy*

Joseph Bonanno
Vito Genovese
Michele Miranda
Vincent Rao
Carlo Gambino
Joseph Profaci
Paul Castellano
John Bonventre

Sicily/Italy

Pepi Cotroni
Luigi Greco
Giuseppe Settecasi

Philip Buccola
Frank Cucchiara
Frank Falcone
James LaDuca
Steven Magaddino
Russell Bufalino
Anthony Giacalone
Louis Larasso
Frank Majuri
Joseph Ida
John LaRocca
John Scalish
Frank Zito
Frank Balistrieri
Joe Marcello
Santo Trafficante
Sam Giacana
Frank Ferrao
Joe Zammuto
Nick Civella
Joe Civello
James Colletti
Simone Scozzari
Frank DeSimone
Joe Cerrito
James Lanza

Boston
New York City
Utica
Apalachin
Scranton
Philadelphia
Buffalo
Pittsburgh
Detroit
Cleveland
Chicago
Milwaukee
Rockford
Springfield
Kansas City
Dallas
Pueblo
Los Angeles
San Francisco
San Jose
Tampa

"They looked like a collection of George Rafts."
— *Sgt. Edgar Croswell*

"There are strong doubts as to Mafia's existence. Certainly nothing of any substance has ever been shown in this respect; nothing has even come close to doing so."
— *J. Edgar Hoover*

Map of attendees' origins. (Map by Kevin Hein/Metroray Studio)

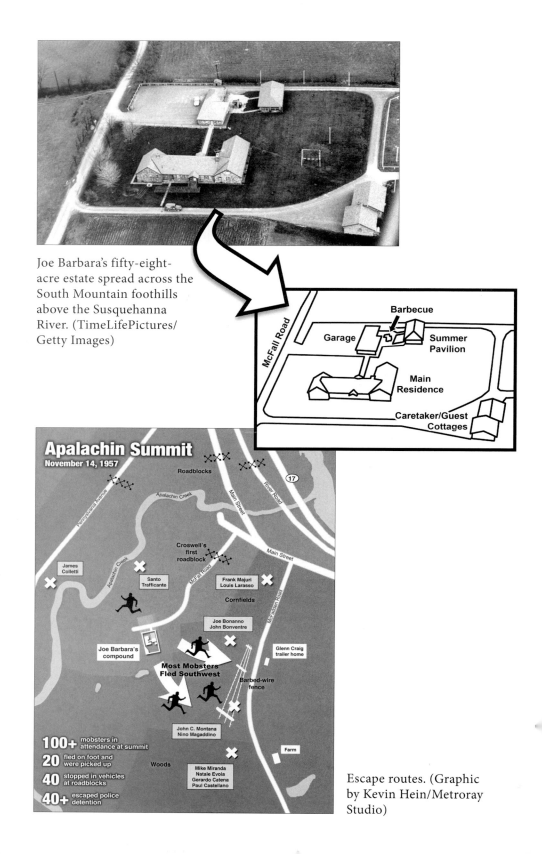

Joe Barbara's fifty-eight-acre estate spread across the South Mountain foothills above the Susquehanna River. (TimeLifePictures/Getty Images)

Escape routes. (Graphic by Kevin Hein/Metroray Studio)

Man-cave spectacular: the bar in Barbara's garage, where Carmine Lombardozzi awaited word on his death sentence. (TimeLifePictures/Getty Images)

Many of the low-level soldiers at the gathering assembled in the screened-in summer pavilion. (TimeLifePictures/Getty Images)

Buffalo's "Man of the Year," John C. Montana after his arrest on federal conspiracy charges in the wake of Apalachin. (Library of Congress)

The iconic barbecue, around which the assembled steak-eaters enjoyed a grill-it-yourself feast. (TimeLifePictures/Getty Images)

Mafia hitman Carmine Galante's murderous activities helped draw police attention to Barbara, and he eventually wound up victim of a mob hit himself. (AP/Wide World)

Attorney General Robert Kennedy clashed repeatedly with J. Edgar Hoover over the FBI's "hands-off" policy toward organized crime, but President John Kennedy laid down the law to his brother: "You've got to get along with that old man!" (National Archives)

Joe Barbara's estate served briefly as a tourist attraction before becoming a private residence once again. (TimeLifePictures/Getty Images)

The question was, how far did the official corruption reach? If there were dirty police chiefs and, like Montana, dirty city councilmen, were dirty governors, congressmen, senators also within reach? If that were the case, the mob did indeed represent a threat to the commonwealth. Perhaps the national security rationale of Hoover's covert surveillance campaign did have logic on its side.

Across town from where the Director played Mafia catch-up in his SOG headquarters, in the hearing rooms of the Old Senate Office Building, Bobby Kennedy and John McClellan developed their own views of the mob threat to national security. "We've got to determine if the government is bigger than the hoodlums," McClellan said.

The first man he and Kennedy turned to, when they decided to train their eyes on the national scope of organized crime, was Ed Croswell.

14

The Watchdogs

SUNDAY, THREE DAYS AFTER THE BUST-UP of the summit, Ed Croswell made another foray to the big stone compound at the end of McFall Road. All was silent as a tomb. The main house was buttoned up. The gravel lot in front of the garage, parked thick the day before, now was empty.

Croswell sought something specific. He cracked open the doors of a barn on the edge of the estate, near the caretaker cottages. Inside, he discovered the pink Lincoln coupe belonging to James LaDuca, the very same vehicle the owner swore was still parked in his driveway in Lewiston, a hundred and fifty miles away.

Performing a quick search of the car's interior, Croswell pulled out a shucked-off suit coat that conveniently identified its owner with a name sewn into the lining. "Stefano Magaddino." The Buffalo mob boss had been at the summit after all. He was one of the quick-swimming fishies, a very big one indeed, who had slipped through the net.

Croswell had Vasisko drive the Lincoln to the Vestal substation. He told the owner that if he wanted it back, he should come and get it. A couple days later, on Tuesday, November 19, LaDuca and his lawyer slunk in. Oh, *that* coral pink 1957 Lincoln. Yeah, that turned out not to be parked back home in the driveway after all.

Snagging the car was to be the last piece of detection, of actual physical hands-on investigating, that Investigator Croswell would do for quite some time. Beginning the week after Apalachin, and for months forward, he would be swept up in an incredible welter of government hearings, grand jury appearances, and courtroom testimony. Over the weekend he had finally gotten some shut-eye, but for the near future he would rarely be allowed to catch his breath. Everyone wanted testimony from him. Through no intent of his own, the Tall Ghost had somehow stepped into the spotlight as the man of the hour.

The '58 elections were still a year away, but they were important—not so much on the federal level, but for the state of New York, where a governorship would be up for grabs. With a Republican-controlled senate and Democrat Averill Harriman in the statehouse, the battle lines were clearly drawn.

The GOP endured heavy losses in local elections the week before the summit. Immediately after the fact, Apalachin became a contested political topic and, by extension, so did organized crime. To have a chance in November '59, the Republicans required a hot-button issue. They seized upon this one, dished up straight from the headlines.

Harriman had been soft on the Mafia, his political opponents charged, allowing mobsters to run wild in New York State. The gathering at Joe Barbara's was proof positive. In Albany, the Republican senators needed a soapbox, so they convened one in the form of the Joint Legislative Committee on Government Operations, otherwise known as the Watchdog Committee.

In early December, only a month after the Apalachin meeting, the committee met in the ornate surroundings of the Senate chamber, a luxe nineteenth-century space featuring Siena marble arches, Scottish granite pillars, and Mexican onyx wall panels. The contrast between the plummy decorative atmosphere of the room and the streetwise crime lords in the dock, with their dees-and-dose diction, was well remarked upon by the press.

Assemblyman William F. Horan, a Westchester Republican whom the *Times* described as "short, stocky and mild-mannered," chaired the proceedings, backed up by the state senator in whose jurisdiction the summit occurred, Daniel Dickinson, Republican of Binghamton. Joseph Corso, a Brooklyn Democrat, was around to correct the pronunciation of Italian names ("I'm sorry," said chief counsel Arnold Bauman after mangling a few, "I thought I was doing well"). But mostly, it was a Republican show.

They kicked things off with Croswell. He told the story he had by now repeated dozens of times to reporters, to his superiors, in courtroom testimony, the tale of busting up the Apalachin summit. He didn't like to use the word "raid," he said, because he had no presentiment of what he was going to find at the top of McFall Road that day in November.

"We were just doing our job, just doing everyday police work," he said. He went out of his way to share credit with Vince Vasisko and the rest of his police cohorts.

The action began, Croswell's boss, State Police Superintendant Francis McGarvey said, as a "routine check of strangers moving into the area. We never dreamed that a mob like this was out there in the mountains."

Via Bauman, committee members pronounced their interest in what was then one of the main concerns surrounding the summit: why State Police so quickly released the Mafia chieftains they had detained.

"We had to let them go, because under the present law we couldn't hold them," Croswell testified, his voice still a little hoarse from the workout it had gotten over the past weeks. He looked pale and, well, ghostly. His gut was bothering him, an ulcer flare-up exacerbated by stress, long hours, and on-the-run eating. The *Times* had him down as "phlegmatic."

Croswell registered a plea to the legislators for new laws, mandating more time to process detainees. "If we could have held them twenty-four to forty-eight hours," he said, articulating not a civil libertarian's but a lawman's fantasy, "we would have had time to check them out."

When Croswell finished, mobster after gangster after crime lord appeared in the Senate Chamber to face the Watchdog Committee, dozens in all, and all detained at Apalachin.

Some of the witnesses were less than stellar but provided comic relief, like sixty-six-year-old fishmonger Bartolo Guccia, who in heavily accented English related his porgie-and-mackerel order on the day in question. The funny little man in the horn-rim glasses proved garrulous, telling the committee about his fish business, what his wife said, even where his mother was buried.

His lawyer leaned over to advise him to "just answer the question."

"I got to tell the truth, you know," Guccia responded, drawing laughter. (His response was rendered in the press as "I gotta tella da truth, ya know.")

Guccia's talkativeness was the exception, not the rule. Most of the participants at the summit showed up in Albany only to repeat one phrase, over and over. "On the advice of counsel, I respectfully decline to answer the question on the grounds that it may incriminate me." Joe Profaci, walking with a limp and chewing gum manically, read his Fifth Amendment catechism off a scrap of yellow paper. Vito Genovese would oftentimes repeat it even when he wasn't actually asked a question.

The communal citing of the Fifth Amendment represented a modern incarnation of the ancient principle of *omerta*, often rendered as a code of silence but actually an untranslatable prescription for a wide range of behavior. Not talking is part of it, yes, but *omerta* also mandates a surly intransigence to all authority outside the clan and an adherence to the principle of the vendetta. Sicilian courts, when faced with *omerta,* labeled it "muteness of malice."

The press called the Watchdog Committee appearances a "Parade of Silence," and kept a sort of running box score on how many times the witnesses pleaded the Fifth. Summit cohost Russell Bufalino, fourteen times. Staten Island boss Joseph Riccobono, thirty-six. Yonkers boss Vincent Rao, forty-four. Vito Genovese, a whopping 206. On a single day, December 13, mobsters cited the guarantee against self-incrimination 410 times.

The all-time batting champion proved to be Harlem drug lord John Ormento, dutifully responding "I respectfully decline . . ." 250 times (including to the question, "Where were you born?"). Ormento invoked the Fifth Amendment twice on every question, once when asked and again when committee chairman Horan directed him to answer.

The Watchdog investigators were nothing if not thorough. By their own tally they combed through over sixty million separate documents on the trail of the Apalachin mobsters, checking with 3,600 separate government offices, from correctional bureaus to liquor boards to such sprawling federal entities as the Securities and Exchange Commission and the Housing Authority. The Committee found that one of the participants at the summit turned up in the records of almost two hundred police departments around the state of New York.

John T. Cusack, a Federal Bureau of Narcotics agent who once busted jazz saxophonist Charlie Parker for heroin, appeared before the Watchdog legislators to scare them silly about the drug threat. He viewed the Apalachin meeting strictly through the lens of his own preoccupations, stating that dope trafficking "had a prominent place on the agenda."

"Important" seemed a favorite word of Cusack's to describe the summit mobsters. John Ormento, he said, was "one of the most active and important" traffickers in the whole country. Joe Civello of Dallas and Dominick D'Agostino of Niagara Falls, linked respectively to Carlos Marcello of New Orleans and Steven Magaddino of Buffalo, were fingered by the agent as dope peddlers of "major importance." Cusack likewise termed Carmine Galante "an important figure in illicit narcotic traffic."

A lot of smoke, but no fire. The Watchdog Committee set the trend for every subsequent government investigation of the Apalachin summit. Be it the Watchdog Committee's Arnold Bauman or the Rackets Committee's Robert F. Kennedy, the chief counsel would pose a question. Then the crime boss witnesses would cite the Fifth Amendment in declining to answer. The stalemate would be chipped away at—jail terms handed out, immunity offered—but never fully breached.

"The committee might never find out what happened [at the summit]," admitted chief counsel Bauman, striking the first note of the "mystery of Apalachin" theme that would eventually swell to a widely accepted soundtrack for journalists writing about the gathering.

Getting hauled up to Albany on a legislative subpoena was bad enough, but the Watchdog Committee was merely one investigation among an even dozen that were mounted by year's end. Along with the formal inquiries, there were myriad small regulatory assaults on the summit participants, the kind of penny-ante nickel-and-diming that the government could effortlessly accomplish whenever it decided to target someone.

The state suspended the notary licenses of a couple of the Apalachin mobsters (that'll learn 'em!). They withdrew prestigious low-numbered automobile license plates, including James LaDuca's 62JL. More seriously, the State Liquor Authority (SLA) stripped the summit mobsters of whatever liquor permits they possessed. Joe Barbara saw his bottling plant lose its license to distribute beer. Rather than fight the loss, he gave up on a $600,000-a-year component of his business because, he sent word to the SLA, his doctor said he might be near death.

Quite a few summit participants had pistol permits, and those, too, were summarily withdrawn. "The revolver has reposed in a cabinet in my office for the past many years," wrote Montana, adopting a comically seigneurial tone when giving up his. "I have no use for the same, and I am pleased to deliver to you herewith both the permit and the revolver."

Joe Profaci's brother-in-law, driver, and underboss, Joseph Magliocco, fifty-nine, who put up a straight front as a Brooklyn beer distributor, had a gun permit issued to him by NYPD Captain Joseph Workman, identified as the "worst grafter in the police department." Magliocco lost both carrying permit and beer license. Joe Barbara's weapons license, the one he carried when he'd first encountered Ed Croswell, dated back to 1938.

Quoth Joe, in a written statement via his attorney: "If there is any criticisms of me having a gun, I will voluntarily surrender it." There were, and he did.

New York City detectives revisited the still-unsolved Albert Anastasia killing, summoning one summit mobster after another to see if questioning them could shake anything loose. Joe Riccobono, Carmine Lombardozzi, and Mike Miranda were all hauled back in. Reporters asked Joe Profaci, leaving Brooklyn police headquarters after a grueling twenty-hour third degree, what the cops were after. "They apparently want me dead," responded Profaci, identified as a "frightened man" in newspaper accounts.

Paul Castellano was equally demonstrative with newsmen waiting for him after his interrogation. "You're as bad as the cops," he said. "Have a heart, I have a family to think about. What do you want to do, get me knocked off?"

The specter that the mob feared most, however, came not from any traditional law enforcement entity, but from the Immigration and Naturalization Service (INS). Many of the Apalachin participants—including, most notably, cohost Russell Bufalino—found themselves wrapped up in interminable and hard-to-defend deportation proceedings. The rules were perplexing at INS hearings, and the bureaucracy could be maddeningly opaque.

The rain of subpoenas continued. The public was treated to the spectacle of another mob boss tamed: on December 2, Vito Genovese sat alone and forlorn, wearing his trademark eyeglasses with darkened amber lenses, in the foyer of a New Jersey courthouse, waiting to be called by a Mercer County grand jury. He showed up without bodyguard or lawyer, twenty-five minutes late for a nine a.m. appointment with the court.

"I wish to be left alone, if you guys don't mind," Vito said to badgering newsmen. "Your guess is as good as mine why I'm here."

Trenton might be pretty far afield from Apalachin, but Vito's presence there indicated the ripple effect that occurred after the bust-up of the summit. Genovese's official residence in Atlantic Highlands put him squarely in the sights of the New Jersey district attorney. Other Jersey boys who had been present at the mob gathering, including Jerry Catena, Joe Ida, and Dominick Oliveto, were also called to testify.

Another Garden Stater found himself busy elsewhere. Frank Majuri, the gambler who gave police an unlikely story when picked up at Apalachin ("Just up there looking over some real estate"), faced County Judge Milton Feller in Elizabeth, New Jersey. By leaving the state without informing his parole officer, Majuri had violated the terms of probation on his July 1956 bookmaking beef.

Croswell and his fellow state police sergeant Joe Benenati traveled to Elizabeth to testify in the Majuri proceedings, with Benenati recounting that Majuri "had burrs on his overcoat" when he was picked up. Croswell noted obvious flaws in the story the gambler gave about his activities that day. A realtor he named turned out not to exist. He said he and his cohort Louis

Larasso had come to the area via the Pennsylvania Railroad, but the closest station on that line is in Elmira, eighty miles away from Binghamton.

Majuri's lawyer Ed Cohen posed a plaintive question to the court, assumably rhetorical: "Where would men like Majuri fit into the picture of a gathering of the top men of the underworld, the powerful, intelligent overlords?" By the end of the hearing Majuri's relative level of intelligence, at least, was no longer in question, given the howlers he was wont to tell police.

The ultimate outcome of the proceedings was also never in much doubt. Judge Feller tossed Majuri back in prison for a two-year stretch. The small-time bookie thus held the distinction of being the first Apalachin participant to see jail time as a result of the bust-up of the summit.

The next two casualties were, oddly enough, not mobsters at all, but a pair of mobbed-up cops. As the furor surrounding the meeting rose in the pages of the press and the halls of government, the year-old bribery attempt that occurred during the Carmine Galante traffic stop reared its ugly head again. Sergeant Croswell's old supplicants for justice, Captain Christopher Gleitsmann and Sergeant Peter Policastro of the West New York force, the same ones who had offered a thousand dollars to slip Galante off the leash, were now officially charged with malfeasance.

Croswell went to West New York to testify. He felt "embarrassed," he said, to take the stand against a fellow officer. He described Gleitsmann as "nervous" as he proposed the transaction. Croswell also hauled out something new, a never-before-revealed tape recording of the bribe attempt that he had made at the Five Points station at the time.

Both West New York cops were doomed. Gleitsmann, Policastro, Commissioner Modarelli, and the West New York chief of police were indicted for the bribe attempt. The others suffered only administrative punishments, but the courts convicted Gleitsmann and he served time. Apalachin notoriety, if not the summit itself, claimed another victim.

The Watchdog proceedings in Albany. A grand jury in Trenton. A probation hearing in Elizabeth. A corruption trial in West New York. Another grand jury ramping up in Tioga County, New York. In the last month of 1957 and the first few months of the following year, Ed Croswell found himself constantly on the move, constantly in demand as a witness. His gangster shadows trooped after him on the same circuit, dozens of them served with subpoenas and compelled to appear.

New York State's investigations of the summit mobsters resembled out-of-town tryouts. The show was ready to hit Broadway, with the federal government about to get involved, and Bobby Kennedy acting a star turn.

On November 24, ten days after Apalachin, Dwight Eisenhower, the president who took J. Edgar Hoover's word at face value, and thus never evinced much interest in the plundering of America by the Mafia, experienced a mild stroke. He recovered, but the administration had clearly entered its sunset phase. For the first time, not only tradition but a constitutional amendment prevented a chief executive from seeking a third term. Jockeying over who would become Ike's replacement began in earnest.

When reporters wanted a comment on the bust-up of the summit from Estes Kefauver, they had to reach out to Paris, where the senator was attending a NATO conference. "Congratulations to the New York State Police," the still-viable presidential candidate said. "This should do much to disperse the gangs."

In early December, Joe Kennedy scored a coup in the effort to get his son some national publicity for the coming 1960 presidential campaign. "I just bought a horse for $75,000," Kennedy père told Francis Cardinal Spellman in conversation. "And for another $75,000 I put Jack on the cover of *Time* magazine."

The December 2, 1957 issue of the news magazine showed an arty portrait of a handsome, unsmiling JFK in the Senate chambers. Inside, the article labeled him "The Democratic Whiz of 1957."

With his brother's face still gracing the newsstands, Bobby called together thirty-three field investigators on the staff of the Senate Rackets Committee for a closed-door session, their first joint discussion in nearly a year. The agents traded intel, filed reports, established what their investigations had yielded thus far. After that meeting, on December 22, Bobby announced a new Rackets Committee probe centering on the participants at the summit.

"Facets of the information gleaned thus far" by the committee investigators, he said, "fits into the meeting at Apalachin, [in that] a number of them are involved in labor, a considerable number are employers in the garment industry."

Bobby Kennedy planned to serve Senate subpoenas, he said, on every single participant of the summit. Rampant union racketeering on the part of those at the gathering gave him the basis for going after them, since the McClellan Committee was on paper charged with investigating corrupt labor practices.

Apalachin was, among other things, a conference of dressmakers.

Dominick Alaimo had the Jane Hogan Dress Company; Angelo Sciandra, the Dixie Frocks Company and Claudia Frocks; Joe Riccobono, Christine Dresses and Toni Belle Dresses. Anthony Guarnieri served as vice president of Binghamton's Tri Cities Dress Company, and Bufalino's bodyguard, Murph Loquasto, listed his job of record as the Northeastern Needleworkers Association, Pittston.

Beyond Scranton, in New York City, Natale Evola was the "shoulder pad king," effectively controlling the pad trade in the garment district. And it had to be remembered that Albert Anastasia himself was, on the books at least, part owner of a dress factory in New Jersey.

As 1957 passed into 1958, events on the political landscape began to cascade, in a way that would eventually overwhelm news about the motley gathering of mob bosses in Southern Tier New York. It was only by an accident of personality—Bobby Kennedy's personality—that the thread that began on November 14, 1957 was taken up and followed during the tumultuous times leading up to the 1960 presidential election, three years later to the month. Even though he was preoccupied running his brother's political campaigns, first for the Senate in 1958, then the White House in 1960, Bobby always kept one eye cocked on the mob.

The realpolitik take on the Kennedy organized crime fixation treated it strictly as a campaign strategy. Jack and Bobby had learned from Kefauver what a potent issue it could be. In addition, the Kennedys had to distance themselves from their father's unsavory underworld associates.

The old Prohibition-era divide of American politics, with urban Roman Catholics facing off against rural Protestants, might have been changing, but still remained in place. The Kennedys were hyper-aware that JFK would be the first viable Catholic presidential candidate since the Al Smith debacle in 1928.

"If I were governor of a large state, Protestant and 55, I could sit back and let [the nomination] come to me," Jack Kennedy said in late 1957. "But if I am going to get it, I'll have to work for it—and damn hard."

Rightly or wrongly, the public perceived organized crime within an urban-immigrant-Catholic context. Never mind that the Kennedys were Irish and the Mafia was Italian, to a lot of voters the distinction didn't make much difference. Via his work on the Rackets Committee, Jack Kennedy could demonstrate his tough-on-the-mob bona fides, and thus help allay the fears of those leery of his background.

Committee work proved to be a publicity bonanza for the brothers.

Look magazine alone took some eight thousand pictures of the photogenic Kennedys for feature spreads in the widely popular publication. With the backdrop of that fusty Senate Caucus Room, many Americans recognized for the first time that with Jack and Bobby the country had a couple of politicians with movie star good looks.

Given Bobby's hard-nosed approach to getting his brother elected, his motivations no doubt had purely pragmatic elements. But a funny thing happened on the way to the White House. If he initially perceived the Rackets Committee as a vehicle for Jack's political ambitions, beginning with Apalachin he began to see racketbusting as a righteous cause in and of itself. The mob offended Bobby's sustaining ideal, his sense of justice. What started out as a strategy became a passion.

The second session of the Rackets Committee convened on June 30, 1958, a sultry, sopping day in Washington, with the outdoor temperature nearing ninety degrees and the humidity over eighty percent. Since the Old Senate Office Building was the first structure on Capitol Hill to have air-conditioning as part of its original equipment, the atmosphere inside the Caucus Room was cooler, dryer, marmoreal.

As usual during that period when he was laid up with back surgery, Jack Kennedy was absent. Chairman John McClellan opened the proceedings, with Bobby as his point man and Senators Goldwater, Ervin, and Church, among others, present on the panel.

"As a starting point for our hearings," McClellan began, "we intend to focus on the criminal group which held a meeting at the home of Joseph Barbara Sr., in Apalachin, New York, on November 14, 1957. The discovery of this meeting by the New York State Police had the effect of revealing the scope of the interrelationships of some of the leaders of the national crime syndicate."

Then McClellan handed the ball off to his chief counsel. "As we are going into this meeting in Apalachin, Mister Chairman," Bobby said, "the first witness will be Sergeant Edgar Croswell."

More than a half year had passed since the summit, and the Croswell who took the stand in the Caucus Room that day clearly showed the strain. Anyone who had known him pre-Apalachin would have been shocked at the change.

Gaunt, drawn, pale, Croswell popped stomach pills and sipped at a glass of milk throughout his time on the witness stand. His ulcerous gut—a condition he shared, coincidentally, with the other Edgar, FBI Director Hoover, as well as with many members of the Kennedy family and such mobsters as L.A.'s Frank DeSimone and Yonkers boss Vincent Rao—would plague him for the remainder of his life and eventually bring him low.

Croswell struggled but made it through the hearing, recounting the tale of the summit bust-up, not deviating, giving a straightforward, just-the-facts-ma'am rendition. On the subject of Joe Barbara, Croswell went into gory detail about the multiple murder charges the man had dodged. The only Federal violation that had stuck turned out to be the illegal acquisition of sugar moonshining arrest, for which Barbara drew a $5,000 fine and no jail time.

"Among police authorities in the Pittston, Pennsylvania, area where he lived for many years," Croswell said about Barbara, "he was known to be connected with a lot of things that could never be proven."

There were a few light moments during the course of the afternoon, but those were mostly provided by the senators themselves. During a recitation of Carmine Galante's arrest record, Croswell mentioned that the mobster had pulled a twelve and a half year stretch in Sing Sing for assault. "I believe I am correct in this, that was a result of shooting his parole officer." After serving only six years of the initial term, Croswell noted, Galante was paroled.

"Did they find a volunteer to be a parole officer?" Senator Karl Mundt of South Dakota wanted to know. "Having shot the first one it would be pretty hard to get the second one."

Titters in the Caucus Room.

Kennedy had been well-briefed beforehand on the kind of testimony Croswell would give, and repeatedly fed him setup lines to elicit specific points. On the fashion sense of the Apalachin mobsters (a particular fascination of Kennedy's), there was this exchange:

Kennedy: Could you describe what they looked like, some of these people?
Croswell: Before they went in the woods or afterward?
Kennedy: Well, describe both.
Croswell: They were all dressed for the most part in silk suits, and white-on-white shirts, and highly polished, pointed shoes, and broad-brimmed hats, and typical George Raft style.
Kennedy: Was that before they went in the woods?
Croswell: Yes, sir.

Kennedy: What did they look like, the ones you picked up, that came
out of the woods?

Croswell: Some of them lost their hats and they were a little bedraggled,
and they were full of cockle burrs and their shoes were kind of scuffy.

Once again, the hand played out largely as it had in Albany in front of the
Watchdog Committee. Croswell testified first, setting up the Apalachin
mobsters who came after him. Setting them up, yes, but the Fifth Amendment prevented them from being knocked down. The litany of "I decline to
answer on the grounds that it may tend to incriminate me" rang out in the
Caucus Room throughout the summer Rackets Committee session, and
continued on into yet more hearings in 1959.

Bobby became increasingly testy and over the months sharpened his
tone considerably. Off-mike, he would deliver profane asides to the mobsters sitting in the witness stand. "You're full of shit," he'd jeer at them.

During an appearance of Chicago boss Sam Giancana, Bobby faced a
man who, unbeknownst to him at the time, shared a mistress with Jack—
they were quite literally strange bedfellows. As he sparred with Giancana,
Bobby became upset when Momo appeared to laugh after citing the Fifth
Amendment rote, triggering this famous live-on-national-TV response:

"Are you going to tell us anything or just giggle, Mister Giancana?"
Kennedy sneered. "I thought only little girls giggled."

In a rare appearance on the panel that summer, Jack also gave a quote-
worthy performance. "We only have one rule around here," he announced.
"If they're crooks, we don't wound them, we kill them."

The Rackets Committee could not, in fact, string its victims up, but it
did have subpoena power, and it could cite uncooperative witnesses with
contempt of Congress charges. But that was a question of jail time, not
prison terms. The Kennedy brothers finally went away frustrated from the
hearings on the Apalachin summit.

The uncertainty still persisted: What really happened at the mob gathering up on McFall Road? Bobby took it personally. He appeared irritated that
a collection of hoodlums could deny him their secrets. When the Rackets
Committee closed up shop for the season, Bobby petulantly declared, "We
know the reason for the Apalachin meeting."

The mobsters were there, he said, to carve up the territory left behind by
the abruptly departed Albert Anastasia. He was right about that, of course.
But there was a lot more to it.

Bobby's assertion was largely a bluff, an angry young man's assertion that he had not been beaten. He, too, like New York State's Watchdog Committee, had after two sessions of hearings merely battered his head against the brick wall of the Fifth Amendment. A legislative venue once again proved too fine a tool to attack the mob. Bobby didn't need a scalpel. He required a sledgehammer.

The Justice Department, just down Constitution Avenue from the chambers of the Senate Office Building where the Rackets Committee held its hearings, could offer just that. With hundreds of lawyers and million-dollar budgets, Justice was known as "the largest law firm in the world with the richest client, the U.S. government."

Sure, J. Edgar Hoover sat atop Justice like a troll on a gold pile, but to Bobby's way of thinking, somebody had to maneuver around that old man and attack organized crime before it corrupted the whole country. Whatever Hoover said about the Mafia, however hard he worked to dismiss it, the summit at Joe Barbara's proved the danger was real. As one commentator put it, "The Apalachin debacle provided Robert Kennedy with the pretext he needed to wage a national war on crime."

In the fall of 1958, with his brother's help as campaign director, Jack Kennedy easily won reelection to the Senate. He had needed a good showing to set himself up for a run at the White House, and he got one, garnering 73 percent of the vote. The future looked rosy. Robert could dare to look ahead toward a possible role in Jack's administration.

There was one Apalachin gangster that the Watchdogs, the Rackets Committee, and all other government entities had failed to reach. Joe Barbara, the man best able to inform the world about what went down at the summit, was protected by a weak constitution of his own. He remained unwilling and, according to doctors, unable to talk.

Shut up in the stone house on McFall Road as though he were preparing for a long siege, Joe Barbara allowed Joe Jr. to take over the day-to-day operations of the bottling plant. The family beverage firm wobbled noticeably in the unwelcome light of scandal. The State Liquor Authority continually dogged it. Its parent company, Canada Dry, attempted to quickly distance itself from its wayward franchisee.

But the only legal repercussions to hit the family so far were Junior's contempt of court beef, and a perjury charge flowing from it. He spent fourteen months inside for refusing to tell what he knew about the summit, and copped a deal on the perjury rap.* But the government had so far proved unable to lay a glove on his father.

By the fall of 1958, authorities had been trying to get at Joe Barbara for a full year. While Genovese, Profaci, Bonanno, and the other bosses endured hearing after hearing, the actual host of the gathering somehow remained immune. His doctors always pled a weak heart, allowing him to avoid court appearances.

Was his condition real or was he malingering? Eventually, the state began throwing doctors at Barbara, teams of them, recognized heart specialists such as Binghamton internist Ronald L. Hamilton, Dr. Charles K. Friedburg, Chief of Cardiology at New York's Mount Sinai and Dr. Richard H. Lyons, professor of internal medicine at Syracuse University Medical School.

On the government's dime, they assembled at the house on McFall Road, where Josephine had installed her husband in a rented hospital-style bed in the formal living room. The physicians likened Barbara's condition to the congestive heart disease of President Eisenhower.

You didn't need a specialist to diagnose poor Joe. All that was necessary was a stethoscope, and if you didn't have one handy, you could just look at the guy. The gray pallor gave him away. His heart was a sluggish pump. Myocardial infarction, the doctors diagnosed, a condition that rendered the patient "a complete cardiac cripple." Too weak to travel. Possibly could be questioned at home.

"He had a coronary thrombosis in January 1957," said Josephine Barbara. "He can't even reach up and blow his nose without feeling pain." The minor attack on the day of the summit laid him up for good. His son told the Watchdog Commission in Albany that after November 14, 1957, his father had never left the fifty-eight-acre estate. Throughout 1958, Barbara took the sacraments of the church weekly in his home, just to be safe.

There were a few things wrong with this picture of a sick, secluded mobster. Earlier that year, in May 1958, Joe Barbara Sr. managed to apply for an extension of his driver's license. An Endicott cop named Charles Wilcox swore he had seen him in town in the fall of 1958, riding in a car driven by his son.

Croswell's State Police cohorts, his immediate boss, Inspector Robert

---

* When police came to arrest Junior at the McFall Road house, he was in his pajamas and bathrobe, but refused to allow the officers inside, fearing they would use the occasion to confront his father. Instead, he had his sister and mother pass clothes to him outside, and dressed in thirty-degree weather in full view of the cops.

E. Denman, as well as the head of the Bureau of Criminal Investigation, chief inspector Martin F. Dillon out of Albany, and Vestal commander Lieutenant Kenneth E. Weidenborner, huddled to decide on strategy. They had to breach Fortress Barbara somehow, to serve a subpoena on the reclusive gangster at the center of the whole affair.

The job should naturally have gone to Croswell. He owned Apalachin. He even sent out Christmas cards that year with an Apalachin postmark, in a sly reference to the summit. But he had been hard at it for a year, and suffered from the severe peptic ulcers that would soon put him in the hospital ("an occupational disease," he said).

Denman thought the Tall Ghost could use a rest, so for the subpoena mission he decided to send Sergeant Joe Benenati, like Croswell also BCI, out of Troop C's Sidney headquarters. The sergeant had been assigned to the new Criminal Investigation Unit, targeting organized crime and formed in response to Apalachin.

On September 20, 1958, a Saturday, Benenati dutifully drove up to the McFall Road house, determined to succeed where others before him had tried. Luck was not with him. He failed to surprise Joe the Barber puttering around outside, trimming the verge. The house was closed up tight. The kitchen door displayed a wrought-iron decorative gate, accented by white-metal bird sculptures, beyond which, through a glass window, Benenati could see Joe lying in bed in the downstairs living room. Then the woman of the house approached and drew shut the curtain.

From behind the closed door, Benenati explained his business. Josephine Barbara declined to open up, saying, "Joe had a rough night, and I'm sick, too."

Benenati answered back that he had to serve the subpoena somehow, keeping to the calm police politesse.

"You're wasting your time if you think you are ever getting into this house with that piece of paper," Josephine told him from inside. "I haven't been served." She then retreated out of the statie's line of sight.

All right, Benenati thought, considering the many ways to skin a cat. He put the subpoena in an envelope, addressed it to Barbara and added $16 in travel expense money, at the going rate of eight cents a mile for the roughly two hundred miles from Apalachin to New York City. He taped the envelope to the door, partially impaling it on one of the bird ornaments.

Then the sergeant returned to his squad car, took out a bullhorn, and proceeded to read portions of the subpoena at top volume, broadcasting the words in the general direction of Joe Barbara, who still lay abed inside the residence.

"Come out, come out, there's a subpoena on your front door," Benenati announced, feeling a little foolish repeating the phrase to the closed-up house.

Later, lawyers would debate the fine legal points of Benenati's service and question if the target had been served at all. Did the amplified outdoor announcement count? Was the $16 sufficient?

It didn't matter, since Barbara always pleaded illness to avoid subpoenas and court appearances. He never summoned up the heart to testify in front of the Watchdog Commission, Manhattan grand jury, or any other government committee or court, until a single last public appearance the following spring.

The notes sounded by Benenati's bullhorn probably didn't float all the way down the hill to the little village at its base, but the locals had already put up with a year of nonstop notoriety. Much to the consternation of Joe Barbara's neighbors, the name of their home hamlet had become synonymous with organized crime in the nation's newspapers.

"If only they'd mention that Apalachin is not a den of thieves," said one native, interviewed by a New York tabloid. "We're decent people down here. We have churches, good schools, nice homes. And then, of course, there's the Barbara place."

Developments had by now totally eclipsed the namesake village to play themselves out on the national stage. Between Jack's senatorial re-election campaign, a book project, and his job as the Rackets Committee chief counsel, Bobby found himself a little busy as summer 1958 passed into fall. He might not have noticed a hard-charging lawyer, a U.S. attorney working, yes, for the Justice Department, who wielded a sledgehammer of his own against the Apalachin hoods.

From a base in New York City, the attorney was in the process of proving he didn't necessarily need to know every single detail of what happened at the summit to be able to bust the chops of every mobster who had been there. In fact, he would eventually demonstrate the truism that if the Federal government ever decided to fuck anybody, the target should just as well resign themselves to getting absolutely, irrevocably, and with utter finality, fucked. No matter how big a mob boss they were, or how bulletproof they had seemed in the past.

The crusading district attorney zeroed in on the biggest of the Mister Bigs at Apalachin. And he didn't play nice.

15

The Feds Take Down Vito

WHEN THE SUMMIT BUST-UP OCCURRED, Paul W. Williams, the United States Attorney for the Southern District of New York State, could marshal a whole array of legal resources in response, including a sitting grand jury. He immediately subpoenaed, just for starters, the tax records of every mobster caught in Croswell's net. Ever since Al Capone went down on tax evasion charges in 1932, the "bookkeeper strategy" had become a shibboleth in law enforcement and mob circles both.

Williams already recognized the majority of the sixty summit mobster names listed by the New York State Police. He had been running rackets investigations since taking office in September 1955. The Southern District, based in the Federal Courthouse in downtown Manhattan's Foley Square, extended from the Battery all way up to Albany. Williams juggled cases in six courtrooms at once, with a staff of sixty-four assistant U.S. attorneys (AUSAs), recruiting the best and brightest from the nation's law schools.

He rattled off his bailiwick to a reporter: "I am the lawyer in all court matters for the F.B.I., the Secret Service, the Bureau of the Internal Revenue, the Army, Navy and Air Force, and the S.E.C., F.C.C., I.C.C. and F.H.A."—somehow neglecting to include that poor orphan of the Treasury Department, the Bureau of Narcotics. Odd, since it would be a heroin bust that figured in his greatest triumph.

Eisenhower's attorney general, William P. Rogers (who would go on to become Richard Nixon's pre-Kissinger secretary of state), had cut his teeth as an AUSA working in the same Southern District office during the late thirties and early forties under the most famous racketbuster of them all, Thomas E. Dewey. Dewey was riding high when he had Rogers on his staff, having put Charles Luciano in prison for what was supposed to be a thirty-year stretch.

Now it was Rogers's turn as attorney general to mentor his own underling, Williams. Rogers formed the first organized crime group within the Justice Department. It was small and only weakly supported, but it was a start. Apalachin gave the initiative a boost. Most of all, what the bust-up of the summit supplied to Rogers and Williams was a target list. And at the head of that list floated a single name, a man who had always emerged unscathed from past prosecutorial campaigns by the Feds.

Vito Genovese.

If you were going after the summit mobsters, picking them off one by one, why not start at the top? Post-Apalachin, Genovese wore a big bull's-eye on his back. In 1959, he got hit with no less than a dozen subpoenas (he always hissed out the word, pronouncing it "sub-penis"). Williams joined in on the scrum, serving paper on Vito and dozens of other summit participants to appear as witnesses before his grand jury. But he didn't stop there.

In the annals of government prosecutions of mob bosses, perhaps only Charles Luciano's trumped-up "direction of harlotry" charge in 1936 rivaled the frame that Williams and company put on Vito Genovese in 1959. Consciously or unconsciously, Paul Williams modeled himself on Dewey, the gangbuster and former New York governor who rode his crime-fighting pedigree all the way (if the early edition of the *Chicago Daily Tribune* was to be believed) to the presidency.

Son of a Baptist minster, the Rochester-born, Maine-raised, and Harvard-educated Williams wore a thin mustache similar to Dewey's, and just as Dewey used questionable tactics to put Luciano away, Williams clearly cut corners on Genovese. It wasn't so much that Vito wasn't guilty of plentiful wrongdoing, from dope trafficking to murder to you-name-it. It's just doubtful he was culpable in the particular case that Williams brought against him.

Genovese's narcotics trafficking charge rested upon the testimony of a single jailhouse snitch with the odd moniker of Nelson Silva Cantellops ("a name that sounded like a musk melon" wrote one mob commentator). He had fallen in with the Genovese mob while seeking backing for an electronic device for cheating at a Spanish card game.

The FBN snared Cantellops by the usual method, with narcs proceeding up the chain of supply from junkie to dealer to supplier, busting people as they went. A heroin addict arrested by FBN agent Anthony Consoli fingered Cantellops as his dealer. Another FBN agent, Steve Giorgio, went undercover and twice copped dope from Cantellops, who proved to be frightened and talkative when arrested ("laboring under fears of personal harm," is how court papers put it). Originally from Puerto Rico, he had been muling heroin and cocaine from Cuba, he said, under the direction of Joseph Di Palermo.

In the incestuous world of organized crime in New York, the same names had a bad-penny way of cropping up again and again. Di Palermo had been by Carmine Galante's side when he shot the anarchist Carlo Tresca, and was also with him during the 1956 traffic bust that reignited Ed Croswell's interest in Joe Barbara.

Along with John Ormento, Galante and Di Palermo managed a majority slice of the Mafia's heroin distribution.

They would never dirty their hands retailing smack themselves. That job they left to cheap punks like Cantellops, a street hustler afflicted with a stubborn case of syphilis, a mere courier who transported drugs all over the country, not only to New York but also Miami, Las Vegas, and El Paso. Cantellops operated out of East Harlem, which was nominally Ormento territory, but he was run by Di Palermo.

Both Ormento and Di Palermo were underbosses in the Lucchese family, though when it came to narcotics, the organizational schema of the mob was nothing if not fluid. Increasingly, given his lockgrip over Manhattan nightclub distribution, Genovese ruled over all of them.

The dope trio of Galante, Ormento, and Di Palermo wanted Cantellops to develop the narcotics market in his native Puerto Rico. Once he was jailed and under pressure from the FBN, the dealer readily gave up not only the three underbosses but Vito Genovese himself—whom, he said, had "personally blessed the [Puerto Rico] deal."

Unlikely as that scenario was, Paul Williams and his AUSA, William Tendeske, went with it. The pressure to get Vito in the wake of Apalachin was intense. Tendeske handled a lot of narcotic cases for the Southern District, heading up the so-called "Junk Squad" at the office. He had been burned before, basing prosecutions on the testimony of a single dealer who had been turned by the government. He directed the FBN agents to corroborate the Cantellops story.

With undercover narcotics officers sitting at nearby tables, Cantellops and Genovese met in a German restaurant in Midtown. Over schnitzel, Genovese acknowledged that Cantellops should proceed with the move into Puerto Rico. Author Douglas Valentine interviewed Francis E. Waters, one of the eavesdropping FBN agents who supposedly overheard Genovese in the restaurant that day, and who subsequently provided the corroboration in court that AUSA Tendeske required.

"I was a rookie agent at the time," Waters told Valentine, "and I probably would have said it, if asked to."

Not exactly a ringing affirmation, but as the phrase goes, good enough for government work. United States Attorney Williams performed the sign of the cross over the case that Tendeske and the FBN had developed, and in early July 1958, agents swept up a raft of big-name mobsters.

Genovese, Ormento, Galante, Di Palermo, and Natale Evola made the list, plus the Frank Costello shooter, Vincent Gigante, as well as thirty others. The action represented one of the biggest Mafia busts of the decade. The charge? Trafficking in heroin "in excess of 160 kilograms."

Genovese appeared in court looking like a conservative banker, wearing a custom gray suit, a matching light gray tie, his usual white-on-white shirt and white pocket square. Williams took pains to connect Genovese with his sidekick muscle, Gigante: "Their participation in the conspiracy seems to be invariably together and simultaneous." Gigante, it was said, was the one who had ushered Cantellops into the presence of the "Right Man," which was the Mafia's code-phrase for Genovese.

Not everyone was convinced. Another, more skeptical FBN agent, Frank Selvaggi, said later, "I didn't believe that Nelson Cantellops ever met Vito Genovese," who was, in Selvaggi's judgment, "the smartest of all the bosses." Selvaggi once met up with Genovese in New York's Tompkins Square Park when Vito was out on bond. Selvaggi asked him why he didn't duck prosecution by fleeing to Italy.

"Generals don't run," Genovese said. Then he told Selvaggi to get a haircut.

Enraged and jealous at the FBN for taking down such a high-profile target, J. Edgar Hoover himself characterized the case against Vito Genovese as a "frame-up" and a "travesty of justice." With the advent of Apalachin, Hoover would see the first crack in the walled reality he had constructed around himself. Events spun out of his control. He was being left behind.

Knocking down all those big shots on the word of a single syphilitic street dealer would perhaps never happen in a different age, particularly in a post-Watergate era of greater public awareness about government malfeasance. But no one was going to squawk over the railroading of a gangster like Genovese. If he wasn't in jail, he should be, or so went the formidable logic of the man in the street.

Vito did all he could to derail the case against him, up to and including murder. On the night of July 17, 1958, one of his prime dope couriers, a Luciano pawn named Cristoforo Rubino, stood on the front sidewalk outside the People's Regular Democratic Club on Central Avenue in Bushwick, Brooklyn. With him was his brother-in-law, Charles La Cascia, also heavily involved in the narcotics trade.

A gunman approached and fired four shots, two of which hit Rubino in the head and shoulder, killing him instantly. A third bullet took La Cascia in the mouth, while a fourth went wild.

Why Rubino was killed: he was about to spill secrets to Paul Williams and the Junk Squad of the Southern District D.A.'s office.

District Attorney Williams had indicted Rubino, a father with three children, on narcotics charges back in 1955, but he had only surrendered the previous December. Because he was out of jail on a $10,000 bond, Rubino could indulge his stupidity by standing outside a political club in Brooklyn—the last place a potential witness against the mob might want to be. On the night of his death Williams had him scheduled to give testimony, a week later, to the same grand jury that had delivered the indictment of Genovese.

It looked as though Rubino would be unable to make that date. Neighborhood junkies were also set for an extended period of disappointment. An FBN agent fingered Rubino as responsible for an eighth of all the heroin distributed in New York City. One of Williams's AUSAs, Joseph Soviero, told the media that Rubino had been set to give "a full blueprint on the operations of the narcotics racket, including names and places."

Vito got indicted, and Rubino had to die. As usual, no witnesses came forth to give police details regarding the murder. The shooter was only vaguely identified as a male around fifty years old. La Cascia, the wounded brother-in-law, wouldn't have talked even if his jaw hadn't been wired shut.

Without Rubino's testimony, Genovese was still going down. There was something valedictory about the hit, a swan song of a mob boss. His last kill. Vito would still be a potent force after Williams got through with him, but he would never again be a free man.

Genovese didn't stop at Rubino's murder. During his appeals, he tried to get at the government's prime witness. Paroled because of his cooperation with Williams, Cantellops set himself up with a sandwich shop in the Bronx. Genovese sent out emissaries to bribe him to recant, $3,000 up front with a promise of $27,000 more. In the presence of a priest, a notary, and three attorneys at a church in the Bronx, the amenable Nelson Cantellops declared major portions of his testimony false. A tape of the recanting, sent to the United States solicitor general, received no response.

Williams labeled Vito's narcotics bust "the most important development linked to Apalachin." It would not be the last.

By the time of Vito's 1958 indictment, the heroin parasite had wormed itself deeply into urban America. The number of addicts nationwide climbed, tripling from its postwar low. The junk-equals-crime equation took hold as rates of muggings, burglaries, and robberies increased. Author Selwyn Raab:

> The Cosa Nostra's variegated crimes—its murders, loan-sharking, extortions, gambling, brutal beatings, prostitution, political fixes, police corruption, and union and industrial racketeering—created immeasurable costs and pain for America. None of these illicit activities, however, inflicted more lasting distress on American society and damaged its quality of life more than the Mafia's large-scale introduction of heroin.

None of that pain, cost, and distress stopped the trade. The mob simply could not give up its love affair with dope. In the mid-fifties, a kilo of opium base to be had in Turkey for $15 could be turned into number four heroin with a street value (at a dollar a gram) of $340,000—a markup of over two million percent. Those were numbers dear to any mobster's heart.

What Vito Genovese had that no other mob boss could rival was a way to get the dope to the addicts on a retail, street level. His network, from which the boss was well insulated by layer upon layer of underbosses and flunkies, operated out of nightclubs he controlled in Greenwich Village, Harlem, and elsewhere: the Black Cat, the Hollywood, the 19th Hole, Club Savannah, the Moroccan Village.

Vito Genovese helped kill Billie Holiday. The heroin that the jazz singer injected into her arms, legs, toes and—in a disturbing image of a junkie in extremis—her vagina came to the singer not directly but ultimately from Genovese. During her descent into addiction, Lady Day availed herself of Vito's distribution network. The mob had a firm grip on the famous Swing Street district on Fifty-second between Fifth and Seventh Avenues, of which Holiday was considered the queen. The doormen at Vito's clubs used to hold her drugs. She copped from Chin Fu, the cook at the famed Onyx Club, founded by bootlegger Joe Helbock and into which Genovese later sank his tentacles.

Yes, the mob loved dope, but it was a love that dared not speak its name. The hierarchy of the Mafia habitually piously washed their hands of heroin. Joseph Bonanno always strenuously denied any involvement in narcotics. Genovese himself instituted a "no drugs" rule after Anastasia's hit on Frank Scalise. A mob-wide ukase against dope deals supposedly ordered death for any made man caught trafficking. But like most Mafia "laws," this one proved pure lip-service hokum.

"What the edict against narcotics really meant was that if you're involved, don't compromise any other made guys by being seen with them when you are making drug deals," said detective Ralph Salerno. "That was the main message to the troops—work alone without endangering the family."

There existed no doubt whatsoever that Vito Genovese did the crime. Over the years, he profited enormously from the illegal trade in narcotics. Now, courtesy of his Apalachin notoriety and the work of crusading United States attorney Paul Williams, he had to face the time. On April 3, 1959, after the jury stayed out for twelve hours, it returned guilty verdicts for Vito and fourteen others on narcotics conspiracy charges.

Two weeks later, on April 17, Genovese stood in court to receive sentencing. Several of his codefendants, desperate to avoid the stiff punishments mandated by the Narcotics Control Act of 1957, offered to take polygraph or truth serum tests to demonstrate their innocence.

Federal Judge Alexander Bicks appeared unmoved. To incredulous whistles and audible groans in the courtroom, he handed the sixty-two-year-old Genovese a fifteen-year prison term, effectively sentencing him to death inside. Natale Evola, a Brooklyn cousin of Josephine Barbara, drew a ten-year stretch; Di Palermo, twenty.

"All I can say, Your Honor," Genovese said to Bicks, "is that I am innocent."

A very bad day for the Mafia leadership, but a good day for others. Indirectly, Ed Croswell's actions at Apalachin had brought down the highest ranking of all New York mob bosses. It wasn't pretty, but it was done.

Some of Williams's targets managed to evade capture, at least for a while. Carmine Galante ducked police for a year before finally being cuffed after an eight-hour cat-and-mouse chase that wound up at a rain-swept rest stop on the Garden State Parkway in New Jersey. The stumpy, bald-headed mobster had been living on Pelican Island, near Genovese's home in Seaside Heights, in a Barnegat Bay retreat stocked with expensive fishing gear, a huge TV, and a cellar full of choice wines. He made frequent trips into Manhattan, hiding in plain sight right under the nose of the feds.

Nineteen fifty-nine looked to be a dark year for the mob. In Cuba, Castro had stormed down out of the hills and entered the capital. Gamblers and casino operators started to flee the island, taking only their clothes, money, wives, and girlfriends. Everything was coming crashing down around everybody's ears. You couldn't blame the summit for all of it, but you could point to Apalachin as the time when it all began to hit the fan.

Repercussions, political and otherwise, continued to spin off from the affair. The day after his office indicted Vito Genovese, United States attorney Paul W. Williams announced his candidacy for governor of New York.

Hard on the heels of its successful narcotics convictions, the federal government leveled a new series of indictments targeting the Apalachin racketeers.

This was the one that everyone had been waiting for, a conspiracy charge that flowed directly from the meeting at Joe Barbara's, busting the hoods simply for being there. It satisfied the knee-jerk response of the American public when they first heard the news of the gathering: well, can't you arrest them for *something*? The Feds would try to prove that the summit itself had violated the law.

The indictments, announced in May 1959, had a tortured genesis. A year previously, Attorney General William Rogers had organized the task force within the Justice Department (called, in a stroke of nomenclature genius, the "Special Group") specifically to mount charges against the Apalachin participants. Deputy Attorney General Lawrence E. Walsh, who as a special counsel would later prosecute the Iran-Contra affair, named an antitrust lawyer from Wall Street named Milton Wessel to head up the new task force.

The Special Group supposedly had unprecedented reach, with liaisons to the IRS, the FBN and, yes, even to Justice's own investigative arm, the FBI. It didn't exactly work out that way—Justice would have to wait for Bobby Kennedy's generalcy before that level of interagency cooperation would develop—but the intent was there.

FBI agents were still in the process of playing catch-up. Hoover was breathing down their necks, demanding results, pronto. The Top Hoodlum wiretaps had been put in place, but information on the summit mobsters was at a premium. Recalled narcotics agent George Gaffney, headquartered at the FBN offices in downtown New York: "No less than a dozen FBI agents rummaged through our files at 90 Church trying to find out who the [Apalachin] arrestees were."

Eventually, Hoover put the brakes on the Bureau's cooperation with the Special Group. Testifying before Congress, Hoover characterized Wessel's initiative as a "fishing expedition," adding, "Obviously, we have neither the manpower nor the time to waste on such speculative ventures." Even after Apalachin, the Director still proved recalcitrant when asked to cooperate with any antimob campaign outside the Bureau.

Wessel had a hard time coming up with a legal strategy to use against his targets, the mobsters whom the government had determined were at the summit, now officially tallied at seventy-two. What, exactly, had the boys done wrong?

Essentially, Wessel faced the same quandary as Ed Croswell in the immediate aftermath of the gathering, trying desperately to find a law that had been broken. Croswell had twelve hours to come up with something, and couldn't. Wessel had months, and almost failed, too.

What he finally settled upon proved to be a novel approach that would have a far-reaching legal legacy. He concentrated on the approximate half hour at Apalachin between Croswell's arrival at the Barbara estate and the exodus of the mobsters through the woods and down McFall Road, from 12:40 p.m., in other words, until 1:20 p.m. During that crucial period, Wessel surmised that the summit participants got together and prepared to meet (and circumvent) the law. They divested themselves of weapons, discarded all documentation apart from their drivers licenses or personal IDs and, most pertinently, settled upon a story they would tell police.

This last would prove critical. In agreeing upon the fabulist tale of just happening by Joe's house to wish him well in his time of illness, the mobsters had conspired together against law enforcement officers. Obstruction of justice made it a felony charge, the grail that the government had been seeking ever since the summit went down.

Wessel cautiously trotted out this strategy to a collection of eminent jurists, asking them if a conspiracy rap would hold up in court. It would, came back the consensus. Theoretically at least, the summit participants could be found guilty of conspiracy to obstruct justice, punishable by up to five years in prison and $10,000 in fines. That the approach was pioneered by Wessel, a legal mind intimately familiar with the closed-door shenanigans of Wall Street, lent it added weight.

"Under the interpretation [of the law]," Wessel stated, "the meeting at Apalachin could have been a tea party. As long as they conspired to lie about its purpose, they are guilty. We will prove that they did."

When it came time to make the busts, Wessel became tangled in bureaucratic infighting over the question of who would actually handle the task. Predictably, the FBI wanted in, despite Hoover's dismissal of Wessel's work. The Special Group responded by demanding that FBN agents do the deed. The assault had to be timed exactly in order that the summit conspirators not be tipped off by previous arrests. That meant going in at three a.m. on the West Coast to match the six a.m. raids in the east.

In order to establish where the mobsters might be at such an early hour, narcotics agents surveilled their targets for weeks to get to know their daily routines. They watched family boss Joe Bonanno sunbathe on his Tucson patio, and dope dealer John Ormento tend his flower garden in his yard at Lido Beach, Long Island.

In the early morning hours of Thursday, May 21, 1959, eighteen months after Apalachin, Federal agents fanned out across the country in a coordinated assault to arrest the summit participants. Some of them, anyway. Wessel's Special Group managed to indict twenty-seven, and of those, twenty-one got picked up in the initial sweep.

Most of them were rousted from bed. The irrepressible Sam Scozzari offered his arresting officers an eye-opener of Scotch, then tried to give them all boxes of candy. Joe Profaci's wife called the cops on the cops, thinking they were burglars. Her husband then used his one phone call to dial up his doctor.

"Don't you think you ought to order me to bed?" Profaci asked hopefully.

"Just take it easy and you'll be all right," was the doc's disappointing response.

Federal agents went for John Montana, only to have his wife slam the door in their faces. They went in through the window instead, nabbing the Man of the Year as he sat on the edge of his bed in long underwear, sipping a cup of hot water.

The judicial battering of the Apalachin mobsters reached a climax that spring. The indictment described a conspiracy in which the summit mobsters agreed to "corruptly influence, obstruct and impede" the administration of justice "by giving false, fictitious and evasive testimony and by other contumacious conduct."

Headline writers indulged themselves. U.S. TRIES NEW CLAM OPENER,

INDICTS 27 APALACHINITES, read the New York *Daily News,* with a similar tag for a photo feature, A SECOND GATHERING OF THE CLAMS, with pics of mobsters from New York to Scranton to Los Angeles getting swept up.

For the Federal court actions on the part of Williams and Wessel, J. Edgar Hoover acted primarily as a bystander, as to some extent did the Kennedy brothers. Jack and Bobby, at least, had the excuse of becoming embroiled in a nip-and-tuck presidential election campaign, the success of which would put them increasingly at loggerheads with Hoover over organized crime.

16

The Brother Within

JOE BARBARA WASN'T ONE of the Apalachin mobsters charged with conspiracy. He had fallen increasingly on hard times since the summit. In 1959, the family was forced to sell the McFall Road estate at a fire-sale price of $130,000.

Bedeviled by tax liens, his business under assault by several different government agencies, Barbara moved to his old house in Endicott, the same humble Union neighborhood digs he had left in 1948 when he relocated to the estate in Apalachin. A picture of downward mobility, the Barbara clan crammed themselves back into the two-story stucco at 405 Loder Avenue. They left behind the family cats when they moved.

That spring, after seventeen months in seclusion, Barbara made his one and only post-summit public appearance, traveling to Syracuse for an arraignment in an IRS tax case. His doctors said he was well enough to be "questioned gently." His son drove him the ninety miles north, not in a Cadillac limousine for this trip, not anymore, but in a green 1956 Pontiac.

Barbara had become the mystery man at the center of the summit, the short ghost to Croswell's tall one. Stalked continually by reporters, he and Josephine stayed overnight on the eighth floor of the Hotel Syracuse. Joe emerged alone with his lawyer at two p.m. on April 28 and took a seven-minute taxi ride in the rain to the hearing, held in the main Syracuse post office building. Arriving at the venue, he climbed into a collapsible wheel chair. The chair, with Barbara in it, had to be hefted up the stone steps to the lobby of the building by two volunteer newsmen.

As they bumped him up the stairs, Barbara murmured, "I don't feel good," his hand over his heart. He wore a dark blue overcoat, a blue suit, a large-brimmed gray hat, black alligator shoes, white shirt, gray necktie and glasses. After the ordeal of getting to court, he popped three nitroglycerin pills for heart pain. He looked thinner, more gaunt, his round baby face reduced and sunk into itself.

Waiting for the judge, he licked his lips and examined his fingernails. It might have looked as though Barbara were inspecting a recent manicure, but it was something different. The relative blueness of the skin beneath his nails was an easy, readily visible gauge of his heart health.

In the high-ceilinged, wood-paneled courtroom, Barbara's formal appearance before Judge James T. Foley lasted for all of two minutes, during which he pled not guilty to eleven counts of evading $14,000 in Federal taxes.

And that was that. Joe Barbara disappeared once again into seclusion. The only news emanating from McFall Road came from LaRue and Phyllis Quick, realtors and contractors who had purchased the former Barbara estate. Apalachin residents professed themselves to be "up in arms" over rumors about making the Barbara place into what they termed a "crime shrine." The Quicks planned to open the place for public tours, then transform it into a restaurant, "Joe's Barbecue Pit."

The man himself didn't last long enough to see it happen. On May 31 he suffered another heart attack. Doctors admitted him in critical condition to Wilson Memorial Hospital in Johnson City. He lingered in and out of consciousness for two weeks, dying in Room 210 at 7:35 p.m. on June 17, 1959, the family gathered at his bedside. Josephine collapsed into a faint when he passed.

"Was he a good patient?" reporters asked a nurse on Barbara's floor.

"Well, he didn't talk much," came the reply. *Omerta* to the end.

The family had a requiem mass said at St. Anthony of Padua's Roman Catholic Church in Endicott, with a wake at the Loder Avenue house. Of the summit mobsters who once pronounced themselves so concerned about poor Joe's health, only four, all locals, attended the funeral: Zicari, Guarnari, Turrigiano, Guccia.

Nineteen-year-old Angie did not allow her father to go gently. "Murderers!" she shouted at reporters assembled across the street from the little stucco house where Barbara's body had been taken.

Mourners passed in front of the open silver-plated casket set up in the dining room, with a candelabra and an illuminated picture of Christ. The deceased was dressed in the same clothes he wore at his recent arraignment: dark blue-gray silk-and-wood suit, plain white shirt, light gray tie, and pearl stick pin, with shoes of blue suede and black alligator leathers.

In death, Joe the Barber achieved some small measure of vindication that had eluded him in life. He hadn't been faking it after all. Like the old joke epitaph: "I *told* you I was sick."

A floral tribute, in the traditional broken-wheel arrangement signifying a death in the family, displayed the words, "From Angela." When the funeral cortege left for the Calvary Cemetery in Oakdale, the grieving daughter again addressed the crowd of news reporters.

"Don't you have a guilty conscience?" she called over to them. "You call us murderers, but you're the biggest murderers of them all."

Graveside in an October-like rain, she acted out a little more, upset, weeping, crying out, "Oh, Daddy, my daddy, I want to kiss my daddy good-bye!"

In a last will and testament that had been dated March 24, 1957, Joe Barbara left his entire $300,000 estate to his wife Josephine.

Over the dog days of summer in 1959, with Jack Kennedy's poll numbers indicating a tight race ahead for the presidency, Bobby found a chance to take some time off from the political fight and pen a book-length account of his Racket Committee work.

He retreated to his family's Hyannis Port summer compound on Cape Cod, his parent's house on Marchant Avenue, between the yacht club and the golf course. Jack and Jackie had just purchased their own adjoining place on Irving Avenue with a common backyard. Amid the controlled chaos of the battle-to-the-death touch football games and sailboat races in Nantucket Sound, Bobby scratched out the manuscript in longhand.

His brother's *Profiles in Courage* had been published in 1955, and though it won the Pulitzer Prize, it had been attacked as a ghostwritten creation. Bobby was determined to write his first book on his own.* The two approaches to authorship underscored the differences in the two personalities: Jack reserved, holding back, cynically detached, Bobby diving in, committed, a shade reckless.

Bobby began the Apalachin section of the resulting book, *The Enemy Within,* with a sly joke: "There'll be fifty-eight for tea, Mrs. Barbara." That sarcastic and irreverent approach likewise displayed the personality of the author, an aspect of himself he had exhibited numerous times during his questioning of the mobsters appearing before the committee. Bobby took

---

* After RFK wrote a draft, his friend and administrative assistant, Nashville newspaperman John Lawrence Seigenthaler, pitched in on editing.

pains to give the lie to the claim of summit participants that the gathering at Joe Barbara's was unplanned and spontaneous.

> It was not a chance meeting [he wrote of Apalachin]. It had been well-organized beforehand. Subpoenaed telephone toll tickets proved that they had been in close contact with each other for weeks before. Reservations had been made in neighboring motels and lodges; huge amounts of food had been ordered.

The Enemy Within did not concern itself much with the summit itself. Bobby's bête noire was front and center, his obsession, his evil other, International Brotherhood of Teamster's president James Riddle Hoffa. Kennedy's fixation on Hoffa indicated how personally he took the crusades upon which he embarked. Apalachin might have provided a window into the seamy underworld of organized crime. But with Hoffa it got close in the clinches. Robert Kennedy tackled Jimmy Hoffa as though he were still on the football field at Milton.

Some of the antics were indeed straight out of prep school. Kennedy would engage in staring contests with Hoffa, who disconcerted him by holding the stare for several beats before giving him a broad wink. Hoffa's cold-eyed gaze ranked up there with that of a real gangster, when Kennedy faced off with him during the hearings. Antonio Corallo, known as "Tony Ducks" for his ability to duck prosecution, was a labor racketeer said to be able to freeze a shop full of workers with a simple glare. Bobby didn't believe it.

> It seemed to me rather funny at the time—almost comic book material. But when Tony Ducks appeared on the witness stand and turned his gaze on us, I changed my mind. The only thing worse for sheer evilness that I have ever seen was that look of Hoffa's.

The focus on Hoffa can obscure Bobby's larger commitment to rooting out organized crime in all its guises. He performed body slams in *Enemy* upon such disparate targets as Joey Gallo ("dressed like a Hollywood Grade B gangster") and Johnny Dio ("his lips curled in an angry snarl, a cigarette dangling from his lips").

Bobby went in very deep, to the degree of checking church records to see if Jimmy Squillante was, in fact, the godson of Albert Anastasia (unconfirmed, Kennedy said). The Rackets investigation team tracked down one Professor C. Don Modica, the tutor of Anastasia's son, or, as Kennedy termed it, "Albert's boy." Modica, instructor in philosophy of education at New York University, also taught the children of Vito Genovese and those of the gap-toothed pretty boy, Joe Adonis.

Of the goodfellas in Hoffa's entourage, Kennedy wrote:

> They have the look of Capone's men. They are sleek, often bilious and fat, or lean and cold and hard. They have the smooth faces and cruel eyes of gangsters; they wear the same rich clothes, the diamond ring, the jeweled watch, the strong, sickly-sweet-smelling perfume.

There are shades here of the well-off Irish-American Harvard kid thrilling at being able to face off with street thugs. The title of *The Enemy Within* might be unintentionally revealing. The enemy within Bobby himself? Within his family's background?

To mark the book's publication Jack and Jackie Kennedy presented Robert with a custom-bound copy of *Enemy*. Jack inscribed it to "the brother within," which again could be read as unintentionally revealing. (Jackie wrote a less ironic inscription, a phrase probably referring to Robert's work putting Jack in the White House: "For Bobby—who made the impossible possible and changed all our lives.")

The Enemy Within did well when it was published by Harper & Row, was even, briefly, on the bestseller lists. It's a feisty, topical book, today read more for what it reveals of its author rather than for insight into labor racketeering. By the time it hit the bookstores, Robert Kennedy had resigned as chief counsel of the Rackets Committee to devote himself full time to getting his brother elected to the presidency of the United States.

But the concerns that *The Enemy Within* voiced did not recede from the young crusader's mind, and he was ready to take them up again when, a year later, in January 1961, Jack summoned Bobby to Washington to become attorney general.

Promoting "the brother within" to a post as the nation's chief gangbuster proved controversial, and was almost derailed from the start. The strongest opposition came not from Jack's political opponents, who screamed nepotism (and eventually pushed through a law prohibiting the practice at cabinet level). No, the real opposition came, oddly enough and most ferociously, from within the Kennedy family, and within Bobby himself.

If innocent parties stumbled into federal court in the late 1950s, the last person they would want to see on the bench was a Brooklyn-born jurist named Irving R. Kaufman, infamous for sentencing convicted nuclear spies Julius and Ethel Rosenberg to the electric chair. While not exactly a hanging judge (he later would rule against the immigration service in its campaign to deport the Beatle John Lennon), Kaufman was known for harsh sentences, an active and interfering presence in court, and stinging trial statements.

When the Apalachin mobsters drew Kaufman for their collective conspiracy trial, it didn't bode well. At 10:30 on the morning of October 26, 1959, almost two years after the summit, twenty-two defendants stood before Kaufman, with phalanxes of lawyers in attendance, until the dock seemed to outnumber the gallery.

Pinning his reputation on the success of a chancy, never-before-tried legal strategy, Milton Wessel stood for the prosecution. Four fugitives were absent: Salvatore Falcone, one of the two brothers who ran the Utica rackets; Joe Ida out of Philadelphia; and Nino Magaddino and James LaDuca from the Buffalo area.

The conspiracy trial represented a reunion of sorts. Police and summit mobsters had faced off many times before, in Albany, in Washington, at grand juries. The two-year-long process had worn on everyone. The *New York Daily Mirror* termed Ed Croswell "cadaverous-looking" when he appeared in Kaufman's court, appearing "pale, inaudible, drawn, peaked."

Croswell had been in and out of the hospital. He popped ulcer pills and, as he had in front of the Rackets Committee, sipped milk.

The conspiracy defendants themselves had begun to drop like flies. Brooklyn beer salesman Salvatore Tornabe went first, dead in December 1957 of a heart attack. Five days before the federal conspiracy charge was filed against him, a heart attack hospitalized Joe Bonanno. A self-styled Sicilian-born aristocrat who was always hesitant to mix with the riffraff, Bonanno managed to petition successfully for a separate trial.

John DeMarco of Shaker Heights also had his trial severed from the others, also because of a heart attack. Carlo Gambino got hauled away from a deportation hearing on a hospital stretcher around this time, an oxygen mask strapped to his face.

Joe Barbara, whose own weak heart had prevented him from being charged by the Feds at all, turned out not to be alone employing the "cardiac defense." The mobsters had demonstrated at the Apalachin barbecue itself what voracious red-meat eaters they were. That kind of diet had its consequences.

The score of summit participants whose hearts did not fail them duly reported to the Foley Square courthouse day after day for the trial. Before a jury of eight men and four women, defense team lawyers tried to take apart Ed Croswell. He elicited laughs in the court with the following rueful response to John C. Montana's attorney, Frank G. Raichle of Buffalo:

Raichle: You're an experienced witness, aren't you?
Croswell: I'm beginning to be.

Raichle hammered Croswell over inconsistencies in his various testimonies at the Watchdog Committee hearings, the Rackets Committee hearings, and the court trials (such as Majuri's and Captain Gleitsmann's) involving Apalachin.

Did Croswell give varying descriptions of the clothing he said Montana wore when picked up? On the morning of November 14, 1957, did he or did he not stop for a late breakfast between the time he met revenue agents Ruston and Brown and when they drove up to Barbara's house?

"After you've been worked over by attorneys for two years, you can forget a lot of things," Croswell said wearily.

Raichle protested the phrase "worked over."

"Well, I'm sorry," Croswell softly replied. "I should have said 'cross-examined.'"

"Have I confused you?" Raichle said, pressing the attack.

"Not so far," the sergeant answered. The courtroom again erupted in laughter. Advantage, Croswell.

The accused mobsters settled upon a virtually unassailable strategy. They based their testimonies upon facts that could be backed up by other witnesses, although strangely, all those witnesses seemed unavailable for corroboration.

Thus Vito Genovese testified that Joe Ida could verify his testimony, but Ida had fled to Italy. Paul Castellano cited Carlo Gambino, who was out of commission with a heart attack, recovering at his summer home in Montauk. Vincent Rao did them one better, naming as his corroborating witness a dead man, Salvatore Tornabe.

Other dodges: Mike Miranda said he took a long, alcohol-induced nap at the summit. Carmine Lombardozzi swore he had come up to hunt deer, even though he had no license, rifle, or proper clothing, a story so ludicrous his interviewing officer did not even write it down.

Most other witnesses stuck to the "just happened by to visit a sick friend" defense, as insipid as it was.

Staten Island boss Joe Riccobono triggered laughter in the court when he told his tale: "I had half a sandwich, then they said the state troopers were there and I lost my appetite." Angelo Sciandra said he hitchhiked home in the rain to Scranton after the bust-up of the summit.

Robert Kennedy did not manage to stay entirely on the sidelines for the duration of the conspiracy trial. In early December 1959, he appeared as a witness for the government. Defense attorney Henry G. Singer questioned him, starting things off by saying, "I'm a Republican and you're a Democrat."

Kaufman broke in with one of his trademark interruptions. "I didn't think politics would rear its ugly head in this courtroom."

"Of course it has to," Singer responded. To Kennedy, he continued, "You are actually engaged in furthering your brother's ambitions to get the presidential nomination, isn't that right?"

Wessel objected, Kaufman sustained the objection, but Singer barged ahead anyway. "You appreciate that by appearing here today," he said to Bobby, "there would be some publicity concerning your appearance which benefits your brother in his search for the nomination?"

"Objection," Wessel said again, and again, Kaufman sustained.

"No, I want to answer that," Bobby said. "That didn't enter my head. That didn't enter my head at all."

RFK told a story that, prior to Joseph Profaci's Senate Rackets Committee testimony, the mob boss approached him in a corridor outside the Caucus Room, a doddering old man tugging on the chief counsel's sleeve. His hands trembling, he showed Bobby pictures of his three grandchildren.

"I love the Church," Profaci said, one good Catholic to another. "I love God and I love my grandchildren."

Bobby's point in recalling the anecdote was that the witnesses at the conspiracy trial would attempt any stratagem to win sympathy.

Sympathy proved in short supply on the part of jury and Judge Kaufman both. Just before Christmas, on December 19, 1959, after a fifty-three-day trial, the jury returned a verdict of guilty for twenty of the twenty-one conspirators. (Kaufman directed an acquittal for one of the mobsters, sixty-two-year-old Boston cheese man Frank Cucchiara, saying the government had not proved a case against him.*)

The judge praised the jury for its "intelligent" verdict. Three weeks later, on January 12, 1960, it was his turn, and Kaufman passed sentence on the twenty guilty parties.

His judgment measured up to his harsh reputation. Most of the Apalachin hoods received five-year maximum prison terms and $10,000 fines. Kaufman said their probation reports "read like a tale of horrors." He provided a series of thumbnail portraits of the convicted mobsters, acid assessments of their characters and misdeeds, sentencing them alphabetically, nailing them to the wall one after another with fine Kaufman rhetoric.

- Russell A. Bufalino, fifty-eight years old, of Kingston, PA, five years in jail and a $10,000 fine. "A man devoid of conscience. One who poses as a legitimate business man. Everything in his record indicates that society would be better off if he is segregated."
- Ignatius Cannone, thirty-five, of Endwell, NY, three years, no fine. "A rather intelligent fellow who played a minor role in the underworld. Loyal to the criminal element and could be trusted by the underworld."
- Paul C. Castellano, forty-nine, of Brooklyn, five years, no fine. "Marked with antisocial patterns. Willingly spent one year in jail in order not to answer any questions, even though given immunity."
- Joseph F. Civello, fifty-nine, of Dallas, Texas, five years, no fine. "A high-ranking criminal who cloaked himself with the facade of legitimate business."
- Frank DeSimone, fifty, a lawyer from Downey, CA, four years, no fine. "Hostile and arrogant toward law enforcement and his bar associates. Lived with individuals of ill repute, and after Apalachin resided in the home of such an individual."
- Natale J. Evola, fifty-four, of Brooklyn, five years, $10,000 fine. "A most important member of the underworld. His five-year sentence to be served following the ten-year sentence imposed last year after a federal narcotics conviction."

---

* This despite the fact Cucchierra had perhaps the most intriguing rap on his arrest record, a 1925 bust for "unlawful possession of morphine and dynamite."

- Louis A. Larasso, thirty-four, of Linden, NJ, four years, no fine. "A person devoid of emotion whose first loyalty was to the underworld."
- Carmine Lombardozzi, forty-six, of Brooklyn, NY, five years, $10,000 fine. "His probation report reads like a who's who in crime. An important member of loan-shark and gambling rackets in Brooklyn and an associate of premier criminals for most of his life."
- Frank T. Majuri, fifty-eight, of Elizabeth, NJ, five years, no fine. "A bootlegger and gambler who would do anything for a fast dollar."
- Michele A. Miranda, sixty-four, of Forest Hills, Queens, NY, five years, $10,000 fine. "Elected to serve sixteen months in civil jail rather than betray his loyalty to the criminal elements. A close friend of the top dogs of the underworld."
- John C. Montana, sixty-six, of Buffalo, NY, four years, $10,000 fine. "Apparently an important factor in the political life of that city. Was apparently leading a double life, which was exposed by events at Apalachin. Respected on the one hand, some law enforcement agencies suspected him of being a power in the underworld. His presence at Apalachin apparently confirmed that suspicion."
- John Ormento, forty-seven, of Lido Beach, Long Island, NY, five years, $10,000 fine. "Has several narcotics convictions. A veteran criminal with nothing but contempt for constituted authority."
- James Osticco, forty-six, of Pittston, PA, five years and $10,000 fine. "A strong-arm man and associate of high-ranking members of the underworld."
- Joseph Profaci, sixty-two, of Brooklyn, NY, five years, $10,000 fine. "Has tried to present himself as a much maligned and humble man, when he is in fact a notorious member of the underworld. The perfect example of the trinity of crime, business and politics that threatens the economy of the country."
- Anthony P. Riela, sixty-three, of West Orange, NJ, four years, $10,000 fine. "Shrewd, cunning and conniving."
- John T. Scalish, forty-seven, of Cleveland, OH, five years, $10,000 fine. "Feels that everybody has a price, including public officials. Tried to bribe a probation officer. A high liver, contemptuous of society."
- Angelo J. Sciandra, thirty-five, of Wyoming, PA, five years, $10,000 fine. "An important man in the underworld since 1946. Has attempted to cloak himself in legitimate business. Tried to invade the union field by using force and violence."

- Simone Scozzari, fifty-nine, of Rosemeade, CA, five years, $10,000 fine. "Has made a mockery of the law since he arrived in this country as a stowaway in 1923."
- Pasquale Turrigiano, fifty-three, of Endwell, NY, five years, no fine. "Had two prior convictions for illegally manufacturing alcohol. A man with little respect for law-abiding citizens."

All through Kaufman's sentencing recitation, groans and cries of despair emanated from the defendants. Montana wept openly. Profaci blurted out, *"So n'innocenca! So n'innocenca!"* repeatedly: "I am innocent!"

Attorney General Rogers hailed the case a "landmark." 20 APALACHIN HOODS GUILTY ran the front-page headline in the *New York Daily Mirror*. In their editorial pages, newspapers professed themselves satisfied, congratulating Wessel for his innovative legal strategy.

The verdict "is a victory for law enforcement," Wessel said. "It proves that the threat posed by syndicated and organized crime in this country can and will be met by coordinated attacks of all law enforcement groups acting together."

The Apalachin summit, it seemed, had been laid to rest as sure as Joe Barbara's body lay in Calvary Cemetery.

17

General Kennedy Goes After the Mob

IT WAS OVER. Was it over?

In a sure sign of closure of some sort, Hollywood began to embalm Apalachin. *Inside the Mafia,* a fictionalized account of the summit, opened in September 1959, with the iconic B-movie actor Cameron Mitchell as "Tony Ledo."

Ads for the film splashed exclamation points across typically lurid banners: RIPPING THE LID OFF THE FAMOUS GANGLAND MEETING! THE WORLD'S #1 SECRET SOCIETY OF CRIME! THE RAID THAT RIPPED THE "CRIME CONVENTION" IN APPLE LAKE, NY! The flick itself featured something missing from the real summit, a climactic gunfire exchange that left bodies sprawled and blood flowing.

On January 17, 1960, immediately after the conspiracy guilty verdicts and sentencing, *Desilu Playhouse* debuted a more sedate "Meeting at Apalachin," a TV production the program had in the can but delayed at Kaufman's request so as not to influence the jurors. THE NOTORIOUS CONFERENCE STRAIGHT FROM TODAY'S HEADLINES! read an ad for the show, a docudrama narrated by Bob Considine and starring, once again, the durable Cameron Mitchell.

Ed Croswell got a little taste of media fame, too. On January 15, 1960, he appeared on the popular CBS game show, *To Tell the Truth.*

On the program, three guests—two imposters and one who was the real thing—faced a panel of minor celebrity actors who asked questions and attempted to discover which of the three was telling the truth. Croswell managed to fool only one of the four panelists, Kitty Carlisle. The others, Tom

Poston, Dana Andrews, and Polly Bergen, correctly sussed him out as the cop who busted up the Apalachin summit.

In the wake of Joe Barbara's death, Joe Jr., Josephine, and Angela moved from the Loder Avenue house to a three-bedroom home on North Road in the Greenlawn Acres Subdivision in Vestal.

The old place on McFall Road opened to the public on Thursday, April 14, 1960, with a grand opening celebration the following Sunday. For an entry fee of two dollars, the public could traipse through the stone ranch house, with most furnishings and decorative touches left intact. By the following month, LaRue Quick said he was hosting two to three hundred tourists a week.

Vito Genovese, "gritting his teeth and fighting back tears" according to news reports, went to prison. A three-judge Court of Appeals panel had unanimously turned down his bid to have his conviction overturned. He surrendered himself on May 18, 1960, in the chambers of Judge Sidney Sugarman of the New York's Southern District, to begin serving his fifteen-year narcotics trafficking sentence.

Always natty, Vito dressed his best simply to be loaded roughly into a Black Maria with ten other convicted criminals. U.S. Attorney Paul Williams was not there to witness his triumph, having failed in his gubernatorial bid and entered into private practice.

On November 8, 1960, John F. Kennedy squeaked out the narrowest of election victories over Richard Nixon in the national presidential race.

Did Kennedy receive crucial help from mob ballot-box stuffing in Illinois? Was there vote fraud in Texas? Hard evidence has been difficult to nail down, and the verdict of historians is still out, despite Sam Giancana's later boast that he helped put JFK in the White House.

Closer to the subject of the Apalachin summit, did the high-profile battles against organized crime by Bobby and Jack on the Rackets Committee make any difference for Kennedy the candidate? The question remained moot, although what wasn't arguable was what happened in the wake of the Democratic win, with Bobby brought in to head the Justice Department.

Predictably, but somewhat lost amid the post-election news flurry, reporters filed stories on the third anniversary of the summit. The by-now familiar theme: "Apalachin Mystery Still Unsolved Three Years Later." But the reports were shorter now, in the manner of fillers rather than articles.

The "mystery" theme would recur with a vengeance later in that anniversary month of November.

In a sweeping "never mind" judgment, the three-judge Appeals Court for the Second District vacated the conspiracy verdicts of the Apalachin defendants. Special prosecutor Wessel, who had gone back to private practice on Wall Street by then, saw his innovative legal confection melt in the face of withering scorn by Appeals Judge Charles E. Clark.

"After all these years," Clark said, announcing the reversal, "there is not a shred of legal evidence that the Apalachin meeting was illegal or even improper." Croswell's "we didn't have the law to hold them" comment, made in the immediate aftermath of the summit, was turned against him. If the gathering wasn't against the law, what was he doing breaking it up?

Clark gave a sinister spin to Croswell's pursuit of Barbara. "For thirteen years prior to the meeting, as a modern Javert, State Trooper Croswell pursued Barbara Sr. in all ways possible."

The "Javert" reference, invoking Victor Hugo's epic of law versus justice, *Les Miserables,* no doubt displayed the range of Judge Clark's learning. But it also cast Joe Barbara in the role of Jean Valjean, a stretch for even the most romantic imagination. A bootlegger, moonshiner, whoremaster, and mob muscle-boy, linked to at least four murders, who robbed a payroll on the way to his wedding, who was set up to masquerade as a legit businessman with mob money—the comparison to the saintly and thoroughly reformed hero of Hugo's novel rings false.

Croswell reacted to Clark's Javert slur with characteristic blandness. "I've been called many things," he told reporters with a shrug. "I don't feel either complimented or insulted by it."

But government figures could not hide their disappointment with the reversal of the conspiracy verdicts. It appeared that Wessel's legal approach represented just another dead end in the battle against organized crime. Vito Genovese and others would remain in prison on narcotics trafficking convictions. But the idea of nailing mobsters just for their presence at the summit proved unworkable.

And yet . . . Even though it had been vacated, the conspiracy case against the Apalachin mobsters continued to send out sympathetic vibrations throughout the legal community. One of the eternal struggles in the law is to bring the actual statutes on the books in line with common sense. Despite the appeals court's brusque dismissal, there remained a stubborn faith that there should be some method to get at mob bosses who did not, themselves, commit crimes but only planned, directed, and authorized them.

Eventually, the law found a way, and it had its legal antecedents in Milton Wessel's strategy. The Racketeer Influenced and Corrupt Organizations Act—or RICO, when Congress passed it as part of 1970s omnibus Organized Crime Control Act—harkened back to the prosecutions of the summit mobsters. Essentially, RICO closed the loophole that gang bosses had been able to exploit by insulating themselves from the direct commission of crimes.

Notre Dame law professor G. Robert Blakey, author and primary proponent of RICO legislation, stumbled across a reference in a paper of one of his students that cited the reversal of the Apalachin conspiracy convictions. Intrigued, he read up on the history and formulated a successful legal response to the conundrum of prosecuting criminals who did not commit crimes, merely ordered others to do so. RICO had Apalachin thoroughly embedded in its DNA.

The law gave prosecutors the tool to dismantle the nationwide organized crime network. The scheme set in place by Charles Luciano, with a national commission of bosses mediating and regulating the competing families across the country, would finally fall. Every major racketbusting initiative, including the spectacular cases that decimated the Five Families of New York City in the mid-1980s, flowed directly from RICO, and thus, from Apalachin.

"Now you can get arrested just for talking," said Vito Genovese, observing the legal revolution from prison.

Professor Blakey worked under two figures already familiar as nemeses of the summit mobsters: Senator John McClellan and Robert F. Kennedy. In the early 1960s, Kennedy would usher in a golden age of government action against organized crime. In his own mind, at least, his initiative would come back to haunt him with bitter and tragic consequences.

On January 20, 1961, Robert Kennedy was sworn in as the sixty-fourth attorney general of the United States. He took charge of a Justice Department recently disheartened by its inability to convict the mob bosses who had gathered at Joe Barbara's more than three years previous. There were other concerns at Justice, to be sure, but racketbusting held a special place in the heart of the new AG.

The nomination of the president's little brother to a top cabinet post raised eyebrows, hackles, questions. First and foremost, both brothers strongly resisted the idea. The press "will kick our balls off," Bobby told Jack. He bridled at being considered his brother's tool, of being always in his shadow. He thought of running for the governor of Massachusetts. Something, anything that would allow him his independence.

Every trial balloon president-elect Kennedy sent up about Bobby becoming his attorney general promptly got shot down. *The New York Times* editorialized against it. Such eminences as columnist Drew Pearson, congressional power Sam Rayburn, and Cold War warrior Dean Acheson argued against it. But others to whom the post was offered demurred, including Democratic leading light Adlai Stevenson and Connecticut governor Abe Ribicoff.

Ribicoff turned it down explicitly in favor of RFK. "I have now watched you Kennedy brothers for five solid years," he told Jack. "I noticed that every time you face a crisis, you automatically turn to Bobby. You're out of the same womb. There's an empathy. You understand each other. You're not going to be able to be president without using Bobby all the time."

Ultimately, it was the father who brought the sons around. "Nobody's better qualified," Joe Kennedy told Jack.

Anyone who had seen Bobby's performance as chief counsel on the McClellan Committee, as unpolished as it was, did not doubt his fierce work habits or his commitment to excellence. The fact was, though, not that many people had witnessed him in action—all they saw when looking at Bobby Kennedy was the president's sibling.

Even RFK's near-miraculous work as campaign manager could be overlooked because it had been accomplished behind the scenes: fending off challenges by such Democratic darlings as Hubert Humphrey and Adlai Stevenson, co-opting Lyndon Johnson, then going on to get a Catholic elected in mid-twentieth-century America. Not everyone realized it, but Bobby was Jack's best asset.

"All of us worked our tails off for Jack," Joe Kennedy told Clark Clifford, one of the many Washington insiders who warned off the elder Kennedy from pushing his younger son for attorney general. "Now that we have succeeded I am going to see to it that Bobby gets the same chance that we gave to Jack."*

Joe Kennedy was never one to be swayed by opposition. For him, the natterings of press commentators and political opposition always amounted to mere background noise. Nothing would change his mind. It had to be Bobby.

---

* Clifford would later write of Robert Kennedy and the attorney generalcy: "To my pleasant surprise, Bobby was to perform well in that position."

Joe managed to sway Jack, but his younger son still had strong doubts. "I was never dying to be attorney general," he told friends, a locution that, as events played out, gives off a slight chill. He finally acceded at the behest of his brother and father. Even on the morning of the announcement, he was glum and reticent.

"Well, General," Jack said, "let's grab our balls and go." Then he told Bobby, in preparation for walking onto the national political stage, to go comb his damn hair. The news conference announcement featured the "give him a little experience" quip that so offended RFK.

Later, after he was sworn in with his family in attendance in a ceremony in the private second-floor living quarters at the White House, Bobby led his troupe of children downstairs—by sliding down the banister. Not the kind of behavior that would soothe doubts about his youth and inexperience.

During the election campaign, JFK's anti-Catholic opponents fretted over the undue influence they imagined the Pope might have in his administration. The strings in the White House, critics said, would be pulled by Rome.

But the power of the Pope could not compare to the power of Papa. Especially at its inception, Joe Kennedy shaped his son's presidency deeply and indelibly, and one of the major ways he did so was by absolutely insisting on Robert Kennedy as attorney general.

The setup had an uncanny ring of underworld familiarity. Any mob boss worth his salt would recognize it. Bobby, in his father's arrangement, would act as Jack's consigliere.

The decision process hadn't been particularly neat or without conflict, but in the end, an Apalachin-inspired racketbuster took the reins at the Justice Department. Which meant—horror of horrors in the halls of SOG— that Bobby Kennedy became the boss of J. Edgar Hoover.

Between Sam Giancana, say, and Hoover, it would have been difficult to gauge who was more dismayed by RFK's ascendency to the nation's top law enforcement position.

When Bobby called around, making a quick temperature check to see how his nomination would be received, only Hoover, among all the political and media luminaries he contacted, had encouraged him to take the job. Kennedy suspected this was simply more of the Director's bad faith, and his suspicions proved out. From the moment he took office, Hoover opposed Kennedy covertly and, to some extent, overtly, too.

Some of this was simply a clash of styles, the yawning gap between a thirty-five-year-old and a sixty-six-year-old. Until Bobby halted the practice,

FBI tour guides at headquarters snidely noted, "Mr. Hoover became the Director of the Bureau in 1924, the year before the Attorney General was born."

Bobby might call himself "the General," but only in an ironic sense, while Hoover's "the Director" was dead serious. It was sitcom-like, a fussy old man having a college-age grandson come to work with him, messy, headstrong, disruptive of routine. Kennedy did not observe the forms. The channels of bureaucracy were holy for Hoover. Bobby was too impatient and too undisciplined to go through channels. He barged.

And he brought his dog to work. Kennedy was Silicon Valley casual before the style was created. Brumus—the name is Latin for "winter"—a black Newfoundland prone to spittle-flinging and random rambunctiousness, howled inconsolably if left alone at the Kennedy house at Hickory Hill, Virginia, so Bobby took him into Justice.

Such "damnably undignified conduct" (Hoover's words) set up friction between the General and the Director, who convened a day-long meeting with a dozen aides to see whether a regulation against dogs in Federal buildings could be invoked in Brumus's case.

Bobby could be viciously sarcastic about "J. Edna," his homophobic tag for the FBI director. When Hoover's companion Clyde Tolson went into the hospital, Kennedy wondered if it could be for a hysterectomy. He repeated Churchill's gibe about Clement Attlee and applied it to Hoover: "He looks like he sits down to pee." Hoover's sartorial fastidiousness clashed with RFK's shirtsleeve informality. The Director worried that schoolchildren, visiting the FBI offices, might encounter an attorney general in relative dishabille.

The Director had a dictator's love of protocol and ceremony. When visiting a police academy, for example, he insisted that his loyal agents line the halls for his grand tour. He loved to receive gifts from his underlings and was peckish toward those who did not pony up. Robert Kennedy would have none of this. There wouldn't be any presents to Hoover from Bobby, nor invitations to Hickory Hill, either.

Part of the face-off went deeper than style. Bobby was determined to bring Hoover to heel. As journalist Victor Navasky stated it: "It was apparent that if Robert Kennedy was going to make any headway in his war on organized crime, he first had to win a bureaucratic war within the Federal government."

RFK installed a direct telephone line from his office to Hoover's. When once an FBI assistant answered, Bobby coldly told him, "When I pick up this phone, there's only one man I want to talk to." He insisted that as attorney general he was the Director's boss. In past administrations, Hoover had become accustomed to dealing directly with the White House.

When, after a minor dustup between Hoover and Bobby, Jack chewed his younger brother out, he shouted, "You've got to get along with that old man!" Hovering in the background, and the reason the Kennedys didn't simply ease Hoover out, were the blackmail files, which contained plentiful entries on Jack's philandering.

In fact, Hoover doled out bits and pieces of these reports to Bobby, suggesting he forward to the president some of the filthy things FBI agents were turning up. Just on an FYI basis, of course. The Director would never *do* anything with the dirt. Heaven forefend.

The salacious, keyhole activities of the Bureau dismayed John Kennedy. Through Bobby, he informed Hoover he no longer wished to see bulletins from the files. He simply didn't want to know what it was that the Director knew.

All his life, RFK could summon a special fury against bullies and being bullied, a common characteristic of a younger child in a large family. The prospect of Hoover's blackmail failed to intimidate Bobby. Most particularly, he refused to allow Hoover's long-standing denial of the Mafia to prevent his assault against organized crime.

18

Bobby Goes Too Far

TWO WEEKS INTO HIS ATTORNEY generalcy, Kennedy announced a major anticrime initiative at Justice. In Bobby's mind, anticrime meant antimob. He helped pass an omnibus bill that attacked the main cash cow of the racketeers, gambling, by outlawing interstate transport of betting equipment and use of telephone lines and wire services for sports and racetrack wagering.

A photo of the crime-bill signing ceremony displays the dynamics of the new administration. Bobby hovers behind Jack, who is seated and in the process of placing his signature on the legislation. The sibling AG looks as though he is about to reach in and sign on the dotted line for the president. Standing to the rear, his bulldog head rendered microencephalitic by a backlit penumbra of window light, J. Edgar Hoover appears thoroughly marginalized.

Bobby inherited a bureaucracy shaken by the reversal of the Apalachin conspiracy verdicts. The last best hope in the war against organized crime appeared to have been dashed. The new attorney general proceeded as though undeterred. The turf-conscious Hoover blocked his dream of creating a national crime commission. So RFK in effect created his own mini-crime commission within Justice, coordinating the attack on mob figures with other units of the Federal government, including the IRS, the Immigration and Naturalization Service, the Labor Department, Treasury—even the Wildlife Service.

This was something new under the sun. It was the first time an interdepartmental approach had been effectively used against the mob. Bobby's relationship with Jack was vital in this respect, as was his willingness to face off with Hoover, who had always put the kibosh on such government-wide strategies in the past.

RFK enlisted Jack's college roommate and future Supreme Court justice Byron White as his deputy attorney general. He rejuvenated the moribund organized crime Special Group, increasing its staffing by a factor of four and recruiting such energetic young attorneys as veteran New York prosecutor Ed Silberling, "Get Hoffa" investigator Walter Sheridan, and future RICO innovator G. Robert Blakey. He brought in Kenneth O'Donnell, his hero at Harvard and a handsome, athletic quarterback and big man on campus, poached from his brother's staff, much to Jack's irritation.

The old Harvard crowd voiced concern that Kennedy and O'Donnell courted danger in taking on the mob. "We were worried that Kenny and Bobby didn't really know who they were screwing with," recalled classmate Wally Flynn, son of an Irish-American cop admitted under Harvard's new egalitarian admission policies. Another member of the school's football team, now working as a labor relations consultant in the steel industry, passed along a death threat to Kennedy, relating that a union rep had said Bobby should "back off or he'll end up in the river."

Bobby blew right past those concerns, too, just as he barged over, under, and through J. Edgar Hoover. He was effective. The year before RFK took up the reins at Justice, 1960, nineteen mobsters were indicted by the Feds. In its first year, the Kennedy-led team indicted one hundred twenty-one and earned ninety-six convictions.

Sixty percent of the cases were IRS-based prosecutions. Bobby went after Santo Trafficante with a $200,000 tax lien, and hit New Orelans boss Carlos Marcello with a monster $835,000 IRS bill. Other charges were flimsier. The Park and Wildlife Service mounted a case against Chicago racketeer Joseph Aiuppa for violating the Migratory Bird Act, for the high crime of having 563 mourning doves in his freezer.

"As attorney general," author Anthony Summers wrote about Bobby, "his fight against organized crime was to be more than a just cause, almost an obsession."

Bobby held weekly staff meetings in his own cavernous space on the fifth floor at Justice, alternatively assembling the troops in Ed Silberling's offices on the second floor. He'd summon whatever staff lawyers weren't in the field at the time, crowd the room with clerks, attorneys, and specialists, then launch right in, eliciting status reports on the myriad cases the Federal government had going on against the rackets. The meetings were spicy, entertaining, and fun, studded with outrageous mob stories from the front lines.

More than anything else, Kennedy proved his competency and probity to his staff of young go-getters. Time after time, the attorney general impressed the cadre of eager young lawyers with his command of the facts, his energy, and his vision. They came to respect and trust him as their leader.

"I wouldn't characterize Bobby as an intellectual," stated longtime Kennedy observer Theodore White. "I'd characterize him as something more important, a guy who can use intellectuals."

It is characteristic of an obsessive to at times push things too far. Perhaps as a vestige of his work on anticommunism with Joe McCarthy, RFK often displayed a quite casual disregard of civil liberties. His approval of the FBI wiretaps on Martin Luther King, for example, would forever stain his record as attorney general.

In the realm of organized crime, Kennedy also tended to ride roughshod over the rule of law. The political cartoonist Jules Feiffer once created a strip with the "good Bobby" fighting it out with the "bad Bobby." In the Special Group, the latter showed up regularly, and RFK's notorious "ruthless" personality shone through.

Perhaps the most severe example of this came in the pursuit of the powerful New Orleans mobster Carlos Marcello, whose brother Joe had acted as his representative at Apalachin. A full-fledged Mafia Commission member, partner with Frank Costello in his Louisiana coin machine empire, smuggler, and conduit between the States and Cuba, Marcello found himself targeted by the Special Group, and suffered for it.

On the morning of April 4, 1961, mob boss Marcello headed to the Immigration and Naturalization Service (INS) in New Orleans to perform a mandated visit, required every three months of all legal aliens. He made the mistake of leaving his lawyer outside the Masonic Temple on St. Charles Avenue, where the INS offices were located. As soon as he appeared for what should have been a routine registration, an INS agent confronted him with a notice written on Justice Department letterhead.

As a citizen of Guatemala who had overstayed his visa, the letter stated, Marcello would be immediately deported. The mobster indeed had previously furnished himself, at great expense, with a false Guatemalan passport, all in an effort to avoid being deported to Italy. He had gone to tiny San José Pinula, bribed officials there and essentially created a false paper trail. Now, that tactic backfired.

Two other agents appeared and put Marcello in manacles. "Can I use the telephone?" Marcello asked. "I'd like to talk to my attorney."

No, came back the answer.

"Can I call my wife to get a toothbrush and some money?"

No, once again. "Let's go," said the agents, leading him away.

His lawyer, Phillip Smith, and his brother Joe Marcello furiously attempted to head off Carlos's impending deportation to the country of his false citizenship. They were too late. Courtesy of Bobby Kennedy directly, one of the highest-ranking Mafia bosses in the United States experienced what amounted to a bum's rush. Whisked in a car with curtained windows to New Orleans International Moisant Airport, Marcello found himself rudely dumped off in Guatemala City and left at the mercy of the authorities in a strange country.*

Robert Kennedy and Carlos Marcello had faced off previously during the Racket Committee hearings. Bobby had been quoted as saying he would deport Marcello once he became attorney general. Which is what he did—cutting corners, sidestepping legalities, ordering, in a memo, "his deportation effected before Marcello's attorney could institute court action to delay this."

Two months later, Carlos Marcello slipped back into the Unites States carrying an extra bit of baggage: a burning hatred for Robert F. Kennedy. "Don't worry about that little Bobby son of a bitch," he told an associate. "He's going to be taken care of." Marcello effortlessly transferred his enmity to all Kennedys, including the one sitting in the White House.

"A dog will continue to bite you if you cut off its tail," Carlos told the same associate. "Whereas if you cut off the dog's head, it would cease to cause you trouble."

The face-off worked both ways, with the Kennedys as obsessed with Marcello as he was with them. "No Mafia figure," writes one historian, "received more concerted attention from the Kennedy administration than Carlos Marcello of New Orleans."

As a young man, Carlos Marcello had proved quite capable of violence, and now as a boss commanded the criminal apparatus to easily order a

---

* According to Marcello, his first night in the country bordered on the surreal. He later told an INS hearing that a certain Miss Jinks, an English-speaking secretary of a Guatemalan colonel, put him up in her apartment in her own bed, sleeping (chastely) beside him while Marcello remained wide awake, certain the whole strange arrangement was a setup for his murder.

killing. All of which has furnished fodder for legions of conspiracy theorists eager to link the Mafia to the murder of Jack Kennedy. Two government commissions investigated JFK's death, and one—the 1976 House of Representatives Select Committee on Assassinations—seriously took up the question of participation by organized crime.

In an ominous finding, the House Committee concluded that the Mafia possessed the fundamental trifecta that investigators always seek in murder cases: means, motive, and opportunity. Robert Kennedy himself had provided motive with his high-handed handling of the Marcello deportation, if not his sneering dismissal of witnesses at the Rackets Committee hearings. He was a thorn in the mob's paw, and the bosses would naturally seek to pluck it out. His brother's death would not be the first political hit that the Mafia carried out.

At the same time, the Select Committee found no direct evidence of either Marcello or any of his Mafia cohorts directly involving themselves in JFK's murder. Overheated commentators might disagree, but more circumspect historians have generally discounted the possibility. Elaborate conspiracies and concomitant cover-ups seem, on the whole, unlikely accomplishments in a human animal chronically unable to keep secrets. The concatenation of events necessary to kill a president probably remained beyond the reach of ad hoc street organizations such as the Mafia.

But whether organized crime was involved in the assassination or not, Robert Kennedy came to think it was, which given his expertise in mob matters is no small thing. Reeling, distraught, plagued by a deep sense of guilt, Bobby in the aftermath of Dallas began reading Greek tragedy and meditating on the vagaries of fate and destiny.

"Doom was woven in your nerves," runs a line in Robert Lowell's poem about RFK, and after the loss of his second brother, the weave ran deeper.

Robert Kennedy believed that the Mafia in general and Marcello in particular was to blame for Jack's assassination. A morose RFK told his aide Richard Goodwin that he thought "that guy from New Orleans," meaning Marcello, had murdered his brother.

JFK's death killed something in Bobby. His role had always been one of protecting Jack, and in his own view he had failed miserably. His life as racketbuster seemed vain to him, or worse, an evil that had infected his family.

Having been roughly thrown from the horse, Robert Kennedy would never ride that particular mount again. For the rest of his short life, he left the mob alone. Indeed, he would not really come alive as a political animal until he immersed himself in the cause of social justice. This came years later, courtesy of a 1965 tour of poverty-stricken areas of the South and a friendship with migrant crusader Cesar Chavez.

The president's murder set back government efforts to attack organized crime for perhaps a full decade. The pressure at the neck that the gangsters had long felt emanating from RFK and the Justice Department suddenly eased. If Dallas was not, in fact, the Mafia's doing, it effectively accomplished the mob's goals.

Senator McClellan, who would go on to mentor Blakey on the development of RICO legislation, pronounced the public eulogy on RFK's campaign against the mob. "When Bob Kennedy left the Department of Justice," he said on the floor of the Senate in March 1969, after Bobby's murder, "the organized crime program seemed to leave with him. It just seemed to fall apart."

Apalachin's twin legal legacies—Bobby's work with the Special Group at Justice and the passing of RICO legislation—would eventually demolish the national operational framework of organized crime. The mob, like the poor, might always be with us, but it will never again enjoy the same reach and power it had in the middle years of the twentieth century.

Robert Kennedy believed another Apalachin legacy played out in Dealey Plaza in November 1963. No "extraordinary evidence" suggests this is so, at least, not in any direct quid pro quo. Yet in the ebb and flow of history, every action triggers reaction, so moves against the mob could conceivably set off moves against the movers against the mob.

The drumbeat about the summit had largely died away by November '63, the repetitive questions and the retrospective newspaper features. Incredibly enough, given all that had transpired, Hoover reverted to his denial-of-the-Mafia mode, stating that "no single individual or coalition of racketeers dominates organized crime across the nation."

In the chaos of time, amid the Vietnam incursion heating up, the fight for civil rights exploding, and the tragic interrobang of the assassination, what happened at Joe Barbara's home six years before largely faded from the communal memory.

Although snowed under by subsequent events and rendered less insistent by the passage of years, the question still lurked:

What *really* happened at the Apalachin summit?

19
November 14, 1957

THE WHOLESALE MEAT TRUCK violates the Sabbath to deliver its load on Sunday, November 10. Twenty ten-pound boxes of steaks, two of veal, a $432 purchase, which in current-day terms is $3,500.

Turns out the local Binghamton butchers can't supply what Joe Barbara wants, so the beef comes special order from the Armour Company out of Chicago, halfway across the country just to wind up in the big refrigerator in the McFall Road compound's garage.

Perhaps, for the religious minded, the desecration of the Abrahamic day of rest is the source of all the bad luck afterward. At any rate, the meat delivery gives the lie to the unplanned nature of the gathering, not that the feeble cover story needs much help in order to collapse. The meeting is extremely well planned.

The barbecue structure itself stands as a thing of beauty. It's a barbecue in the sense that the Great Pyramid of Giza is a mausoleum. The grillwork is fabricated out of welded stainless steel, very expensive. Sited in the yard between the garage and the summer house, a massive, blocky pile constructed out of quarried stone to match the house, the edifice boasts its own awning to shield the cook from the elements.

Like the Dude's rug in *The Big Lebowski*, the barbecue really ties the whole compound together. Three large buildings surround it. The main house sits back off the road, regal and impressive across the yard.

To the east of the barbecue, a screened-in pavilion lends a recreational air to the arrangement, with a pair of illuminated Gibbons Beer and Ale clocks glowing in the dim interior. The back of the big four-bay garage completes the composition of the central compound, everything in field stone, everything country-gentleman rustic.

Other buildings orbit the perimeter, a guest house, a stable for Joe's seven horses (with an attached apartment for the stable master), a hay barn, an equipment shed banged together from old Canada Dry metal highway signs, a couple of small caretaker cottages. The whole place has been raked out and spiffed up by Mel Blossom and Norm Russell, the two laborers whom Barbara employs.

If one is looking for omens, a minor mishap the night before the big meet might answer. Earlier in the evening, Steven Magaddino and Jimmy LaDuca come by, just a brief visit, but Joe can tell the Buffalo boss is checking things out, making sure all the I's have been dotted.

After they leave, Joe and his Endicott subordinate, Pasquale "Patsy" Turrigiano, sit around watching television—the prime-time programs on WINR, the new NBC channel that had just began broadcasting a couple weeks before. *You Bet Your Life, Dragnet, Ernie Ford,* then, on CBS's *Playhouse 90,* something called "The Jet-Propelled Couch." The TV weather guy calls for a wet day tomorrow, drizzly and cold.

Around the time Turrigiano gets up to go at eleven o'clock, Joe discovers that the water pump that supplies the whole estate has stopped working. He feels like the Biblical Job, assailed by troubles when all he wants is to do right by God. Trying to throw a nice party for friends, and this happens.

Barbara telephones Russell Bufalino, and Russ calls Jimmy Osticco—a good guy, he and Bufalino went to Bimini together once, and Jimmy works in a motor pool in Pittston. Bufalino tells Jimmy to get up to Apalachin and fix Joe's pump.

Jimmy tells Bufalino that it's eleven o'clock in the pee-em. Russ says he knows what time it is. Jimmy says he'll go first thing in the morning.

"When you head up there," Russ tells him, "wear a suit and tie."

"Wear a suit to fix a water pump?" Jimmy says.

There's going to be a lot of important people around, Russ says, and hangs up.

Joe can't sleep, worried about how things will go the next day. How can he throw a party with the water off? He heads out to the garage to visit his beef. Sunday through Wednesday, he lets the stuff sit there, resting in the big cooler he has installed, transported over from the bottling plant.

Beautiful, well-aged, well-marbled prime meat such as this, it has to be handled correctly, you can ruin it if you don't know what you're doing.

Carlo Gambino's guy, Paul Castellano, owns a string of butcher stores. He's going to show up, he will know a good cut of beef when he sees one, although an old Mafia scam is to treat meat that is beginning to turn bad with formaldehyde, keep it looking fresh and rosy-red, the customers none the wiser.

Joe leaves the garage and crosses the yard to the main house to try to get some sleep. Overcast, no stars, the weather's been lousy all day. At night, up here, the silence is complete, no highway noise, no squealing tires, no nothing. Maybe the horses nickering in their stalls.

Inside, too, the rooms are quiet. TV's off the air, his wife's already in bed in the big master suite in the new wing, still called the new wing even though it's eight years old now. Peter is away at college, on the dean's list at the University of Buffalo. Joe Jr. has the boy's bedroom down the hall all to himself. Angie is on a sleepaway at a friend's.

The bedroom he enters is plush, furnished in antique, ivory-painted French Provincial furniture, tiered tables, a scarlet love seat. The floral pattern on the chairs echoes a similar one on the drapes and bedspread. Light gray carpeting contrasts with the handpainted walls of deep rose. There's a painting hanging over the double bed, depicting the Christ child in the arms of his father, Joseph.

Off the bedroom, an eight-by-eighteen private bathroom, its wall-to-ceiling mirrors alternating with red, white, and blue panels of plate glass.

Joe doesn't think he can sleep, but he does.

The next day dawns raw and wet, just like the weather guy said. Jimmy O arrives to fix the pump.

"You wearing a suit to do plumbing?" Joe says, and Jimmy just shakes his head and heads over to the equipment shed next to the barn.

Joe's locals arrive early, too, his helpers, Patsy Turrigiano back again, Guv Guarnieri, Emanuel Zicari, all of the Triple Cities, Angelo Sciandra, up from Pittston. You begin to hear snatches of Sicilian dialect in among the phrases of accented English. You look around, you see this gorgeous estate up in the Susquehanna hills, you think, we're a long way from Palermo.

Jimmy O gets the water back on by replacing the pump hose. Zicari sets up a coffee station on the picnic table in the summer house. If there's one thing made guys like just behind booze, it's cigarettes, and after that, it's coffee. Especially the drivers, bodyguards, and assorted flunkies, all they do is sit around waiting for the big boys to decide where they want to go next, and as they wait they run coffee through their bladders like it's the finest champagne.

For them and for others who haven't yet breakfasted, in the summer pavilion there's coffee, pastry, brandy. When Barbara passes through, busy as a buzz saw, the boys ask him how he is feeling. The host throws his hands in the air and says, "Ah, how you gonna feel?"

Nervous, Joe makes a few runs that morning in the big seven-passenger Caddie with the fold-down jump seats in the back. He picks up the Jersey boys, Gerardo Catena and the others, at the Tri-Cities Airport. He really shouldn't leave the compound, there's a lot to keep an eye on, but to Catena at least, respect must be paid.

Around ten o'clock, Magliocco shows up with the big boss, Profaci, the first of the real New York godfathers to arrive. Only nobody says "godfather." If you say anything, you say, *compare,* which in Sicilian dialect comes out sounding like "goomba." Profaci is sixty but aging tough, like old leather. Beginning a procedure common to all the bosses as they arrive at the summit, his brother-in-law Magliocco leads Profaci into the main house and deposits him in the formal living room to the right of the entryway.

The big, well-furnished space is where all the men of major respect will be seated. It's where the real business of the summit is conducted. Casement windows look out onto the forested foothills. Hundreds of feet of mauve and green drapes, encased in wooden valences, line the east and west walls. Sometimes it's good to have friends in the drapery business.

Richie Rich stuff is carefully positioned around this end of the living room, a baby grand, a heavy oak corner hutch displaying Royal Bayreuth Bavarian china, a 22-carat bar service, an enameled parrot displayed on a four-foot pedestal. All the glitz clashes somewhat with the walls, what can be seen of them amidst all the drapery, done in imitation knotty-pine paneling.

The newly arrived Profaci greets the just-back-from-the-airport Joe Barbara, and expresses surprise to see the host "looking like a dead man."

"How do you feel?" asks Profaci.

"A miracle I live," replies Joe Barbara, a.k.a. Job the Afflicted. The two aging men exchange verbal catalogs of their aches and pains.

By eleven o'clock, the arrivals come one after another, Paul Castellano driving up accompanied by Carlo Gambino, Bufalino chauffeuring the California guys, Vito Genovese arriving with Joe Ida from Philly.

Joe Bonanno, the man who wasn't there, is there, so is Sam Giancana,

Carmine Galante, Steven Magaddino. The Cuban gambling-and-smuggling cartel is well represented by Santo Trafficante and Carlos Marcello's brother Joe.

Bosses, and underlings. Heroin rides in on a white horse in the person of John Ormento. Man of the Year John C. Montana shows up with Steven's brother Nino. Carmine Lombardozzi car pools with Natale Evola from Brooklyn, Joe Riccobono from Staten Island, and Frank Cucchiara from Boston.

Land boats line the road, crowd the garage lot, and spill out into the field.

While the members of the Commission gather in the living room of the main house, the underbosses, soldiers, and random hangers-on congregate in the summer pavilion and, despite the morning drizzle, beneath the barbecue canopy in the middle of the yard.

At noon, Mel Blossom gets the coals going. The boys eye the beefsteaks, spread out on a wooden table like a votive offering.

There's other meat around, too, a boiled ham and a spiced luncheon loaf, some nice veal, a little fish course for anyone whose gut is bothering them, Guccia is bringing mackerels and porgies. But the beef is the main event. And no chicken, chicken is for fanooks.

Joe the host announces a surprise treat for his guests. The steaks, he lets the word out, will be a grill-it-yourself style of deal. Pick your slab, lay it on the fire yourself if you want, or if not one of the boys will do it, the point is you can watch it burn and have it burn exactly the way you like it burned.

In the midmorning that Thursday, as hellos are made and backs are slapped, the assembled gangsters have a brief opportunity to drink, to enjoy the (shitty) country weather, to marvel at the mammoth feast Barbara lays on.

A hundred-plus men, mostly middle-aged, in a stone manor up in the mountains, about to assault their already hardened arteries with another dose of saturated animal fat.

Magliocco, always a big eater, acts as coffee sergeant. Tornabe and Sciortino trot back and forth from the main house to the summer house, barbecue pit, and garage, acting as couriers, carrying messages, delivering this or that summons from this or that boss.

By half past noon, the steaks are just about ready to go on the grill. The food comes, and keeps on coming. Joe Barbara knows how to put on a spread. Since he runs the local Canada Dry distributorship, the assembled brethren know his liquor is top shelf.

His cohost Bufalino describes him: "He always does things big. If he is sick, he has fifty or so doctors. He has a nice place and likes to have people there."

First, a little business. In the living room of the big ranch house, Commission members Genovese, Profaci, Bonanno, Giancana, Steven Magaddino, and Trafficante (included by virtue of his connection with Lansky and Cuba) have gathered.

On the agenda: heroin, Cuba, divvying up Albert Anastasia's piece of the pie. Also, the elephant in the room, how best to recognize Vito's status in the overheated, competitive world of the Five Families of New York City.

Genovese's presence overwhelms the gathering. The "Right Man" is sitting right there. He wants to be crowned. He wants *capo dei capi*, the boss-of-bosses title. With Costello wounded and out of the way, and Anastasia dead, who is there to deny him?

It doesn't look as though a simple "godfather" label is going to do it for Vito. Maybe just plain "God"? How about that? Would that satisfy his unquenchable thirst for power?

The boys outside half expect to see *fumata bianca,* white smoke, gush from the chimney of the stone house, just like at the Vatican when a Pope is elected.

The other Commission members can be forgiven if they feel a sense of foreboding at the prospect of Vito's elevation. A couple of them, Bonanno and Profaci, might even have a thought that it would be great if the hand of fate simply reached down and swept Genovese away. Otherwise, all the bosses present are going to have Vito sitting on top of them like some voracious giant, flexing his muscle, taking his percentage, calling the shots.

Does Profaci say a private novena for Vito's demise? Mobsters, like everyone else, should be careful what they pray for.

Unwilling to face the big issues, the Commission bosses dither a bit. They take care of a minor problem before moving on to the main items of the agenda. Waiting out in the garage's recreation room is Carmine Lombardozzi, sometime Brooklyn stevedore, shylock, gambler, mob captain and, when it comes down to it, Albert's guy, left hanging in the wind when his boss got whacked.

A shylock and extortion specialist who is deep into boiler-room stock market scams, Lombardozzi stands accused of playing fast and loose with all his coin from a jukebox racket, not kicking a sufficient percentage up the ladder to the bosses.

For him, at least, this is the serious part of the summit. Lombardozzi is under a sentence of death. He doesn't really think anyone is going to ace him right there at the barbecue, but even so, it can upset a person's equilibrium.

After a sleepless night at the Dell Motel in Vestal he's worn out, and sits glumly in the carpeted den of the garage, the smell of smoke drifting in from outside.

His surroundings are man-cave spectacular, featuring a bar that would do justice to a small tavern, with a hundred glasses neatly lined up at the bartender's station. A collection of souvenir swizzle sticks rest in a cup on the counter, from all over—the Sans Souci in Havana, the Latin Quarter in New York City, the Hotel Casey in Scranton. A tricked-up old-style telephone is actually a radio, with a crank to tune the stations.

Forgive Lombardozzi if he notices none of this. After an interminable wait, Magliocco brings news of the decision of the bosses: death sentence commuted, fine of $10,000 levied instead.

Ten large? Jesus. Lombardozzi has a flicker of doubt that maybe he might prefer death instead. He heads outside to grill himself a steak. The boys welcome him back into the fold. Nobody ever seriously thought he was gonna get whacked. The guy's too good an earner.*

That small matter taken care of, the bosses inside the house take up the issue of the heroin trade.

The new Narcotics Control Act passed the previous year is on everyone's mind. Serious prison time—years, not months—now await anyone caught dealing dope. The bosses want no part of that, of course, but somehow cannot quite see giving up the enormous profits at the other end of the equation.

Vito has already announced his "no dope" policy. But there's wriggle room. Joe Bonanno, just back from Sicily, the man with the most experience in the Marseilles-to-Montreal narcotics route, comes up with a compromise, one already sketched out at the Hotel et des Palmes meet.

Spin off the importing and smuggling business onto foreigners. The Corsicans, Bonanno means, the "sixth family" he dealt with in Montreal. On the American Mafia's end, the boys will stick to retail on a case-by-case basis.

Even though, with his string of nightclubs, he's Mister Retail Heroin,

---

* Two weeks after the summit, sure enough, two cash payments of $5,000 exit from Lombardozzi's bank account, payee carefully left unspecified.

Vito says he doesn't like it. But Magaddino and Bonanno, the two La Marese cousins, gang up against him, and the vote goes their way.

Henceforth, the American Mafia gets out of the wholesale heroin smuggling business as just too damn liable to bring heat from the Feds. Retail street distribution, that's another matter. It's every made man for himself.

They're about to move on to another item on the agenda, the question of who inherits Anastasia's Brooklyn fiefdom. Carlo Gambino waits in the wings. It's his moment.

Second-level guys like Jerry Catena, John Ormento, Carlo himself, captains and underbosses, drift in and out of the house all the time, but unless a boss calls them over they mostly stay at the opposite side of the house from the Commission.

The other end of the expansive, twenty-five by forty-five-foot-wide living room is more informal, dominated by an enormous, twelve-foot-wide stone fireplace, twenty tons of gray stone, unlit even though the day is chilly.

Next to the hearth stands the combination TV-radio-hi fi in light wood, as well as two octagonal tables in dark oak. The boys all admire how the inlays on these tables lift out to display slots for poker chips and drinking glasses.

Since the second-level guys are the ones who are nearest the kitchen, they're the ones who get the news first.

Josephine Barbara sits with her housekeeper Marguerite Russell in the breakfast nook, both of them at a large round dining table with an inlaid sunburst design. Open to the nook is the kitchen, all hospital-white tile accented by red Formica countertops.

Another illuminated Gibbons Beer clock gives the time, a little after 12:30. The arrangement allows the two women at the sunburst table a partial view outside, to the north, where McFall Road is parked thick with cars.

"Hey, it's that state trooper," Josephine Barbara says.

She doesn't shout it out, either, just states it like it's an ordinary everyday fact. A shiver goes through the assembled mobsters, similar to one that might pass over a herd of antelope, say, when a lioness is sighted far off over the savannah. There isn't a stampede. Not yet. Just a nervous stirring.

At that same moment, two things happen outside in the compound yard. Bartolo Guccia, the fishmonger and jack-of-all-trades who has just dropped off a delivery, drives his little panel van out of the compound and up McFall Road.

And a group of mobsters comes around the corner of the garage, having just fetched Carmine Lombardozzi from his man-cave exile. They're laughing and congratulating him for slipping out from under a death sentence.

Lombardozzi is in the middle of the group. Moving forward, they pull up short, getting a clear view of what their friends around the barbecue pit and inside the summer pavilion don't see.

The law. They spot the pair of staties standing just where the asphalt runs out and the road turns back to dirt. Two more cops join the first two, so now there are four, staring across the twenty yards of road and field and compound, just like they're looking down a rifle sight.

The group around Lombardozzi sees the cops allow Bartolo to pass them by. The police are jotting down plate numbers of the cars parked along McFall. They're in plainclothes, but nobody at the summit has to have a badge shoved in his face to know exactly what they represent.

A short but excruciating period of waiting ensues. The mobsters mill, uncertain. Are the staties busting people? Or are they just checking license plates?

Gangster discipline is notoriously hit or miss. The gathering quickly descends into an every-man-for-himself situation, a variation on Joe Barbara's grill-your-own approach to barbecue.

Who will go, who stays, who drives out and in which car, who heads for the hills on foot, it all shakes out by itself. No one needs to be told to dump weapons and get rid of anything extraneous and incriminating.

There's some getting straight on the "visiting a sick friend" story that will be repeated, in the coming hours, ad nauseam. Mixed-up carloads start to form, Jersey and Brooklyn and Scranton jammed in together, nobody knowing who's who or what's what.

"Don't worry, don't worry," Joe says, passing through the gathering, trying to stanch the panic. "Those knuckleheads come around here all the time. They never do nothing."

Then Bart Guccia rattles back down the road in his piece-of-shit fish truck, pulling up next to the garage, leaning out of the window to utter the horrible, magic word.

"Roadblock."

It's over.

EPILOGUE
Apalachin in the American Imagination

A HISTORY OF THE MOB in America, arranged in a three-act screenplay structure.

Initiating incident: January 16, 1920. The Volstead Act becomes law, making alcohol an illegal commodity in the United States. Streaks of homicidal violence mar a decade of enormous profit-taking during Prohibition.

First-act turn: the 1931 Chicago conference, when Charles Luciano and the assembled bosses codify the Commission hierarchy of the mob, which leads to . . .

Act two: A golden age of organized crime, over a quarter century of relative peace wherein a stable national syndicate, largely unhampered by any pressure from the law, left alone especially by J. Edgar Hoover and the FBI, rakes in billions of dollars in revenue from gambling, loan-sharking, extortion, prostitution, labor racketeering, and narcotics smuggling.

Second-act turn: November 14, 1957, the bust-up of the Apalachin summit, which leads to . . .

Act three: Thirty years of increasing government pressure on the mob, RICO legislation, the dismantling of the national crime syndicate, the end of the underworld as Charles Luciano envisioned it. The last national mob commission meets in 1985.

In the history of organized crime in America, the Apalachin summit is a game-changer, a watershed moment, a big noise that continues to echo. The centrality of Apalachin persists in books, movies, and popular history. In particular, the comic trope of mob bosses fleeing into the woods still holds sway in the creative imagination.

Here's how the 1999 Billy Crystal-Robert DeNiro movie comedy *Analyze This* opens, with an old mobster, Dominic Manetta, reminiscing in voiceover:

MANETTA (V.O.)
1957 was a big year. The Russians put that Sputnik into outer space, the Dodgers played their last game at Ebbets Field, "that guy" shot Frank Costello in the head, and missed, and the Gallo brothers whacked Albert Anastasia in that barber shop in the Park Sheraton Hotel. It was total chaos. With Anastasia gone, Vito Genovese figures he's king shit, but Carlo Gambino and "Joe Bananas" both want to be boss of all bosses. So they call a meeting—a big meeting.

EXT. UPSTATE NEW YORK - DAY
In FADED 16mm documentary-style, we see a country road winding through rolling hills. At the top of the hill, a black '57 Cadillac appears and sweeps through the peaceful landscape.

MANETTA (V.O.)
It was the first time the whole Commission was ever gonna meet face to face. Bosses and wiseguys were comin' in from all over the country, and all the New York families, too—maybe sixty bosses, the whole wiseguy world—all headin' toward this little town upstate to figure out what's what.

EXT. ROADSIDE - DAY
A sign reads, "Entering Apalachin, pop. 342." The black Cadillac speeds past the sign, then another black Caddy, then a black Lincoln, then another Caddy, a Lincoln, etc.

MANETTA (V.O.)
I don't know what anybody was thinking, but some asshole thought it would be a good idea to have this meeting at Joe Barbara's farm in the country where nobody would notice.

EXT. RURAL GAS STATION - DAY
A local state police deputy is gassing up his motorcycle when the parade of shiny black cars rolls by. He looks up and scratches his head at the unusual sight.

MANETTA (V.O.)

Turns out the local cops were watching Joe Barbara like a hawk. So now you got about fifty Caddies and Lincolns pullin' into Apalachin and some deputy sheriff with cow shit on his shoes notices all the traffic and calls the Feds.

EXT. JOE BABARA'S ESTATE - DAY

The Caddies and Lincolns are all parked around a rambling country manor. Bosses and wiseguys are meeting and greeting each other on the big front porch.

One WISEGUY is trying to shoo a cow away from his car.

WISEGUY

You wanna be a ribeye? Get away from the fuckin' car.

EXT. WOODS - SAME TIME

Federal agents start moving in quietly, heavily-armed, wearing big FBI arm bands.

MANETTA (V.O.)

The meeting never even got started. The Feds moved in—

EXT. HOUSE - DAY

Agents with weapons drawn charge the house and start breaking down the front door.

EXT. BACK OF HOUSE - SAME TIME

MANETTA (V.O.)

—and we moved out.

Gangsters in shiny suits are squeezing through windows and leaping off balconies.

It's interesting to notice, in the screenplay by Peter Tolan, Kenneth Lonergan, and director Harold Ramis, the mix of fact and fantasy. A generally accurate summary of the run-up to the summit is followed by such obvious falsehoods as "some deputy sheriff with cow shit on his shoes" and "Federal agents start moving in quietly, heavily-armed, wearing big FBI arm bands."

The scene is played for comedy, for the ludicrous image of city-mouse gangsters fleeing into country-mouse fields, but also for something else, too. Manetta the wise old wiseguy attempts to teach the younger Robert DeNiro character, Paul Vitti, the lessons of history. Spanked at Apalachin, the modern underworld has learned to forgo large-scale meets as too risky.

For anyone paying attention, the manifold ironies of the summit continued to unspool long afterward. To pluck just one example from many: Bobby's family found itself ravaged by narcotics, as though the ghost of mobs past would obtain its revenge, in whichever twisted way it could.

In 1983, Robert Kennedy Jr. was taken off a commuter flight after calling out for help in the plane's bathroom, and a search of his baggage turned up heroin. David Kennedy died in 1984 in a Palm Beach hotel room, over a gram of cocaine in his wallet, a cocktail of coke and prescription drugs in his bloodstream. Other Kennedy children, including Christopher Lawford and Ted Kennedy's son Patrick, also struggled with drugs.

Writes one commentator, blaming the father, "The 'Kennedy stomach,' the tranquilizers, illicit drugs, and alcohol were but manifestations of the culture of deceit that Joe created." No one much bothers to trace the thread, narcotics-Mafia-Apalachin-RFK, so a lot of these odd historical connections go unremarked.

America's image of the mob, and its recollection of the Apalachin summit, is colored by overweening romanticization. In the hands of the great Damon Runyon, the murderous gambler and dope pusher Arnold Rothstein gets played for laughs as Nathan Detroit in *Guys and Dolls*. Mario Puzo and Francis Ford Coppola transform the crabbed, miserable Joe Profaci into the majestic Vito Corleone in *The Godfather*. The process continues, with Rothstein, Luciano, and Lansky appearing most recently as characters in HBO's *Boardwalk Empire*.

Who writes this stuff? English majors, film students, garret-stranded authors. They're the bookish nerds looking across the playground at the bullies, the tough corner boys, the ones who victimized them with repeated beat downs and random humiliations, and in response the nerds create an underworld of their own imagining. They invent the figure of the noble mobster.

Likewise, the revisionist view of Apalachin. A single bland-mannered state police sergeant could not possibly have brought down a summit of Mafia bosses. That narrative simply does not fit the mythology. This other mob boss did it, or that one, it was all an inside plot, a fix, wheels turning within wheels of dark, poetic conspiracy. That may be someone's idea of a better tale, but it's one that is further from the truth.

Once in a while, the publishing world and Hollywood get it right. The tawdry universe of *Goodfellas* is a little more clear-eyed than the rose-colored idealizations of *The Godfather*. Not that Coppola's epic is less of a grand, world-class drama, it's just less of a realistic portrait.

After *The Godfather* came out, street wisdom had it that mobsters studied the film to learn how they were supposed to behave. Life imitated art imitating life. James LaDuca, whining at the box office of a theater where *The Godfather* was sold out: "You've got to let me in. This movie is about my family!"

It wasn't. He only wished it was.

VITO GENOVESE died in *confino* at Atlanta Federal Penitentiary on February 14, 1969, having run his crime family with varying levels of effectiveness and reach from inside prison. The cooking scene in the movie *Goodfellas* is widely believed to reflect Genovese's life as a Federal inmate.

Olive Oil King JOE PROFACI never lived to see himself immortalized as the model for Vito Corleone in *The Godfather* movies. He died of liver cancer in 1962, having survived a takeover attempt of his family by the upstart Gallo brothers.

SAM GIANCANA, turned by prosecutors to testify as a prospective government witness, was killed by a mob hit in his Chicago home on June 19, 1975.

In 1984, SANTO TRAFFICANTE JR. died at the Texas Heart Institute in Houston, where he had gone for heart surgery. He remained tightlipped to the end, with the hospital making public a statement: "At the request of his family, no information at all will be released."

CARMINE GALANTE died with a cigar in his mouth, killed by a fusillade of bullets from a trio of hit men on July 12, 1972, on the open-air terrace of an Italian restaurant in Brooklyn.

CARLO GAMBINO died of natural causes while watching TV at his home on Long Island.

The last Apalachin mob boss to go, JOE BONANNO, died of a heart attack in Tucson, Arizona in 2002, at the advanced age of ninety-seven.

Summit cohost and pillar of the community RUSSELL BUFALINO inherited leadership of the mob in the Pittston-Scranton-Wilkes-Barre area. Resisting repeated deportation efforts, as well as prosecutions for extortion and homicide, he died of natural causes in 1994 at age ninety.

Another community pillar, JOHN C. MONTANA died of a heart attack at

Buffalo General Hospital on March 18, 1964. His son Charles, married to the daughter of Steven Magaddino, resided in the same Lewiston, NY "Mafia Row" neighborhood where the extended Magaddino clan lived.

After the death of his father and the sale of the family bottling company, JOE BARBARA JR. left New York to take up residence in Detroit, where he entered the waste-hauling business, establishing a near monopoly with his Tri-County Sanitation. In 1968, police arrested Barbara on rape and extortion charges. He was acquitted of rape but drew a seven-to-twenty-year prison term for extortion. Upon his release from prison, by then approaching three hundred pounds in weight, he was arrested for income tax fraud in 1979 and sentenced to a four-year prison term. His brother, PETER R. BARBARA, came to grief after a successful career as a Detroit medical malpractice attorney crashed and burned in a mail-fraud conviction.

The Kennedy brothers both fell to assassin bullets, with ROBERT F. KENNEDY slain by Sirhan Sirhan at the Ambassador Hotel in Los Angeles on June 6, 1968, the evening of his primary election triumph in California. The victory would have cleared RFK's path to the Democratic nomination for the presidency.

On the morning of May 2, 1972, J. EDGAR HOOVER's housekeeper discovered him slumped on the floor next to his bed, dead of a heart attack.

State police sergeant (afterward county sheriff) JOSEPH BENENATI died in 2011 at age ninety-seven in a Veterans Administration hospital, where the walls of his room were hung with Apalachin memorabilia.

EDGAR D. CROSWELL continued his racketbusting career, attacking corruption in the mobbed-up city of Utica, New York. He retired from the state police after twenty-five years of service with the rank of captain, then worked as an inspector general for New York City's Department of Sanitation, helping to clean up the Mafia-plagued waste-hauling business. During the 1970s, he served as Executive Assistant to the Attorney General on the New York State Organized Crime Task Force. A lifelong smoker (Salems, Merits), he died of emphysema at the age of seventy-seven on November 17, 1990, thirty-three years and three days after the crime summit he helped to expose.

After the tourists stopped coming and Joe's Barbecue Pit restaurant never materialized, the estate on McFall Road changed hands several times. It was held for a time by a local furniture magnate who furiously excluded sightseers and reporters. The property currently exists as a horse ranch. People in the village still occasionally refer to Joe Barbara's old place as "the Mafia house."

APPENDIX

The histories, activities, and associations of the participants in the Apalachin summit as contained in records of federal and state law enforcement agencies.

ABBREVIATIONS

S.P.: State Police
P.D.: Police Department
D.C.I.: Division of Criminal Identification, New York State Department of Correction
F.B.I.: Federal Bureau of Investigation
H.N.A.: Harrison Narcotics Act, Federal Bureau of Narcotics, U.S. Treasury Department
A.T.U.: Alcohol Tax Unit, U.S. Treasury Department

DOMINICK ALAIMO, 6 CHERRY STREET, PITTSTON, PA.

Born: January 28, 1910, in Pittston, PA

Occupation: Co-owner and manager of Jane Hogan Dress Co., Pittston, PA. Acts as committeeman for Local 8005, United Mine Workers of America, Scranton, PA.

Reputed Associates: Herman Stromberg (narcotics suspect), Angelo Sciandra, Pittston, PA, Russell Bufalino, Kingston, PA, Jimmie Doyle, Frankie Garbo, Emanuel Zicari, James A. Osticco, Pittston, PA.

Arrests (Department of Corrections, Division of Criminal Identification ID #654700X):

12/17/32: Robbery (Scranton, PA); not guilty, 1/30/33.

11/6/33: Suspicion of theft (Wilkes-Barre, PA).

8/16/40: Violation, Internal Revenue Act (Wilkes-Barre, PA), suspended sentence, one year probation.

Apalachin: Subject was riding in car with Emanuel Zicari of Endicott, NY. Questioned on highway seven miles west of Vestal, NY, and released. Subject stated he came to Apalachin with James Anthony Osticco and Angelo Joseph Sciandra.

JOSEPH MARIO BARBARA JR., MCFALL ROAD, APALACHIN, NY.

Born: March 24, 1936

Occupation: After one year of college, subject went to work for his father, Joseph Barbara Sr. During the three years prior to the summit, Barbara Jr. was active in his father's Canada Dry bottling plant in Endicott, NY. He drove a truck and worked in the bottling room of the plant. When his father suffered a series of heart attacks in early 1957, subject assumed the duty of operating the company.

Arrests: No criminal record.

Apalachin: On November 14, 1957, Barbara Jr. drove from the Endicott plant to his home for lunch. In doing so, he passed through Sergeant Croswell's road block. Upon arriving at his home, he did not have his lunch but turned around to drive back down the road. At the bottom of McFall Road he was stopped by the road block. On November 13, upon the request of his father, Barbara Jr. made the following reservations (and picked up the keys): Community Motel, Binghamton, one room; Parkway Motel, Vestal, three rooms.

JOSEPH MARIO BARBARA SR., MCFALL ROAD, APALACHIN, NY.

Born: August 9, 1905, Castellammare del Golfo, Sicily

Aliases: Joseph Barber, Joseph Barbaro, Joe the Barber

Occupation: President, Endicott Canada Dry Bottling Co., Inc., of Endicott, NY

Arrests:
1/5/31: State Police, Wyoming, PA (arrest ticket #2954): Suspicion of murder; discharged.
8/1/31: NYPD (#E8291): Possession of revolver; dismissed.
2/21/33: Police Department, Scranton, PA (#3146): Suspicion of murder; discharged.
6/13/46: Office of Price Administration, U.S. Marshall, Utica, NY (#7864): Illegal requisitioning of sugar; 6/27/46, $5,000 fine.

Reputed Associates:, Joseph Mangino; Pasquale Turrigiano, Endicott, NY; Vincent Coppola; Tony, Carmel, and Joseph Morreale (in connection with suspicion of murder in Wyoming, PA on 1/5/31); Santo Volpe and Angelo Polizzi (in connection with suspicion of murder in Scranton, PA, on 2/21/33).

At subject's wedding, automobiles registered in the following names were identified by State Police, New Milford, PA: Louis Consalvo, Joseph Genovese, Ernest Sesso, Joseph Ciliberto, Nicola Genovese, Sam Galente, Vincent Arceri, Guiseppo Polizzi, Joseph Pinto, Pasquale "Patsy" Turrigiano.

Business Associates (Notes due, according to corporate books):
Charles Bufalino: $2,500 (7/31/45)
Louis Consalvo: $5,000.00 (7/31/45)
Louis Pagnotti: $10,000 (7/31/45
Angel Polizzi: $15,000.00 (7/31/45)
Josephine Barbara (Mrs. Joseph Barbara): $5,000 (2/28/46)
Louis Piciano: $2,714.25 (4/30/48)

Relatives: John and Matthew Vivona (brothers of Mrs. Joseph Barbara), Ignizio Cannone, (nephew of Mrs. Joseph Barbara), Matthew and Mary Vivona, 6 Garfield Place, Endwell, NY (brother-in-law and sister-in-law by marriage).

Persons recommended for gun permits by subject: James Tedesco, Old Forge, PA; Thomas Carey, Old Forge, PA; America Rego, Old Forge, PA; Primo Cesaro, Old Forge, PA.

MELVIN J. BLOSSOM, R.D. 1, APALACHIN, NY.

Born: July 16, 1920, Noxon, PA

Occupation: Employed as caretaker for Barbara properties

Apalachin: Claims he did not participate in the meeting, but was employed on the Barbara property. Fingerprinted 6/19/56, NY State ABC Law, as an employee of the Barbara Enterprises.

Arrests: None.

Criminal Record: None.

JOSEPH BONANNO, 1726 DEKALB DRIVE, BROOKLYN, NY AND 1847 E. ELM ST., TUCSON, AZ.

Born: January 18, 1905, Castellamare del Golfo, Sicily; naturalized U.S. citizen, 5/17/45

Aliases: Guiseppe Bonanno, Joe Bananas

Occupation: Colorado Cheese Co., Trinidad, Colorado, with John Spadero and Robert Dionisio. Formerly, partner in B&D Coat Company, 47-55 Thames St., Brooklyn, NY, and 480 Johnson Ave., Brooklyn, NY, 1/1936 through 8/1942, manufacturers of women's coats.

Arrests (DCI #117101X):

9/16/30: NYC, Grand Larceny and possession of a revolver (detained with two other men in the transporting of machine guns to Capone mob in Chicago; acquitted.

12/10/40: alien registration.

1/12/42: U.S. Marshal, Brooklyn, NY: Violation Wage and Labor Law; fined $400 2/27/42, suspended sentence and eighteen months probation.

2/6/42: U.S. Marshal, Brooklyn, NY: Conspiracy (four counts); 5/1/42: count one, $50 fine paid, count two, suspended sentence; count three, suspended sentence; count four, suspended sentence; six months' probation.

Reputed Associates: Joseph Barbara, John Bonventre (uncle), Louis Volpe, Frank Giaramita, Vincent DePasquale, Pietro Vonventro, Charles DeBenedetto, Joseph Spadero, Cornelius Bertschinger, John Tartanella, Vincent Mangano, Frank Garafalo, Joseph Profaci, Ann Junno (Tucson), James Colletti, Robert Dionisio.

Note: Traveled to Palermo, Sicily, in September 1957 (passport #666676, as Giuseppi Bonanno), where he was seen in the company of Santo Serge.

Deportation proceedings: On 2/6/53, deportation proceedings were instituted against subject emanating from the Kefauver Senate Investigating Committee. Subject was believed to have entered the U.S. illegally.

Apalachin: Was found in a cornfield on McFadden Road adjoining the Barbara property and brought to Vestal Station and questioned by State Police. Admitted being at the meeting and was "visiting" Joseph Barbara Sr. In his possession was the business card of James V. LaDuca, secretary-treasurer, Waiters Union, Local 66. Subject was registered on October 17, 1956 at the Arlington Hotel, Binghamton, N.Y. (room charged to Canada Dry Bottling Company, Inc., Endicott, NY), along with Joseph Barbara Sr. (Endicott), John Bonventre (Brooklyn), Frank Garafalo (NYC), Louis Volpe (L.I. City, NY).

JOHN BONVENTRE, 115 CLEVELAND STREET, BROOKLYN, NY.

Born: April 18, 1901, Castellamare, Trapani, Sicily; entered U.S. from Cuba, 5/10/40; naturalized 8/5/46.

Aliases: Guiseppe Bonanno, Peppin Bananno, Joseph Bonaventre, Joseph Bonaventre, John Bonaventre

Reputed Occupations: Undertaker, cheese business, Pinta Clothing Company, Levine & Bonventre (ladies coats), garment contractors.

Arrests: none known.

Associates: Joseph Bonanno (nephew), Carmine Galante

Apalachin: Picked up in cornfield on McFadden Road adjoining Barbara property by Trooper Sackel and brought to Vestal Station. Bonventre said he came up with Joseph Bonanno "to visit Joseph Barbara, who was sick." Identified him through Social Security Card (094-12-9610.) A person of this name, giving the same address, under Passport #861454 entered the United States October 2, 1956 at New York City from Italy. Stayed at Arlington Hotel, Binghamton, NY, October 17 and 18, 1956 with Frank Garafalo and Louis Volpe (who was registered for October 16, 17, 18, 19, 1956). Room was charged to Canada Dry Beverage Company. Joseph Bonnano and Joseph Barbara were registered at this hotel on October 17, 1956.

RUSSELL A. BUFALINO, 304 E. DARRANCE ST., KINGSTON, PA.

Born: 1903. The U.S Immigration authorities contended that the subject was born in Sicily. Subject contended he was born in Pennsylvania. Month and date are unknown in regard to his birth.

Occupation: Owner of Penn Drape and Curtain Company, 161 South Main Street, Pittston, PA. Believed to be active in Pennsylvania garment industry, operating nonunion shops. Subject and James Osticco were guests of Atlas Chain & Manufacturing Company, W. Pittston, PA, at Bimini, British West Indies, April 1956 and from there went to Hotel Nacionel, Havana, 5/2/56. Subject stayed at Hotel Frederick, Endicott, NY 6/1/56 with son Angelo and stated on registration that he was representing Medico Industries, Inc. Room charged to Canada Dry Bottling Co., Inc., of Endicott, NY.

Arrests (FBI ID #691-589, NY State DCI #656155X):

2/4/27: Buffalo Police Department: Criminally receiving stolen property.

7/22/33: Buffalo Police Department: Possession of machinery with serial number filed off (auto); no bill of arrest.

6/13/35: Buffalo Police Department: Criminally receiving stolen property.

Associates: Joseph Barbara, Apalachin, NY, John C. Montana, Buffalo, NY (uncle of subject); Santo Volpe, Scranton, PA; Dominick Alaimo, Pittston, PA; Angelo Sciandra, Pittston, PA; James Plumeri (alias Jimmy Doyle), New York City; Herman Stromberg (alias Nig Rosen), New York City; John Ormento (alias Big John), New York City; Salvatore Loproto, New York City; Anthony Guarnieri (alias Guv), Johnson City, NY; Angelo Polizzi, Scranton, PA; Samuel de Bella (business partner in PA), Modesto LoQuasto (Pennsylvania), Castra Guimonto (alias Cappy) (Pennsylvania), Jack Paresi (NYC and Pennsylvania), Albert Anastasia (deceased, murdered 10/25/57), John Dio (NYC) serving time for extortion.

Apalachin: Arrived with DeSimone, Civello, and Scozzari in motor vehicle owned by William Medico (alias Greco), owner of Medico Electric Motor Company, Pittsburgh, PA, who is reputed to have been engaged in illicit liquor traffic from 1928 to 1933. At the time the New York State Police checked his car on 11/15/57, 1957 black, Chrysler Imperial (PA registration #256SJ) the following occupants were with him: Vito Genovese, 68 West Highland Ave, Atlantic Highlands, NJ; Gerardo Catena, 21 Overhill Road, South Orange, NJ; Dominick Olivete, 1157 Magnolia Avenue, Camden NJ; Joseph Ida, 108 Lincoln Avenue, Highland Park, NJ. Subject stayed at Arlington Hotel, Binghamton, New York, on March 18, 1957 with Joseph Barbara, Vincenzo Osticco, and Angelo Sciandra. Room bill charged to Canada Dry Beverage Company of Endicott, NY.

IGNATIUS CANNONE, 3634 RATH AVENUE, ENDWELL, NY.

Born: November 12, 1925, New York City.

Occupation: Owner of Nat's Place, 400 North Street, Endicott, NY, and Plaza Lounge, 1 Endwell Plaza, Endwell, NY.

Arrests: Subject admitted to state police to two arrests twenty years ago, both for disorderly conduct; one involved a fight in Endwell, the other was for shooting dice in New York City, for which he was fined $2.

Reputed Associates: Joseph Barbara, Natale Evola (subject's godfather, Mrs. Joseph Barbara's cousin)

Note: Broome County authorities noted subject's automobile at places where crap games were believed to be in progress.

Apalachin: Subject traveled to Barbara's home alone in his own car.

ROY CARLISI, 20 ANDERSON PLACE, BUFFALO, NY.

Born: April 10, 1909, Chicago, Illinois.

Occupation: Owner, Club 97 Restaurant, Buffalo, NY.

Arrests (FBI #1434575):
12/30/37: Violation, Internal Revenue Act, Chicago, Illinois (#15913); discharged.
1/4/43: SOS War Department, #40, C.W.B.; trial, no disposition.

Reputed Associates: Samuel Pittisi, John Termini, Sam Drago, Concerta Acquisto, Michael Constanto, Joe Romano.

Apalachin: Claimed to have been picked up by John Scalish, 11706 East Harrington Street, Cleveland, and John Anthony DeMarco, 3536 Hidane Street, Shaker Heights, Ohio, and James LaDuca, Dana Drive, Lewiston, en route to NYC on business and pleasure trip. Claimed he was not at Barbara house. Brought to Vestal Station by Trooper F. A. Tiffany in car,

Ohio license plate number HM-373, owned by John Scalish. Had $300 on person. Indicted for contempt (thirteen counts) by Tioga County Grand Jury on February 27, 1958.

PAUL CONSTATINO CASTELLANO, 1737 EAST 23 STREET, BROOKLYN, NY.

Born: April 6, 1912, New York City.

Occupation: Butcher, owner EMCEE Meat Markets (six stores), office headquarters at 140 Fort Greene Place, Brooklyn, NY.

Arrests (FBI #824-437, NYC B#125933, NYS DCI #653525X)
7/3/34: NYPD, 1897 PUBLIC LAW, wanted in Connecticut.
8/12/34: Hartford, CN PD, robbery with violence, one year jail, state supreme court.

Reputed Associates: Armand Rava, Carlo Gambino (brother-in-law), Mike Miranda.

Apalachin: Subject stated he was invited by Carlo Gambino, his brother-in-law, to drive him to Joseph Barbara's house. Gambino borrowed an auto from one Peter Ferrara. Castellano said he was introduced to Armand Rava and Mike Miranda and drove them all upstate on November 13, 1957.

GERARDO VITO CATENA, 21 OVERHILL ROAD, SOUTH ORANGE, NJ.

Born: January 8, 1902, Newark, NJ.

Occupation: Employee and stockholder, Runyon Vending Sales Co., 221 Frelinghuysen Ave., Newark, NJ. As of 10/22/56 personnel director (formerly vice president) of Marcal Manufacturing Company, East Paterson, NJ. Reported to have formerly been an officer of Kool Vent Metal Awning Co. of New Jersey and Delaware.

Arrests: (NJ #1639, DCI #194089 X)

8/11/23: Shooting crap, Newark, NJ, suspended sentence, 8/13/23.

12/9/23: Gambling, Newark, NJ, paid $2 fine, 12/11/23.

10/26/24: Interfering with an officer, Newark, NJ, two-year probation, 1/25/25, $50 fine first week, $1 weekly thereafter.

7/27/26: Suspect, material witness, $750 bail for grand jury, 7/28/26.

8/5/26: Robbery, Harrison, NJ, indeterminate term Rahway Reformatory, 1/19/28.

1/15/27: Grand Larceny (truck highjacking), Newark NJ, nine months, Essex County Penitentiary, 4/11/27.

1/24/28: Robbery, Rahway, NJ, state reformatory, transferred to Ann Reformatory, 1/28/29, maximum sentence to 1/19/43, suspended.

11/17/30: Material witness in Pacelli murder case, Newark, NJ, turned over to prosecutor's office, 11/30/30.

11/3/33: Loitering, Orange, NJ, sixty days' suspended sentence, 11/3/33.

1/23/34: Bribery of Federal juror, Hammonton, NJ, $1000 fine and eight months in county jail, 3/12/34.

Reputed Associates: Albert Anastasia, Anthony Anastasio, Eugene Catena, Frank Catena (brothers), Frank Costello, Joseph Doto (alia "Joe Adonis"), James O'Connell, Joe Stracher, Salvatore (Charles) "Lucky" Luciano (subject believed to have met Luciano in Havana after his deportation from United States to Italy), Mike Miranda, Anthony Guarino, Angelo "Gyp" DeCarlo, Vito Genovese, Russell Bufalino, Joseph Ida, Dominick Oliveto, Abner "Longie" Zwillman, Al Dugan, Richard Bordiato, Frank Cardinale (Hoboken, NJ).

Note: During the eight months before the Apalachin summit, subject made numerous trips to Havana, Cuba, where he is alleged to have large financial interests in gambling concessions at the Riviera Hotel. Information indicates that some of the funds used by Catena were supplied by Nevada gambling interests. Special note should be made of Catena's former association with Joe Stracher, who is connected with gambling operations in Nevada.

Note: Subject is mentioned sixty-six times in the report of the Kefauver Committee.

Apalachin: Catena rode in car driven by Russell Bufalino checked at road adjoining Barbara property.

SALVATORE "CHARLES" CHIRI, 2 BRIDLE WAY, PALISADES, NY.

Born: August 10, 1898, Palermo, Italy; citizenship status unknown.

Occupation: Automotive Conveying Co. of NJ, Inc., Mahwah, NJ.

Arrest (INS #5167880):
12/26/40: Alien registration, no charge or disposition shown.

Note: Mentioned three times in proceedings of the Senate's Kefauver Committee.

Apalachin: Registered at Del Motel, Binghamton, with party of three guests on November 13, 1957. Brought to the Vestal substation and initially questioned by Trooper R. C. Geer, who identified subject through operator's license #0600974 NJ.

JOSEPH FRANCIS CIVELLO, 5311 DENTON DRIVE, DALLAS, TX.

Born: February 3, 1902, Port Allen, Louisiana.

Occupation: Importer of food and liquor.

Arrests (DCI #655196X):
7/14/28: Murder, Dallas, Texas, PD #7265, exonerated.
1928: Violation of liquor law, Dallas, Texas, served forty days in county jail.
7/14/28: Violation of Harrison Narcotics Act and conspiracy, Dallas, Texas, PD #7265, sentenced to fifteen years in Leavenworth Federal Penitentiary and five years' probation.

Reputed Associates: John Ormento, Rocco Pellegrino, Frank DeSimone, Los Angeles, California, attorney, (cousin).

Apalachin: Traveled from Scranton, PA, to Barbara's in car operated by Russell Bufalino.

JAMES COLLETTI, 1415 CLAREMONT AVENUE, PUEBLO, CO.

Born: October 3, 1897, Italy.

Occupation: Owner of the Colorado Cheese Company, Pueblo, CO.

Arrests (PD NYC E#8884):
10/7/27: Received stolen goods, discharged.
5/1/33: Disorderly person, Jersey City, NJ, PD #B7149, no disposition.

Reputed Associates: Robert Dionisio (Trinidad, CO), John Spaduro (Brooklyn, NY), Joseph Bonnano, Frank Garafolo, Carmine Galante, John Bonventre.

Apalachin: Picked up by Trooper Teneyck and Trooper Smith on Little Meadows Road, west of Barbara property, and brought to Vestal substation. Identified from Colorado Registration 2-17992, 1954 Cadillac four-door sedan, Colorado operator's license K2-15791. Supposed to have flown to Binghamton and believed to have left by plane. Registered at Airport Hotel, Inc., Port Newark, New Jersey, on November 12, 13, and 14, 1957. (Frank Zito also registered there on these dates.)

FRANK CUCCHIARA, 228 COMMON STREET, WATERTOWN, MA.

Born: March 29, 1895, Italy; naturalized on August 10, 1931, Boston, MA.

Occupation: Since 1938 treasurer and reputed owner of controlling interest in Purity Cheese Company, 55 Endicott Street, Boston, MA.

Arrests (FBI #4477, NYS DCI #654319X):
9/28/15: Assault and battery, Boston, MA, discharged.
10/19/23 (as Frank Cucchiara): Grand Larceny, Manhattan, suspended sentence, 6/27/24.
3/26/25: Unlawful possession of morphine and dynamite, Boston, MA, not guilty, 2/11/25.
7/15/25: Speeding, Concord MA, $10 paid.

10/20/25: Lottery, Boston Municipal Court, $50 paid.

11/26/26: Sale of narcotics, New York City, one year and one day, 12/28/26.

5//1/30 (as Frank Cohara): Forgery, New York Police Department, reduced to grand larceny in the second degree, suspended sentence, 5/16/30.

1/1/32 (alias Frank Caruso): Murder, Police Department, Boston, MA, no bill of arrest, 7/1/32.

7/30/32: Conspiracy to set up lottery, Boston Municipal Court.

7/15/34: Failure to obey stop sign, Concord, MA, $2 paid.

12/20/34 (as John Perneci): Possession of still, New York Police Department, 2nd Division.

5/15/36 (as John Maio): Possession of still, Alcohol Tax Unit, Newburgh, NY, nine months, $1,000 fine, 8/4/36.

10/11/38 (as Joseph Pizzo): Possession of still, Alcohol Tax Unit, New York City, disposition unknown.

12/16/40 (as Josph Pizzo): Conspiracy to erect still, New York City, six months, 5/11/41.

Reputed Associates: Cristoforo Rubino, 114-31 221 Street, Cambria Heights, L.I., NY (fugitive in narcotics case since 1955, murder victim 1958), Carlo Gambino, Frankie Carbo, Phillip Brudela (visited Charles "Lucky" Luciano and Joseph Dato in Italy in 1957).

Apalachin: Subject claimed he came alone to Barbara's by train from Boston to Binghamton, and then by cab to Apalachin. Other evidence indicated that subject rode with Carmine Lombardozzi, Joseph Riccobono, and Natale Evola.

DOMINICK D'AGOSTINO, 2226 ONTARIO AVENUE, NIAGARA FALLS, NY.

Born: December 7, 1891, Italy.

Occupation: Allegedly unemployed, although believed to own a bakery in Niagara Falls, Ontario, Canada.

Arrests (DCI #222824X):

11/2/30: Harrison Narcotics Act and criminal conspiracy, Buffalo, NY. Sentenced to six months in Erie County Penitentiary on conspiracy.

Sentenced U.S. District Court to four years and four days in Atlanta Prison, sentence suspended, and probation on four additional counts of assisting in concealment of drugs, sale, and failure to pay Federal tax.

Reputed Associates: Sam Lagattuta, Rosario Mancuso.

Note: Subject was indicted by Tioga County Grand Jury, April 8, 1958, on seven counts of criminal contempt.

Apalachin: Joseph and Salvatore Falcone traveled from Utica with subject to Barbara house.

JOHN ANTHONY DEMARCO, 3536 HIDANA STREET, SHAKER HEIGHTS, OH.

Born: February 14, 1903, Italy.

Occupation: Real estate broker

Arrests (DCI #654684):
12/13/26: Robbery, Detroit, MI, *nolle prossed*, 1/28/27.
7/31/30: Investigation of criminal conspiracy, Cleveland, OH, *nolle prossed*.
8/13/39: Extortion, Cleveland, OH, convicted 8/10/42.
9/15/42: Blackmail, Columbus, OH, convicted, sentenced one to five years, 9/29/43.
8/23/48: Investigation connected with bombing, Cleveland, OH, no further information.

Reputed Associates: John Scalish.

Note: Subpoena served for subject's appearance before Tioga County Grand Jury, failed to appear.

Apalachin: Riding in car operated by John Scalish. Subject stayed at Parkway Motel with Scalish, Joe Barbara Jr. making reservations.

FRANK DESIMONE, 7838 ADOREE STREET, DOWNEY, CA.

Born: July 17, 1909, Pueblo, CO.

Occupation: Attorney.

Arrests: No record.

Reputed Associates: Michael Polizzo (Detroit), Russell Bufalino (Scranton).

Note: Subject mentioned in the report of Kefauver Committee.

Apalachin: Traveled to Barbara's house with Bufalino, Joe Civello, and Simone Scozzari.

NATALE JOSEPH EVOLA, 792 BAY RIDGE PARKWAY, BROOKLYN, NY.

Born: February 22, 1907, New York City.

Occupation: President-treasurer of Belmont Garment Delivery Company, 242 West 37th Street, New York City; president, Amity Garment Delivery Company (same address), operates Fratelli Berio Distributing Company; subject was believed to exercise control over the shoulder pad industry with the backing of Joseph Stracci, alias "Joe Stretch," and Harry Strasser through a shoulder pad association which manufacturers were required to join.

Arrests: (DCI #198655X)
8/1/31: 1897 P.L, New York City, discharged, 8/7/31.
8/5/32: Coercion, New York City, acquitted, 9/13/32.

Reputed Associates: Carmine Galante, Frank Cucchiara, Boston, MA, Ignazio Cannone (subject's godson), Harry Strasser, Joseph Stracci, John Tartanello (vice president, Belmont Garment Delivery, Inc.), Joseph Barbara, Nicola Gruppo, Joseph Riccobono, Carmine Lombardozzi, Alfred Angelicola (Paterson, NJ), Joseph Profaci, Vincent Rao (Yonkers,

NY), Charles B. Chiri (Palisades, NJ), Joseph Bonanno (Brooklyn, NY), John Ormento (Lido Beach, NY), Joseph Magliocco.

Apalachin: Subject came to Apalachin with Carmine Lombardozzi, Joseph Riccobono, and Frank Cucchiara in Riccobono's car; subject was picked up at roadblock on highway adjoining Barbara's property, driving 1957 Cadillac sedan owned by Alfred Angelicola of 600 Market Street, East Paterson, NJ; with the subject at the time he was picked up was Frank Cucchiara of Boston, MA; subject stayed at the Carlton Hotel, Binghamton, NY, on November 13, 1957; on November 14 subject stayed at the Carlton with Louis Larasso and Frank Majuri, leaving November 15, 1957.

JOSEPH FALCONE, 1623 MOHAWK ST., UTICA, NY.

Born: January 27, 1902.

Occupation: Manager of liquor store.

Arrests (FBI #1697613, DCI #653 529X):
1/24/39: Violation of Internal Revenue Liquor Tax, U.S. Marshal, Utica, found guilty, sentenced two years, penitentiary to be designated, $7,500 fine to stand, conviction reversed on appeal, 6/17/39.

Reputed Associates: Salvatore Falcone (brother).

Note: Joseph Falcone was believed by the A.T.U. investigators to be his brother Salvatore's chief aide. Joseph Falcone was served with a subpoena to appear before the Tioga County Grand Jury. Pleading illness, he evaded appearance. Subject was formerly interested in a pinball machine enterprise in the City of Utica. When he terminated his interest, the enterprise fell on hard times and was liquidated. The bulk of the pinball business thereafter fell to a new enterprise. Subject was known to be on friendly terms with the reputed owner of the new enterprise.

Apalachin: Subject was picked up in an automobile in which the passengers were Salvatore Falcone (brother), Dominick D'Agostino, Sam Lagattuta, and Rosario Mancuso.

SALVATORE FALCONE, 1652 CONKLING AVENUE, UTICA, NY.

Born: August 17, 1891, Italy.

Occupation: Operated grocery store in Miami, Florida.

Arrests (FBI #1697794):
1/9/39: Violation of Internal Revenue Liquor Tax Law, U.S. Marshall, Utica, NY, found guilty and sentenced to one year and five months, enitentiary to be designated and $1,000 fine to stand, reversed, 6/27/39.

Note: In 1939 the A.T.U. agents of the U.S. Treasury Department launched a large-scale investigation of stills in the Utica area. Salvatore Falcone was believed to be the head of all the illicit alcohol manufacture and also reputedly headed the Italian lottery in Utica. He was reported to control the shoe repairmen in Utica and to operate a monopoly in that field. It was reported that other bootleggers operated stills in the area, but were required to pay a tribute of $1 to Falcone for every can of bootleg alcohol made. The A.T.U. agents failed to secure proof. Salvatore never appeared upon the scene of any illegal endeavor; he never visited any of his stills; he never bought any of the necessary products for the making of alcohol, nor did he ever visit any of the Italian lottery drops. The A.T.U. agents estimated in 1937 that Salvatore Falcone was worth from one to five million dollars. In 1936 Salvatore visited Italy and made a large contribution to some public fund and was cited publicly by Mussolini. Upton his return from Italy, he was met in New York City by his brother Joseph and by John Montana. Salvatore and Joseph Falcone have invested in many legitimate enterprises in the Utica area. Salvatore Falcone reputedly was an important leader in the Italian underworld, and after Apalachin resided at 1652 N.W. 62 Street, Miami, FL. Salvatore and Joseph Falcone have invested in many legitimate enterprises in the Utica area.

Apalachin: Salvatore Falcone was one of the participants at the Apalachin meeting, arriving in an automobile operated by his brother, Joseph, and occupied by Dominic D'Agostino, Sam Lagattuta, and Rosario (Russell) Mancuso.

CARLO GAMBINO, 2230 OCEAN PARKWAY, BROOKLYN, NY.

Born: August 24, 1902, Palermo, Sicily, Italy (remains unnaturalized alien).

Occupation: Associated with Schriller, Gambino & Salstein, 141 East 44 Street, NYC, labor relations consultants; reputedly has financial interest in Carrol Paper Products Company, 412 3rd Avenue, Brooklyn, NY.

Arrests (FBI #334450, PD NYC #B 128760, NY DCI #467576X)
11/13/31: Suspicion of burglary, Lawrence, MA, case dismissed.
10/9/34: Grand larceny, Brockton, MA, *nolle prossed,* made restitution of $1,000.
6/17/37: Violation Internal Revenue Act (operation of still) Philadelphia, PA, twenty-two months, Lewisburg (PA) Federal Penitentiary.

Reputed Associates: Santo Serge (Sicily), Joseph Bonnano, Thomas Lucchese (alias "Three-Finger Brown"); subject's son was married to Lucchese's daughter; Charles "Lucky" Luciano (deported to Italy), Mike Miranda, Paul Castellano (brother-in-law).

Note: Subject has several Federal alcohol tax arrests, most of which have been dismissed. Subject's brother, Paul Gambino, fled to Italy to avoid prosecution in a Federal alcohol tax case. Subject was suspected by immigration authorities to be involved in smuggling aliens into Philadelphia, PA, May 1948.

Apalachin: Subject went to Apalachin in borrowed car with Armand Rava, Mike Miranda, and his brother-in-law, Paul Castellano.

MICHAEL JAMES GENOVESE, RD 2, GIBSONIA, PA.

Born: April 9, 1919, Pittsburgh, PA.

Occupation: Owner, Archie's Auto Car Wash.

Arrests (FBI #4373362, DCI #654686X):
9/14/36: Robbery, Pittsburgh, PA, two years probation.

6/16/45: Concealed weapon, PD, Youngstown, OH, indicted 9/13/45, arraigned, pleaded not guilty, *nolle prosequi*, 11/21/45.

Reputed Associates: Gabriel Mannarino, Frank Valenti, Vito Genovese (relative), Sam Russo, Gyp Contaldo, Anthony Visco, Chuck Teemer, Ralph Arcadi, Boots Bellini, Danny Bellini, Michael "Moon Mullins" O'Connor, Richard Ambrose, James Pecora, Joseph Suxia, Charles Brusco, Anthony Febraro, Arthur Rocca, John LaRocca, Anthony LaRocca, Edward Trunick, Fiore Genovese, Chester Grassi (all Pittsburgh, PA).

Note: In 1956 subject in partnership with John LaRocca in the L & G Amusement Company (coin-operated machines), Pittsburgh, PA. In 1956 subject was employed as a salesman by the North Star Cement Company, Pittsburgh, PA. Alleged to be head of numbers racket in the East Liberty district of Pittsburgh, PA. Alleged to have concealed interest in Genovese Cocktail Lounge, 412 Larimer Avenue, East Liberty, Pittsburgh, PA. Concealed interest in the notorious Club 30 restaurant and gambling casino located on Route 30, just west of the Pennsylvania state line in Chester, West Virginia.

Apalachin: Subject was identified in the same car with James Osticco, Gabriel Mannarino, and Angelo Sciandra. Registered 11/13/57 at Arlington Hotel, Binghamton, NY, with John LaRocca of Coin Machine Distribution Company, Pittsburgh, PA. Registration made by Joseph Barbara Sr., on 11/12/57 and charged to Canada Dry Bottling Company.

VITO GENOVESE, W. HIGHLAND AVENUE AND AVE. C, ATLANTIC HIGHLANDS, NJ (FORMERLY OF 130 OCEAN BLVD., ATLANTIC HIGHLANDS, NJ).

Born: November 21, 1897, Resiglino, Napes, Italy; naturalized: November 25, 1936; denaturalized, November 1953, on charges he concealed his criminal record; was scheduled in 1956 for deportation trial in Federal Court, Newark, NJ.

Occupation: Waste Paper Removal, 106 West Houston St., NYC; Erb Strapping Company, 180 Thompson Street, NYC; general manager, Colonial Trading Company (rags and waste paper) 527 Hudson Street, NYC.

Other Activities and Interests Reported: Said to receive $20,000 weekly from Italian policy operation in New Jersey. Believed to have dog track interests in Montauk Beach, Virginia and South Carolina, as well as a stake in the Monte Carlo lottery in Europe. Reputed to have financial interests in the following nightclubs: Moroccan Village, 23 West 8th Street, NYC; Caravan Club, 578 West Broadway, NYC; Savannah Club, 66 West 3rd St., NYC; 82 Club, 82 East 4th Street, NYC, as well as other Midtown and Harlem venues. Alleged to have financial interests in Sea Coast Liquor and Beer Distributing Company, Fairhaven, NJ, operated by his son, Philip Genovese, and the latter's wife, the former Rose Marie Canlendrillo. Reputedly possessed interests in two legitimate power plants in Italy.

Arrests (DCI#166 080):
1/15/17: 1897 public law (gun) , NYC, sixty days in workhouse, 6/4/17.
4/23/18: Felonious assault, Queens, NY, discharged, 4/30/18.
4/25/24: 1897 public law (gun) , NYC, discharged, 4/26/24.
5/13/24: Homicide (auto), Brooklyn, NY, discharged, 6/3/24.
1/17/25: Disorderly person, Hoboken, NJ, discharged, 1/20/25.
7/25/25: Burglary, NYC, discharged, 7/25/25.
10/10/25: Homicide (gun), NYC, discharged, 10/13/25.
1/9/27: 1897 public law, Brooklyn, NY, fined $250 and thirty days, 1/21/27.
1/19/31: Carrying dangerous weapon, Jersey City, NJ, no indictment, dismissed, 2/3/31.
12/4/34: Homicide (gun), Brooklyn, NY (see below, same case).
9/28/44: Wanted for murder, NYC, apprehended (see below, same case).
6/2/45: Murder, first degree, NYC, discharged, 6/10/45.

Note: Subject was reputed to have fled to Italy to escape prosecution for the murder of Brooklyn gambler Ferdinand Boccia. During World War II, Genovese acted as interpreter for numerous American military government officials in Italy. At the same time, he was also active in the black market, stealing U.S. Army trucks, driving them to supply depots, loading them with flour, sugar, and other supplies; the truck was then driven to a place of concealment and unloaded. The trucks were then destroyed. He was arrested by Army officers but never tried on the black market charge. He was returned to the United States and turned over to the officials of Kings County (Brooklyn) to stand trial for the Boccia killing. A witness died in Metropolitan Correctional. Genovese was released. Another witness, Santos, was murdered in the Flatlands section of

Brooklyn. Genovese is #130 on the United States Narcotics List of major violators.

Reputed Associates: Mike Miranda, John Caputo, Frank Ocetallo, Joseph Profaci, Russell Bufalino, Salvatore Chiri, Vincent Rao, Thomas Lucchese, Jerry Catena, Anthony Paterno, Salvatore Moretti, Peter La Placa, Abner Zwillman, James Lynch, George Smurra, John Robillotto, Albert Anastasia (deceased), William Cardinale (chauffeur), Charles Luciano, Angelo "Gyp" De Carlo, Tony Bender (a.k.a. Anthony Strollo), Joseph Doto (a.k.a. Joe Adonis), Andy Richards (owner of bar and package store in Atlantic Highlands, NJ).

Relatives: Carmine Genovese (brother), Asbury Park, NJ; Michael Genovese (brother), 131 Riverside Drive, NYC; Philip Genovese (son), married to Rose Marie Calandrillo, operators of the Sea Coast Liquor and Beer Distributing Company, Fair Haven, NJ.

Apalachin: Subject was picked up at roadblock on highway adjoining Barbara's property, riding with Bufalino.

ANTHONY FRANK "GUV" GUARNIERI, 3619 ROYAL ROAD, JOHNSON CITY, NY.

Born: May 1, 1910, Utica, NY.

Occupation: Dress contractor, vice president of Tri-Cities Dress Company, Inc., Binghamton, NY; president-treasurer of Owego Textile Company, Owego, NY.

Arrests: (FBI#5073273, NYC PD B#319216, NY DCI #208194X)
12/5/45: 974 public law (lottery), PD Binghamton, NY, disposition unknown.
3/12/48: Lottery, NYS Police, Sidney, NY, final charge, Section 580 and Section 1376 public law, fined $1,500, 5/2/48.
3/13/48: Illegal possession of firearms, Broome County, NY, reduced to misdemeanor, sent to Broome County jail for four months, $300 fine, 11/19/52.
10/3/52: Felonious Assault, PD NY 16 Precinct, reduced to assault, third degree, dismissed, 10/7/52.

Reputed Associates: Russell Bufalino, Louis Stromberg (brother of Herman), Herman Stromberg (alias "Nig" Rosen), Patsy Sciortino, Joseph Profaci, Louis Maraconi, Mike Blandia, Angelo Sciandra, James (Doyle) Plumeri, Nick Alaimo, Joseph Barbara, Joseph Lapadura.

Note: Friedman's Express, used by subjects Owego Textile Company to transport goods to NYC, was reported to be owned by Abraham Chait, formerly of the Bronx, a questionable character reputed to be a "muscle" operator in the underworld. Contacts have been established between Bufalino and James "Doyle" Plumeri, a notorious underworld character.

Apalachin: Subject was apprehended in a 1957 Oldsmobile, operated by Patsy Monachino. Other passengers were Sam Monachino, brother of Patsy, both from Auburn, NY, and Joseph Profaci of Brooklyn, NY.

BARTOLO GUCCIA, 202 OAK HILL ROAD, ENDICOTT, NY.

Born: December 28, 1891.

Occupation: Fish peddler, self-employed.

Arrests (DCI #699):
1916: Possession of revolver, NYC, three months in workhouse.
3/30/17: Carrying weapon, indeterminate sentence.
1923: Reported by NY County (Manhattan) in Pennsylvania bank robbery.
1/2/23: Breaking and entering, reported by NY County (Manhattan).
1924: Bootlegging, reported by NY County (Manhattan).
10/22/36: Murder, first degree, Bath, NY, violation section 1044 PUBLIC LAW, not guilty.

Apalachin: Picked up at roadblock on highway adjoining Barbara's property.

JOSEPH IDA, 108 LINCOLN AVE., HIGHLAND PARK, NJ.

Born: July 26, 1892, Tuimare, Italy.

Occupation: Automobile salesman for DeAngelis Brothers, New Brunswick, NJ.

Arrests (FBI #23312A, DCI #654343X):

8/8/36: Public law, section 15-B, chapter 114, Palisades Park, NJ, PD #21169, $10 fine and $3 fine.

Reputed Associates: Ralph Sarceno, Alfred DeMarrco, Mike Clemente, Rocco Pellogrino.

Apalachin: Stopped at roadblock in automobile driven by Russell Buffalino, with Joseph Oliveto, Gerry Cateno, Vito Genovese.

JAMES V. LADUCA, DANA DRIVE, LEWISTON, NY.

Born: October 19, 1912, Buffalo, NY.

Occupation: Secretary-treasurer of Hotel and Restaurant Workers Union, Buffalo, NY (resigned after Appalachin incident); secretary-treasurer of Magaddino Memorial Chapel, Inc.; in 1939, chauffeur employed by Van Dyke Taxi Company (owned by John C. Montana); alleged to have had a concealed interest in Charles Distributing Company, former holder of wholesale beer license, Niagara Falls, NY, through his wife, Angelina Magaddino LaDuca.

Reputed Associates: Steve Magaddino (father-in-law), Willie Moretti (New Jersey), Paul Palmeri (New Jersey hoodlum), Joe Di Carlo (Youngstown, OH and Buffalo, NY), John C. Montana.

Arrests (DCI #653535X):
Twice for traffic infractions in Buffalo, NY; no known criminal record.

Apalachin: LaDuca was stopped on Route 17 near Binghamton, NY, by Troopers F. A. Tiffany and C. F. Erway and brought to Vestal Station. Identified through chauffeur's license (7026569 NY) and registration 62JL (NY plates) for 1957 Lincoln coupe. Subject's car was observed at Barbara's residence on November 13 and at the Parkway Motel on November 13 and 14. Hotel receipts found in wastepaper basket in motel for James V. La Duca from Lexington Hotel, NYC, for November 7–11, 1957, and Utica Hotel, November 12, 1957. While at the Lexington Hotel, he phoned Joseph Falcone on 11/9/57 and 11/12/57, and made four calls on

11/11/57. LaDuca, when picked up on Route 17 after raid, was riding in 1957 Cadillac sedan (registration HM 373 OH, issued for to Buckeye Cigarette Service Co., Cleveland, OH). In the car were John Scalish of 11706 E. Harrington St., Cleveland, OH, and John Anthony DeMarco of 3536 Hidana St., Shaker Heights, OH, both of whom were subpoenad o appear before the Tioga Country Grand Jury, but did not appear.

SAMUEL LAGATTUTA, 555 LAFAYETTE ST., BUFFALO, NY.

Born: April 7, 1897, Italy.

Occupation: House painter, self-employed.

Arrests (FBI #1348437, DCI #12945X):
4/3/33: Arson, second degree, PD Buffalo, NY, #30181, indictment dismissed.
8/13/37: Investigation of murder, PD Buffalo, #30181, discharged by City Court, Buffalo, NY, 11/24/37.
8/14/37: 1897 public law, PD Buffalo, NY, #30181, indictment dismissed.

Reputed Associates: John Montana, Rosario Mancuso, Joseph Falcone, Salvatore Falcone.

Apalachin: Subject traveled to Barbara meeting with the Falcone brothers, Mancuso, and Joe Di Carlo (identified with the rackets of the 1920s).

LOUIS ANTHONY LARASSO, 115 DONALDSON PLACE, LINDEN, NJ.

Born: November 13, 1926, Elizabeth, NJ.

Occupation: Labor foreman. Formerly trustee of Local 394, Common Laborers and Hod Carriers, resigned 12/15/57.

Reputed Associates: Anthony Riela, Vito Genovese, Joseph Ida, Dominick Olivetto, Emanuel Riggi, Albert Doyle.

Apalachin: Registered at Carlton Hotel, Binghamton, NY, at midnight on 11/14/57 with Frank Majuri and Natale Evola.

CARMINE LOMBARDOZZI, 114 STRATFORD ROAD, BROOKLYN, NY.

Born: February 8, 1913, New York City.

Occupation: 1951: Stevedore, Brooklyn docks, Monti-Marine Corporation, King Street and East River, Brooklyn, NY (reputedly afflliated with Mobile Power Company, 624 Coney Island Ave., Brooklyn, NY and Superior Trading Company). 1954: connected with Hi-Tone Amusement Company, Brooklyn, NY (coin-operated machines); public relations, Gray Steamship Lines, Pier 57, North River, NY; owner of Mac Platers, Brooklyn, NY (brass platers).

Arrests (DCI #114397):
10/1/29: Homicide (auto), Brooklyn, discharged, 11/21/29.
6/13/30: Burglary, Brooklyn, Kings County Court, discharged, unlawful entry, 6/24/30.
6/5/31: Abduction-rape, Brooklyn, complaint taken for vagrancy, twenty days, 9/6/31.
11/30/41: 1897 public law, Brooklyn, NY, dismissed.
1/12/42: Application, Coast Guard Explosive Materials Card.
6/1/45: 986 public law, Brooklyn, NY, $75 fine.
8/3/45: 986 public law, Brooklyn, NY, 100 or 60 days.
1/7/46: 986 public law, Brooklyn, NY, 150 or 60 days.
6/2/48: 986 public law, Brooklyn, NY, 150 or 60 days.
10/11/51: Common gambler, Brooklyn, NY, 60 days, 4/15/52.
10/28/52: Disturbing the peace, NYC, thirty days in workhouse.

Reputed Associates: Joseph Klein, Angelo Russo (1015 63rd St., Brooklyn, NY), Al Newman, Michael Scandifia, Louis de Fillippo, Harold Alterman, Arigo Gearasso, Joseph Riccebono, Frank Caruso, Joseph Agone, George Smurra, Frank (The Bug) Caruso, Pat Esposito, Saboto Muro, Max Tanenbaum, Gina Lospina, Natale Evola, Frank Cucchiara, Rocco Pellagrino, Frank Tierri.

Note: In the 1940s, subject is reputed to have been engaged in bookmaking. Between 1938 and 1943 subject was the hiring boss at the army base at 58th Street and First Avenue, Brooklyn, NY. Subject was able to settle labor trouble during 1950–52 when Venti Marine Company was involved in hiring strife with a maintenance local on West Side of New York. In 1953, subject was investigated by Brooklyn Grand Jury as possible payoff man for gamblers during the period 1946–1952. Subject is believed to have made sizable loans to bookmakers and policy operators. Complaints of shylocking on the waterfront were made against him, but not substantiated. Addendum: Lombardozzi went to Utica NY, with Tony Anastasia to attend the wedding of Anastasia's nephew Antonio.

Apalachin: Came to Barbara's with Natale Evola, in a car that also carried Joseph Riccobono and Frank Cucchiara.

ANTHONY "NINO" MAGADDINO, 1528 WHITNEY PLACE, NIAGARA FALLS, NY.

Born: June 18, 1897, Castellemare, Italy; entered United States, November 1, 1923, *S.S. Patria*; naturalized, Niagara Falls, NY, June 21, 1948.

Occupation: Undertaker, vice president of Magaddino Memorial Chapel, Inc., Niagara Street and Portage Road (2404 South Avenue), Niagara Falls, NY.

Foreign Criminal Record: Fingerprinted under the name Antonio Giovanni Margardino at Ventimiglia, Italy, on 2/19/16, on charge of falsifying a passport. In custody at Ventimiglia, Italy, on 3/15/16 for clandestine activities, released 4/16/16, arrested for homicide at Castellamare, Italy, on 8/14/16, discharged 7/23/17, insufficient evidence to prosecute. January 29, 1929, Magistrate of Trapini, received amnesty for using false passport. June 19, 1928, Castellemare del Golfo, denounced for robbery, rape, and extortion committed in 1924. March 1, 1930, Tribunal of Trapani Court of Appeals, traveling without a passport, released. Magaddino's older brother, Pietro Magaddino, was shot and killed by the Buccillate brothers in Italy, particulars unknown.

Arrests (FBI #947466):

2/21/35: Violation U.S. Immigration Laws, U.S. Immigration and Naturalization Service, no disposition.

Note: Anthony and Steven Magaddino were requested to appear before the
Federal grand jury in 1952 at Buffalo, NY, regarding gambling condi-
tions in Niagara Falls, NY. Anthony invoked the Fifth Amendment before the New York State Lquor Authority, 12/19/57. Steven Magaddino is
president, director, and first stockholder of City Distribution Co. Steven
Magaddino's son Peter is married to a niece of John C. Montana's. Steven Maggadino's daughter is married to Charles Montana, a nephew of
John C. Montana's; another Magaddino daughter is married to James V.
LaDuca.

Associates: Frank Valenti, Dominick D'Agostino, Di Carlo (Youngston,
OH, formerly of Buffalo, NY).

Apalachin: Anthony Magaddino was picked up on McFadden Road near
Barbara property by Troopers Sackel and Luthy, brought to Vestal Station and questioned by Trooper Vasisko and Croswell. Anthony claimed
he came to visit Joseph Barbara with John C. Montana.

JOSEPH MAGLIOCCO, BAY VIEW AVENUE, EAST ISLIP, NY.

Born: June 29, 1898, Villahote, Palermo, Sicily; entered the United States in
1924; admitted to U.S. citizenship in Brooklyn, NY.

Occupation: Prior to 1933, Magliocco worked in the olive oil business. In
1933, he commenced operating Sunland Beverage Company, beer distributor, licensed 1933 as sole proprietor.

Arrests: Transporting wine, convicted in Federal Court, Brooklyn, NY,
fined $31.

Reputed Associates: Joseph Profaci, Sebastino Muni, Salvatore Mozzasalme,
John M. Balsamo, Emanuel Commerato, Charles Luciano, Santos Trafficante Sr.

Note: Subject's sister was married to Joseph Profaci. Magliocco attended the 1928 Cleveland meeting of Mafia leaders with Profaci. Subject was a stockholder in the Ward Trading Company, 170 Lawrence Ave., Brooklyn, NY, a holding company which comprises Alpine Wine and Liquor, Ramapa Wine and Liquor, Universal Liquor Corporation, Webster-Lawrence and Company, Inc., 181 Lawrence Avenue Corporation, and the Arrow Linen Supply Corporation, interrelated companies, but subject shows as a stockholder in Arrow Linen Supply only. Arrow Linen serviced most of the nightclubs, restaurants, and bars in New York City. Frank Bonfiglio, former manager of Arrow and its present sales manager, was closely associated with Frank Costello. Bonfiglio had dinner with Costello the evening that Costello was shot.

Apalachin: Subject registered at Hotel Starling, Wilkes-Barre, PA, on November 14 and 15, 1957, following Apalachin meeting.

FRANK THOMAS MAJURI, 629 SOUTH BROAD ST., ELIZABETH, NJ.

Born: April 18, 1909, New York City.

Occupation: Vice president of Labor Local #364, Morris Avenue, Elizabeth, NJ; listed on books as construction worker for C. F. Braun, Linden, NJ.

Arrests (FBI #110 2386, NYS DCI 355 325X):
3/3/33: Conspiracy to commit robbery, Dunellen, NJ, PD, no bill, 6/16/33.
10/12/35: Illegal Possession of Liquor, Long Branch, NJ, PD, fined $150, 10/26/35.
5/11/36: Violation of Section 48 and 84, Monmouth County, NJ, three years' probation, 10/2/36.
12/30/37 (as Frank Gagtaliano): Illicit manufacture of alcohol with intent to sell, eight months in jail, fined $200, 3/11/38.
5/30/50: Disorderly conduct, New York State Police, Troop C, Sidney, NY, fined $50.
10/17/54: Bookmaking, Linden, NJ, PD, one to two years' probation, fined $3000, 7/31/56.

Reputed Associates: Louis A. Larasso (New Jersey), Jack Dragna (Los Angeles, CA).

Note: Because of the raid in Apalachin, this subject was found in violation of his New Jersey probation and, as of 12/3/57, was incarcerated in New Jersey State Prison to serve his remaining probation term.

Apalachin: Natale Evola drove to Apalachin with subject, both registered at the Cartlton Hotel, Binghamton, NY, 11/14/57 at midnight, with Anthony Larasso (no known criminal record). Subject was stopped near Barbara's home, on McFadden Road, driving a 1955 Chrysler (License No. UC 5997), registered to James Merlo, 35 Loomis St., Elizabeth, NJ.

ROSARIO MANCUSO, 926 ARTHUR ST., UTICA, NY.

Born: January 29, 1907, Buffalo, NY.

Occupation: Concrete business, unspecified.

Arrest (FBI #731- 025A):
3/25/51: Assault with intent to committ murder, Hartford, CN (#22826), disposition, not less than two, nor more than five years, 4/17/51.

Reputed Associates: Salvatore Falcone, Joseph Falcone, James LaDuca.

Note: Mancuso has been investigated in connection with gambling activities in the Utica area, as well as at large-scale contruction projects in various localities in New York State. Subject evaded service of subpoena by Tioga County Grand Jury. In November of 1953 elected president of Local 186, International Hod Carriers and Common Laborers Union of America. Anthony Falange was elected secretary-treasurer and Carl Giardino, elected business agent. The territorial jurisdiction of this union extended to portions of Essex and Franklin Counties, as well as throughout Clinton County. On December 4, 1953, after a complaint by Thomas R. North, District Attorney of Clinton County, NY, to Fred Melito, state traveling representative of the Hod Carriers Union, Melito obtained the resignation of Rosario Mancuso and Anthony Falange, as officers of Local 186.

Apalachin: Traveled to Barbara's with Joseph Falcone, Salvatore Falcone, and Samuel Lagattuta.

GABRIEL MANNARINO, 540 CHARLES AVENUE, NEW KENSINGTON, PA.

Born: October 31, 1916, New Kensington, PA.

Occupation: Self-employed, Ken Iron and Steel Company.

Arrests (FBI #854-850, DCI #659 416):
3/31/31: Gaming, Greenburg, PA, #45137.
11/18/34: Violation of the liquor laws, Pittsburgh, PA, PD #30307, not guilty.
4/20/36: Robbery, Greenburg, PA, state police, #5137, discharged.
4/27/43: Fire Arts Act (fireworks), North Kensington, PA , PD, no disposition.
9/12/45: Lottery, Greenburg, PA, state police, #45137, $25 and costs.
5/22/56: U.S. marshal, Pittsburgh, PA, #14901.

Reputed Associates: Gabriel Mannarino and his brothers at one time owned the Sans Souci Hotel Casino, Havana, Cuba. The present owner, Santo Trafficante Jr., was also at Apalachin, NY.

Note: Owner of Nu-Ken Novelty Company, New Kensington, PA (operators of slot machines, jukeboxes, and cigarette machines). Subject and his brother Samuel were reputed to be the controlling gangsters in Westmoreland County, PA, operating various lotteries, pools, and bookmaking enterprises.

Apalachin: When stopped at Apalachin, Michael Genovese was in subject's car, with Angelo Sciandra and James Osticco.

MICHELE "MIKE" MIRANDA, 167 GREENWAY, FOREST HILLS, NY; 629 E. OLIVE STREET, LONG BRANCH, NY (SUMMER RESIDENCE).

Born: July 26, 1896, San Guiseppe Vesuviano, Italy.

Occupation: Auto salesman for Huntsen & Raffo, 238 West 55th Street, NY (Cadillacs, used cars, Cadillac hearses, ambulances, flower and service automobiles).

Arrests (FBI #91524, DCI #166078):

7/10/15: Disorderly Conduct, Manhattan, NY, thirty days.

5/6/17: Suspicious person, Boston, MA.

2/23/18: Vagrancy, Buffalo, NY, ordered out of town.

10/25/19: Vagrancy, Springfield, MA, discharged.

5/12/20: Suspicious person, Pittsburgh, PA, discharged.

11/9/34: Homicide (gun), Brooklyn, NY, dismissed.

9/16/46: Homicide (gun) , Brooklyn, NY, dismissed.

6/24/52: Investigation, Los Angeles, CA, no disposition.

Note: Suspected activities in narcotics (International Narcotics List #229) and gambling. Son, Michael, is in insurance business, as a consultant in union welfare and pension funds.

Reputed Associates: Vito Genovese, Gus Frasco, Anthony Strollo, Anthony Cirillo, Frank Russo.

Apalachin: Picked up on McFadden Road, near Barbara's property. Subject said he came to Binghamton by train with Gambino, Castellano, and Rava, and took a cab to Barbara's residence.

PASQUALE "PATSY" MONACHINO, 14 ORCHARD ST., AUBURN, NY.

Born: January 3, 1907, Italy; naturalized at Auburn, NY, 2/8/41.

Occupation: Wholesale beer business, Super Beverage Co., Auburn, NY (partner with brother, Sam Monachino).

Arrests: No known record.

Reputed Associates: Salvatore Falcone, Joseph Falcone, Patsy Sciortino, Joseph Profaci.

Appalachin: Subject was riding in a Super Beverage Co. car when stopped. Registered on June 26, 1957 at Community Motel, Route 17, Binghamton as Pat Monichino, Auburn, NY; also on March 17, 1957.

SAM MONACHINO, 11 ORCHARD ST., AUBURN, NY.

Born: February 14, 1894, Sicily, Italy; naturalized Auburn, NY, May 28, 1927.

Occupation: Partner with brother Patsy in the Super Beverage Co., 229 W. Geneseo St., Auburn, NY, beer wholesalers and distributors.

Arrests: No record of arrests.

Reputed Associates: Joseph "Socks" Lanza (prints filed at Auburn Prison on 8/20/46 in connection with application to visit Joseph Lanza), Joseph Barbara.

Apalachin: Subject claimed he drove to Barbara's house with his brother Patsy and a friend, Patsy Sciortino, to talk about matter connected with business of Super Beverage Company.

JOHN CHARLES MONTANA, 340 STARIN AVENUE, BUFFALO, NY.

Born: June 30, 1893, Italy; naturalized, July 7, 1921.

Occupation and Activities: President, Van Dyke Taxi & Transfer Company, Inc.; Van Dyke Airport Transport Corporation; Van Dyke Baggage Corporation; Van Dyke Property, Inc.; Frontier Liquor Corporation, Inc.; Buffalo Beverage Corporation; Montana Motors (discontinued 1956); controller, Empire State Brewery Corporation (closed 1940); chairman, Zoning Board of the City of Buffalo, 1942; delegate, NYS Constitutional Convention, 1937; director, Buffalo Baseball Club; director, A.S.P.C.A., Eric County; elected, City Council, Buffalo, 1927, served in that office for four years; director, Buffalo Ball Park; Buffalo Club Member, City of Buffalo.

Arrests: No known record.

Reputed Associates: Joseph Barbara , Russell Buffalino, Joseph Falcone, James LaDuca, Samuel Lagattuta, Anthony Magaddino, Peter Magaddino.

Note: Upon the return of Salvatore Falcone from Italy to NYC in 1937, John C. Montana came from Buffalo to meet him. Montana was closely associated with Joseph DiCarlo. DiCarlo was associated with labor and union rackets and the distribution of lottery tickets in the Buffalo area. DiCarlo was a power in Buffalo politics, and it is alleged he backed John C. Montana in all his political moves.

Apalachin: Subject asserted that because of automobile trouble, he stopped at Barbara's home with Anthony Magaddino en route to Pennsylvania.

DOMINICK OLIVETO, 1157 MAGNOLIA AVE., CAMDEN, NJ.

Born: January 7, 1907, Camden, NJ.

Occupation: Manufacturer, Forest Products, Almonesson, NJ.

Arrests (FBI #2935549):
11/17/30 (as James De Marco): Volstead Hobart Enforcement Act, Camden County, NJ, #618, illicit alcohol, fined $300.
1/12/37: Criminal registration, PD, Camden, NJ, #694, no disposition.
8/7/42: Criminal registration, Delaware Township #12, no disposition.

Reputed Associates: Felix De Tullis, Louis Campbell, Angelo Bruno, Alfred Tezzi, Marco Reginolli (vice and racket king).

Note: Subpoena served, Tioga County Grand Jury, subject failed to appear.

Apalachin: When stopped, subject was in an automobile with Russell Buffalino, Vito Genovese, Gerry Cateno, Joseph Ida.

JOHN ORMENTO, 118 AUDREY DRIVE, LIDO BEACH, NY.

Born: August 1, 1912, New York, NY.

Occupation: Self-employed, Long Island Trucking Company, 240 West 37th St., New York, NY. Prior to 1952, subject was partner in the Roxy Gas Station, NYC, for a number of years.

Arrests (DCI #575371):

Subject has been convicted for violation of the Federal Narcotics Law on three separate occasions during the past 20 years.

1937: Ormento was convicted of violating the Harrison Narcotic Act and sentenced to a three-year prison term.

1941: Ormento again arrested for violation of the Harrison Narcotic Act, convicted and sentenced to an eight-year prison term.

1951: Ormento again arrested and subsequently convicted for conspiracy to violate the Harrison Narcotic Act, and was sentenced to a two-year prison term.

Note: In addition to narcotcs convictions, Ormento was convicted of book-making in 1948, and fined $50. On March 18, 1955, Ormento was arrested in New York City with Salvatore Lo Prate in possession of two loaded pistols, one a .38 caliber and the other a .22 caliber, equipped with a silencer. Both weapons were concealed in an electrically controlled trap built into the front seat of a 1952 Chrysler, bearing New York license 1952, PB3730, listed to Lo Prato's sister, Betty Licatto, 2073 2nd Avenue, NYC. Charges against Ormiento were dismissed when Lo Prato alleged the guns belonged to him.

Reputed Associates: Russell Bufalino, Natale Evola, Vincent Rao, Joseph Barbara, John Dio, Rocco Pellegrino, Salvatore Santora, and Joseph Vento (heroin and opium smugglers), leader of the East 107th Street Mob, Anthony Guarnieri.

JAMES ANTHONY OSTICCO, 156 1/2 ELIZABETH STREET, PITTSTON, PA.

Occupation: Transportation manager for Modico Industries, Inc., Pittston, PA.

Arrests (DCI #659 415X):

2/3/31: Violation of the liquor law, state police, Wyoming, PA, three months, 5/5/31.

11/25/47: Conspiracy, state police, Wyoming, PA, no disposition.

Reputed Associates: Dominick Alaimo, Joseph Barbara , Russell Bufalino, Anthony Guarnieri, Angelo Sciandra.

Note: Subject, with Russell Buffalino, were guests of Atlas Chain and Man-ufacturing Company, West Pittston, PA, at Bemini, British West Indies in April 1956, and from there went to the Hotel Nacional, Havana, Cuba, on May 2, 1956.

Apalachin: Subject drove to Apalachin with Dominick Alaimo and Angelo Sciandra. When picked up, he was with Michael Genovese, Gabriel Manarino, and Angelo Sciandra. The motor vehicle was owned by Wil-liam Medico, alias "Greco" and "Medirico," owner of Medico Electric Motor Company, in Pittston, PA, who is reported to have been involved with illicit liquor traffic from 1928 to 1933.

JOSEPH PROFACI, 8863 15TH AVENUE, BROOKLYN, NY.

Born: October 1, 1897, Villabati, Italy; naturalized, Brooklyn, NY, Septem-ber 27, 1927.

Occupation: Owner-operator, Mama Mia Olive Oil Company, Brooklyn, NY; G & P Coat Co., Brooklyn, NY; United Uniform Corporation, 1578 86th St., Brooklyn, NY; Fratelli Berio Company, 1402 65th St., Brook-lyn, NY; Carmolla Mia Packing Company, Brooklyn, NY.

Foreign Record:
4/18/16: Theft-violation of a domicile and attempted rape, Sicily, Italy, dis-missed.
11/23/20: Theft and false witness of a public document, Palermo, Italy, one year in prison.

Arrests (DCI #219180, FBI #362142):
12/5/28: Investigation, Cleveland, OH, discharged.
9/19/34: Investigated in connection with murder of Ferdinand Boccia in Brooklyn, NY, with Vito Genovese, Michael Miranda, Sebastiano Nami, Gus Frasca, Joseph Smurra, Peter DeFeo; subject was not arrested.
5/9/46: Forgery (auto registration), Brooklyn, NY, acquitted.

4/7/49: Violation of Food & Drug Act (adulterated olive oil) Brooklyn, NY, pleaded guilty, suspended sentence, probation one year.

10/27/52: Violation of Food & Drug Act, Brooklyn, NY, fined $4,000.

9/21/53: Evasion of Income Tax, Brooklyn, NY.

Reputed Associates: Vincenzo Mangano (disappeared), Philip Mangano (murdered), Joseph Magliocco (brother-in-law), Salvatore "Lucky" Luciano, Michael Miranda, Frank Costello, John Oddo, Joseph Bonann, Vito Genovese, Sebastian Nani, Gus Frasca, Joseph Smurra, Peter DeFeo, Joseph Rinaldi, Nicola Impostato.

Note: On June 4, 1955, Profaci's daughter Carmella married Anthony Joseph Tocco, son of William and Rosalina Zirilli Tocco. At Carmella's wedding to Joseph Tocco, the following underworld figures were present: Frank Livorsi, John Oddo (alias "Johnny Bath Beach"), Anthony Anastasio (alias "Tough Tony"), John Dioguardi (alias "Johnny Dio"), Salvatore Mussachia (alias "Sally the Sheik"), Inolla Ercolo (alias "Mr. T."), Vito Genovese, Peter Liquerao, Angelo Polozzi, Mike Miranda, Dominick Ferrato, John Ormeno, Angelo Meli, Michael Robino. Another daughter of Profaci's is married to the son of George Zirili of Detroit, who is a brother of Rosalina Tocco, mother of Joseph Tocco.

Apalachin: Subject was picked up at roadblock on highway adjoining Barbara property. Subject with Joseph Magliocco stayed at Hotel Sterling, Wilkes-Barre, PA, on November 14 and 15, 1957. Subject registered at Arlington Hotel 7/9/56 with Joseph Barbara, Joseph Barrocino, John Culuicca, and Gilo Gelonti, reservation charged to Canada Dry Beverage of Edicott, NY. Culuicca and Gelonti were also registered on 7/10/56.

VINCENT RAO, 192 DUNWOODIE ST., YONKERS, NY.

Born: June 21, 1898, Corleone, Province of Palermo, Italy.

Occupation: Owner (as of December 1957), Five Borough Hoisting Company, 218 E. 116 St., NYC (lathing contractor, in lath hoisting business, hoists lathes for all lathing contractors); owner, Rao's Garage and Parking Lot, East Gunhill Road; owner, four-story building at 2010

Third Avenue, NYC. Located at this address is Regal Wine & Liquor, Inc., owned by subject's son-in-law Joseph Vene (formerly located at 2006 Third Avenue.) Connected with Vin-Sens Paint Company, 309 E. 167 St., NYC; Marcy Rao Fuel Oil Company; Rao Sports Wear, 47 Martene Avenue; White Plains Liquor Store, 1821 First Ave., NY (1952, with Charles Rao, brother); Turao Realty Corporation, 1937 Third Ave, NYC; Garage, 22-23-25 E. 107 St. (since demolished); V&C Realty Corporation (believed to stand for Vincent and Charles); Vinoar Corporation (believed to stand for Vincent-"oar," Rao backward); Gandolfo Motors, 1909 Bruckner Blvd., Bronx NY; Jack Wyn Realty Corporation; 203rd Avenue Realty Corporation; Marino's Restaurant, 716 Lexington Ave., NYC.

Arrests (NYC PD #4857)
1919: Grand larceny, dismissed.
1923: Possession of gun, dismissed.
1925: Possession of gun, dismissed.
1938: Violation, Workmen's Compensation Act, acquitted.

Note: Alleged to have attended 1952 Mafia meeting in Florida. In 1945, Ralph Bellusco—who at that time was a prospective son-in-law of Vincent Rao's—opened Regal Wine & Liquor at 2010 Third Avenue, NYC, with an investment of $77,000, of which $69,000 was borrowed from Rao. From 1946 to 1948, Joseph Vente, who married Rao's daughter, Nina, worked as a clerk in this store. In 1947, Bolluscio, on two occasions, made an application for a corporation liquor license together with Vincent Rao's wife, Millie, as a partner and stockholder (details unclear). Both applications were denied. In 1948, the SLA approved a corporation liquor license with Belluscio's president-treasure, holding one hundred shares, and Joseph Vente as secretary, holding no shares. This arrangement was made so business could be continued as ususal in the event of Belluscio's illness. At this time, Belluscio owed Vincent Rao $34,000 on the original loan of $69,000. As of 1953, the corporation owed Rao $1,854.64.

Reputed Associates: Salvatore Speciale (nephew, narcotics peddler); Joseph "Fix the Blond" Gagliano, narcotic violator who hung himself in Bronx County Jail; John Ormento, Joseph Rosato, Thomas Luchese, Thomas Pappadio.

ARMAND RAVA, 1180 OCEAN PARKWAY, BROOKLYN, NY.

Born: January 7, 1911, New York, NY.

Occupation: Manager of New Corners Restaurant, 2201 8th Ave., Brooklyn.

Arrests (NYC PD #73155):
2/1/29: Extortion, acquitted, 5/8/29.
5/27/39: Violation of Internal Revenue Law, no disposition.
7/27/39: Policy, suspended sentence, 9/28/39.
12/3/41: Vagrancy, discharged, 12/22/41.

Reputed Associates: Anthony Coppola, Joseph "Gus" Colozzo, Joey Randazzo, Albert Anastasia, Joseph Profaci.

Apalachin: Stopped in car with Carlo Gambino. Subject not seen at residence or place of business since November 14, 1957.

JOSEPH RICCOBONO, 781 PELTON AVE., STATEN ISLAND, NY.

Born: April 23, 1894, Italy.

Occupation: Owner of two dress shops: Christine Dresses, 750 Grand Street, Brooklyn; Toni Belle Dresses, 1720 Broadway, New York, NY.

Arrests (NYC PDB #228590, NYS DCI #653526X, FBI #321523):
10/31/30 : Concealed weapon, Jersey City, NJ, PD, no bill, 11/7/30.
11/17/44: Extortion and conspiracy, NYPD, pleaded guilty to extortion, three years' probation, 1/3/45.

Reputed Associates: Charles Salvatore-Chiri.

Note: Subject was part of the Louis Buchalter and Jacob Shapiro mobs.

Apalachin: Subject drove to Joseph Barbara's home with Carmine Lombardozzi and Natale Evola. Frank Cucchiara probably came to Binghamton by train but stayed at a motel overnight and was picked up in the morning by Riccobono.

ANTHONY RIELA, 7 BENVENUE AVE., WEST ORANGE, NJ.

Born: August 5, 1896, Italy.

Occupation: Owner of Airport Motel, Newark, NJ.

Arrests (NYS DCI #654342X):
11/9/55: Maintaining a nuisance and permitting prostitution on premises, Newark, NJ, PD, #67510, dismissed by grand jury on Feb. 1, 1956.

Reputed Associates: Gerry Cateno, Vito Genovese, Joseph Ida.

Apalachin: Riela was undoubtedly one of those who traveled to Binghamton by airplane from Newark Airport and was met by Joseph Barbara Sr.

Post-Apalachin Court Action:
1/29/58: Order to show cause filed with Essex County, New Jersey, for Riela's appearance before the Tioga County Grand Jury.
2/3/58: Subpoena order signed by Alexander P. Waugh, judge of Superior Court of New Jersey.
2/25/58: Indictment of Tioga County Grand Jury filed, violation of Section 600, subdivision 6 of the Penal Law.
2/25/58: Surety bond for $1,000 filed and defendant released from sheriff's office.

JOSEPH ROSATO, 34-31 81ST ST., JACKSON HEIGHTS, NY.

Born: January 4, 1904, Palermo, Italy.

Occupation: Owner of trucking companies: S & R Trucking, 460 W. 35th St.. New York, NY, County Garment Delivery Inc. (same address as S & R Trucking).

Arrests (FBI #4165533, NYS DCI #653524):
7/18/28: Homicide (gun), dismissed, 7/24/28.

Reputed Associates: Vincent Rao, Carlo Gambino, John Ormento, alias
    "Big John," John Dioguardia, alias "Johnny Dio," Thomas Lucchese,
    alias "Three-Finger Brown" (sister is the wife of the subject).

Apalachin: Subject stopped at a roadblock and brought to the Vestal State
    Police Barracks, where he was questioned by Lieutenant K. E. Weiden-
    borner on 11/14/57.

NORMAN RUSSELL, APALACHIN, NY.

Born: October 19, 1915, Pennsylvania.

Occupation: Laborer, employed by Barbara.

Arrests:
4/17/39: Breaking and entering and larceny (burglary), Pennsylvania State
    Police #247198, suspended sentence and costs.

Associates: Barbara family, Leon Doleman (uncle of subject's wife).

JOHN SCALISH, 11706 E. HARRINGTON ST., CLEVELAND, OH.

Born: September 18, 1912, Cleveland, OH.

Occupation: Operator of Buckeye Cigarette Service (vending machines) at
    11219 Superior Ave., Cleveland, OH.

Arrests DCI 654685:
1/19/30: Investigation, Lorain, Ohio.
2/5/31: Burglary, Cleveland, OH, disposition unknown.
4/4/32: Burglary, Cleveland, OH, disposition unknown.
7/28/32: Investigation, Cleveland, OH, disposition unknown.

1/27/33: Robbery, sentenced 10–25 years; pardoned by Governor George White, 1/15/35.

Note: Subpoena served, Tioga County Grand Jury, but subject failed to appear.

Reputed Associates: John Anthony DeMarco, James V. La Duca.

Apalachin: Picked up on highway Route 17, west of Binghamton; riding with subject was James V. La Duca and John DeMarco; all registered to Parkway Motel, Vestal, 11/13/57.

ANGELO JOSEPH SCIANDRA, 108 S. MAIN STREET, PITTSTON, PA.

Born: November 26, 1924, Buffalo, NY.

Occupation: Garment manufacturer.

Arrests (FBI #2185503):
7/12/35: Rape, first degree, Buffalo, NY, PD 33957, reduced to assault, third degree, suspended sentence.

Reputed Associates: Jack Bonfantio (union rackets), Modesto LaQuasto (union rackets), Anthony Guarnieri, Nick Bonfantio (union rackets), Joe Barbara (union rackets); has connections with Anthony Guarnieri, Tri Cities Dress Company, Inc., Binghamton, NY.

Apalachin: Traveled from Pittston, PA, with Dominick Alaimo and Anthony Osticco. When stopped at Appalachin, subject was in same car with Mike Genovese and James Osticco. Registered at Arlington Hotel, Binghamton, with Joseph Barbera, Vincenzo Osticco, and Russell Bufalino on March 18, 1957.

PASQUALE "PATSY" SCIORTINO, 58 HALLEY ST., AUBURN, NY.

Born: March 15, 1915, Italy; naturalized September 11, 1939.

Occupation: Bleach manufacturer, self-employed.

Arrests (FBI #76092):
7/9/51: Violation Immigration Act of 1924, White Plains, NY, PD 6952.

Reputed Associates: Sam Monachino (stayed at Hotel Nacional, Havana with subject 11/5/55), Tony Randazzo, Emanuel Zicari, John Castiglione, Patsy Monachino.

Apalachin: Traveled to Apalachin with Monachino brothers Sam and Patsy, by automobile.

SIMONE SCOZZARI, 61112 N. MUSCATEL AVE., SAN GABRIEL, CA.

Born: January 7, 1900, Palermo, Sicily.

Occupation: Unemployed.

Arrests (DCI 487230):
11/19/42: Suspicion of bookmaking, San Gabriel, CA, released 11/20/42.
7/14/54: Suspicion of bookmaking, Los Angeles, CA, released 7/16/54.

Reputed Associates: John Cerrito, John Civello, James Lonzo, Frank Di-Simone, Russell Bufalino.

Apalachin: Picked up on Little Meadows Road, identified through INS registration card #5113555-2722, Alta Street, Los Angeles, CA.

SALVATORE TORNABE, 1454 SECOND AVE., NEW YORK, NY; SUMMER RESIDENCE, ROUTE 9W, MARLBORO, NY.

Born: May 27, 1896, Italy, citizen.

Occupation: Beer salesman, Sunland Beverage Corporation.

Arrests (DCI 054-061):

1921: New York State Liquor Authority, Albany; subject admitted (in interview in connection with solicitor's permit 14805) that he had been arrested for selling whiskey in violation of prohbition laws.

Reputed Associates: Frank Majuri, Joseph Magliocco.

Note: When picked up at Apalachin, subject had scribbled note in pocket, partially legible, reading: "Call Giovanni Vivona [Barbara brother-in-law], Endicott 5-9197, get together with Lille [prostitute] Monday, Endicott 6-2711, go to Airport Motel take Jimmy and Zito, Riela take Majuri and Johnny, RO 4-1416, Thursday a.m. for Saturday visit with Jerry."

Apalachin: Subject claimed he went to Apalachin by train, but evidence indicated he drove, leaving from garage at 71st Street and Seventh Avenue in New York City.

SANTO TRAFFICANTE JR. (ALIAS LOUIS SANTOS), HAVANA, CUBA.

Born: November 15, 1914, Tampa, Florida.

Occupation: Manager of Sans Souci Hotel and Casino, Havana Cuba.

Arrests (FBI #671194):

5/15/33: Grand larceny, NYC PD, #B114397, pleaded to petty larceny, fined $100, three months probation, suspended.

6/1/33: Unlawful entry, PD NYC, no disposition (warrant).

Associates: Santo Trafficante Sr. (father, Tampa, Florida, suspected of lottery), Joe Rivers (gambling and union activities with subject in Cuba).

Apalachin: Subject picked up in woods near the Barbara property by Trooper Fred Tiffany.

EMANUEL ZICARI, 103 SQUIRES AVE., ENDICOTT, NY.

Born: February 10, 1900, Italy; naturalized, 1925.

Occupation: Shoe worker.

Arrests (FBI #777-05, DCI #464075X):
3/14/34: Violation 263 and 265, Title 1, U.S. Code, Binghamton, NY, PD #2328.
4/2/34: Counterfeiting, Utica, NY, U.S. Marshall, #2153, pleaded guilty 3/26/35 and sentenced to thirty days in Broome County Jail.

Reputed Associates: Sam Monachino, Patsy Monachino, Patsy Sciortino, Joseph Barbara (former employer). Subject is a member of the Society Concordia Castellemmare del Golfo, Endicott, NY.

FRANK ZITO, 1801 ILLINI ROAD, SPRINGFIELD, IL.

Born: February 24, 1893, Italy; naturalized, 9/11/45.

Occupation: Owner and operator of Modern Distributing Corporation, Springfield, Illinois (juke boxes); subject stated he has retired.

Arrests (FBI #1777995):
3/1/33: Conspiracy to violate prohibition laws, two years, U.S. Penitentiary Leavenworth, KS.

Reputed Associates: James Colletti (Pueblo, CO).

Apalachin: Subject stayed at Riela's motel with Colletti, registered at Airport Motel, Inc. Port Newark, N.J. November 12, 13, and 14, 1957. Subject picked up on Little Meadows Road, near Barbara property.

ENDNOTES

Primary sources for information on Apalachin include the archives of Ed Croswell, maintained primarily and most assiduously by his wife Nathalie, and the recollections of the late Joe Benenati. The latter developed a "Deep Throat" for information about the summit, Pasquale Turrigiano, the Endicott grocer whom the state police sergeant dogged for years, eliciting crucial details about the day in question. Both Croswell and Benenati collected photos, maps, clippings, notes, and mementos from Apalachin and its aftermath. The author gratefully acknowledges the help of Benenati and of the family of Edgar Croswell, particularly his son Robert Croswell, in accessing these materials.

PROLOGUE

1   "The Chrysler Crown Imperial . . .": *Interim Report of the Joint Legislative Committee on Government Operations: On the Gangland Meeting in Apalachin, New York,* New York State Legislature, 1955, p. 19.

1   "Sergeant Croswell always had a sharp eye . . .": Most personal details and background on Edgar Croswell's life from author interview, Robert Croswell.

4   "Stated a prosecutor . . .": *Perfect Villains, Imperfect Heroes: Robert Kennedy's War Against Organized Crime,* by Ronald Goldfarb, 1995, p. 30.

5   " 'I should have broken both my legs . . .' ": "Just a Framed Mugg[*sic*], Says Vito," New York *Daily News,* June 17, 1959.

7   "The definitive reference guide . . .": *The FBI: A Comprehensive Reference Guide,* by Athan G. Theoharis, *et. al.,* 1999, p. 121.

7   "By and large, no one had really ripped . . .": "The Day a Lone Trooper Shook Up the Underworld," by Jeffrey Stinson, syndicated, Gannet News Service, reprinted in *The Trooper* (magazine), Nov./Dec. 1987.

8   "Apalachin forced the federal government . . .": *American Mafia: A History of Its Rise to Power,* by Thomas Reppetto, 2004, p. 269.

8   "A book on the alliance between the Sicilian . . .": *The Godfathers,* by Roberto Olla, 2007, (originally published in Italy in 2003 as *Padrini*), p. 137. See also *The Strength of the Wolf,* by Douglas Valentine, 2004, p. 177; *The Last Testament of Lucky Luciano,* by Martin A. Gosch, Richard Hammer, and Lucky Luciano, 1975; and *Lansky,* by Hank Messick, 1973, p. 215.

9   "They would have mobilized . . .": see *Bringing Down the Mob: The War Against the American Mafia,* by Thomas Repetto, 2006, p. 71.

9   "'I don't even like to hear' . . .": "Trooper's Own Story," by Edgar D. Croswell, *New York Mirror,* November 24, 1957.

9   "It becomes almost impossible . . .": *The Mafia Encyclopedia,* by Carl Sifakis, 1987, pp. 19, 138; also *Organized Crime: An Inside Guide to the World's Most Successful Industry,* by Paul Lunde, 2004, p. 163; "Changing of the Guard: Gunsmoke in Gangland, 1957," by Jay Maeder, *Big Town, Big Time,* chapter 127, 1999, p. 133.

1. MURDER ON FIFTEENTH STREET

15   "Carlo Tresca is a name . . .": *Carlo Tresca: Portrait of a Rebel,* by Nunzio Pernicone, 2010; *All the Right Enemies,* by Dorothy Gallagher, 1988; *Who Killed Carlo Tresca?* by the Tresca Memorial Committee, forewords by Arturo Giovannitti and John Dos Passos, 1945.

17   "Carlo Tresca is an archenemy . . .": Gallagher, *op.cit.* p. 24.

19   "Prison psychologists at Sing Sing . . .": *The Sixth Family: The Collapse of the New York Mafia and the Rise of Vito Rizzuto,* by Lee Lamothe and Adrian Humphreys, 2008, pp. 25–26.

22   "Leibe brought his charge . . .": see *Interim Report,* pp. 15–17.

24   "Abco Vending had a direct telephone line . . .": "4 Jersey Police Officials Indicted in Bribe Attempt," *New York Times,* February 4, 1958.

25   "The Speeding Ticket of the Decade . . .": *The Knickerbocker News,* November 4, 1958.

2. THE RISE OF JOE BARBARA

26 "'They thought the world of him at Sears'...": "Former Kingston Patrolman Breaks Up Hoodlum's Conclave," *Kingston Daily Freeman,* November 16, 1957.

27 "'I was always annoyed by them'...": "Final Victory of Apalachin Sleuth," *New York Daily Mirror,* January 17, 1960.

27 "On the road as a trooper during the war...": "Investigation of Improper Activities in the Labor or Management Field," *Proceedings of the Permanent Subcommittee on Investigations of the U.S. Senate Committee on Government Operations,* Eighty-Fifth Congress, Second Session, June 30, July 1, 2, and 3, 1958, Part 32, United States Government Printing Office, Washington, D.C., 1958, pp. 12, 202.

32 "The occasion was yet another gala...": "Arrest of 14 Foils Murder Fete Plan," *New York Times,* Aug. 18, 1932, "Free 14 in Slaying," *New York Times,* August 20, 1932.

33 "On February 21, 1933, he was again...": *Proceedings of the Permanent Subcommittee on Investigations,* pp. 12, 204.

37 "Ten a.m. on the morning of the Barbara-Vivona wedding...": "Reuter [State Investigation Commissioner] Links Barbara to 1933 Payroll Robbery Here, 4 Murders," *Binghamton Press,* May 10, 1958.
"She tooled around town...": "The Lonesome Princess of Apalachin," by Charles J. Pelleck, *New York Post,* November 17, 1957.
"'It's hard to remember'...": "Gangland Confab Viewed Calmly By Most Residents of Apalachin," *Binghamton Press,* July 24, 1958.

3. ALBERT ANASTASIA'S WATERFRONT

39 "Half of all New York longshoremen...": *The Longshoremen,* by Charles B. Barnes, 1942, p. 112. See also, *East Side, West Side,* Block, p. 186.

39 "To the tune of some $350 million a year...": "Duty of the State: The Transit Authority," New York *Daily News,* March 26, 1953.

40 "Agoglia kicked off the melee...": *Capone: The Man and the Era,* by Laurence Bergreen, 1994, p. 156-57; *Mr. Capone,* by Robert J. Schoenberg, 1992, pp. 142–43; also "Three of Gang Slain at Brooklyn Dance," *New York Times,* December 27, 1925. For an autopsy report on the wound to Lonergan's skull, see *Young Al Capone: The Untold Story of Scarface in New York, 1899–1925,* by William and John Basalmo, 2011, p. 204.

44 "Harry Feeney was widely credited . . .": *New York Times,* "Harry T. Feeney, 53, Brooklyn Reporter," September 20, 1960.

45 "Concerns for the safety of the cast . . .": *On the Irish Waterfront,* by James T. Fisher, 2009, p. 256.

46 "There were gangsters watching . . .": *Kazan: The Master Director Discusses His Films,* by Jeff Young, 1999, pp. 124, 136, 150.

47 "NYPD detectives told tales . . .": "Probers Seek Reason for Apalachin Mob Parley," by Tom Cawley, *Binghamton Press,* November 18, 1957.

47 "An example of Albert Anastasia's work . . .": *Where the Money Was,* by Willie Sutton with Edward Linn, 1976, pp. 237–38, 243–55. Also "Public Duty: Arnold Schuster, 1952," by Jay Maeder, *Big Town, Big Time,* chapter 116, 1999, p. 122.

49 "Anastasia was really off . . .": *The Last testament of Lucky Luciano,* by Martin A. Gosch and Richard Hammer, 1974, pp. 391-92.

49 "At one time a billion-and-a-half dollars . . .": *East Side, West Side: Organizing Crime in New York, 1930–1950,* by Alan Block, 2009, p. 184.

4. VITO COMES HOME

51 "Officers of the Allied Military Government . . .": "Fighting the Mafia in World War Two," by Tim Newark, AmericanMafia.com, May 2007.

51 "A car of Vito's, a 1938 Packard sedan . . .": Deposition, September 1, 1945, U.S. Army Criminal Investigations Division agent O. C. Dickey, to United States District Attorney's Office, Eastern District of New York, reprinted in *Mafia,* by Ed Reid, 1952, p. 229.

52 "The AMG employed Vito as a translator . . .": "O'Dwyer Accused of Justice Delay," *New York Times,* October 19, 1945. See also Reid, *op. cit.,* p. 206. Poletti denied knowing Genovese or employing him in any capacity. See "Genovese Link Denied," *New York Times,* December 2, 1952.

52 "In spring 1944, an Intelligence Sergeant . . .": See Reid, *op. cit.,* chapters 11–12; also "Hunting Down Vito Genovese in WWII Italy," by Tim Newark, in *Crime Magazine,* June 2007, http://crimemagazine.com.

54 "'By devious means,' Liebowitz declared . . .": *New York Times,* "Genovese Is Freed of Murder Charge," June 11, 1946.

55 "A half year later, in February 1946 . . .": *Lucky Luciano: The Real and Fake Gangster,* by Tim Newark, 2010, pp. 174, 179.

55 "The basic Turkey-Italy-America heroin route . . .": *The Politics of Heroin,* by Alfred W. McCoy, rev. ed., 1991, p. 44.

55 "Prosecutors claimed that Rothsteins gang . . .": "Rothstein Is Linked with Lowenstein," *The Milwaukee Sentinel,* Dec. 2, 1928.

55 "Brooklyn boss Joe Bonnano once actually attempted . . .": *The Sixth Family,* by Lee Lamothe and Adrian Humphreys, p. 12; *Honor Thy Father,* by Gay Talese, p. 22; *The Last Testament of Bill Bonanno: The Final Secrets of a Life in the Mafia,* by Bill Bonanno and Gary B. Abromovitz, 2011, p. 206.

56 " 'The Italians stepped on' . . .": *Addicts Who Survived: An Oral History of Narcotic Use in America, 1923–1965,* by David Courtwright, Don Des Jarlais, and Herman Joseph, 1989, p. 98.

57 "At the beginning of the Second World War . . .": The Mafia and Politics, by Michele Pantaleone, 1966, p. 52.

58 "Since it is highly concentrated . . .": "America's Habit: Drug Abuse, Drug Trafficking and Organized Crime," *Report to the President and the Attorney General,* by the President's Commission on Organized Crime, 1986, p. 34.

5. GENOVESE HITS COSTELLO

62 "An informer at the meeting . . .": *Vito Genovese: King of Crime,* by Dom Frasca, 1959, p. 109.

63 "A seven-room, eighteenth-floor apartment . . .": *Frank Costello: Prime Minister of the Underworld,* by George Wolf and Joseph DiMona, 1974, p. 137.

64 "Office in the Chrysler Building . . .": Wolf, *ibid,* p. 38.

65 "Those writhing, twisting hands were hypnotic . . .": Wolf, *ibid,* p. 203.

66 "As Rudolph Giuliani analyzed . . .": "The Day a Lone Trooper Shook Up the Underworld," by Jeffrey Stinson, *The Trooper* (magazine), Nov./Dec. 1987.

6. ANASTASIA GETS HIS

69 "Lansky was a great good friend of Batista . . .": *Little Man: Meyer Lansky and the Gangster Life,* 1991, p. 230. The "brothers" quote is from Lansky's Hollywood attorney, Joe Varon.

70 *"Excambion . . ."*: *Le Dain Commission Report: The Commission of Inquiry into the Non-Medical Use of Drugs,* "Appendix B-2, Opiate Narcotics," 1973, p. 15.

72 "On June 17, 1957 . . .": *New York Times,* "Underworld Figure Murdered in Bronx," June 18, 1957.

74 " 'Everybody's getting rich' . . .": *Havana Nocturne: How the Mob Owned Cuba . . . Then Lost It to the Revolution,* by T. J. English, 2007, p. 197.

75 "Other customers sat for service . . .": *The Enemy Within: The McClellan Committee's Crusade Against Jimmy Hoffa and Corrupt Labor Unions,* by Robert F. Kennedy, 1960, p. 244.

75 "Dispatched by Carlo Gambino at the behest of Vito Genovese . . .": *The Valachi Papers,* by Peter Maas, p. 243; *Organized Crime: An Inside Guide to the World's Most Successful Industry,* by Thomas Lunde, 2004, p. 159. The Gallos are likewise fingered in *Hoover's FBI: The Inside Story by Hoover's Trusted Lieutenant,* by Cartha D. "Deke" DeLoach, 1995, p. 305. Due to their later comments, the Gallos remain the best-guess choice for the killers of Anastasia. Other candidates put forth include another set of Gambino underling brothers, the Armones, Steven and Joseph, but since Steven walked with a pronounced limp, a characteristic of the gunmen wholly unremarked upon by witnesses, they are unlikely to have done the job.

76 "One of the bullets tumbled . . .": *The Mad Ones: Crazy Joe Gallo and the Revolution at the Edge of the Underworld,* by Tom Folsom, 2008, p. 40.

7. GENOVESE CALLS A CONFAB

79 "Magaddino had been the one . . .": *Bringing Down the Mob: The War Against the American Mafia,* by Thomas Repetto, 2006, p. 151.

79 "He first set up shop . . .": *Mob Nemesis: How the FBI Crippled Organized Crime,* by Joe Griffin with Don DeNevi, 2002, pp. 69–70.

80 " 'The Arm,' as Magaddino's organization . . .": *The Sixth Family: The Collapse of the New York Mafia and the Rise of Vito Rizzuto,* by Lee Lamothe and Adrian Humphreys, 2008, p. 32.

80 "In the basement of his Lewiston residence . . .": *Mob Nemesis: How the FBI Crippled Organized Crime,* by Joe Griffin, p. 127.

80 "According to an immigration agent . . .": "The Rap Gangsters Fear

Most" [deportation], by Stanley Frank, *Saturday Evening Post*, September 13, 1958.

82   "The first took place October 12–16 . . .": "Police in Sicily Say U.S. Mafia Attended '57 Parley," by Charles Grutzner, *New York Times*, January 2, 1968; *Five Families: The Rise, Decline and Resurgence of America's Most Powerful Mafia Empires*, by Selwyn Raab, 2005, pp. 112–13; *Octopus: The Long Reach of the International Sicilian Mafia*, by Claire Sterling, 1990, pp. 82–86, 88–90. Spirited, detailed, and engrossing as it is, Sterling's largely unsourced account of the Grand Hotel et des Palmes meeting has long been a subject of debate among mob commentators. For one prominent doubter, see *Lucky Luciano*, by Tim Newark, pp. 221–23.

82   "Put bluntly, the Narcotic Control Act . . .": *The Salerno Report. The Mafia and the Murder of President John F. Kennedy: The report by Mafia expert Ralph Salerno, Consultant to the Select Committee on Assassinations*, by John William Tuohy, 2011, p. 37.

83   "Another presummit summit convened . . .": "Chronological History of La Cosa Nostra in the United States," *Organized Crime 25 Years After Valachi : Hearings Before the Permanent Subcommittee on Investigations of the Committee on Governmental Affairs, United States Senate, One Hundredth Congress, Second Session, April 11, 15, 21, 22, 29, 1988*, p. 313. See also *Life*, September 1, 1967.

83   "Wiretaps caught some . . .": "Savagery, greed and a life of crime: meet the real sopranos," by Charles Laurence, *Daily Mail* [London, U.K.], May 7, 2007.

83   "David Chase, creator of *The Sopranos* . . .": "This Thing of His," by Elizabeth Primamore, *New Jersey Monthly*, April 2007, pp. 84–87, 116–17.

8. THE MOB MEETS

87   "The mobsters gathered that day . . .": Most of the information on travel to Apalachin is contained in *Interim Report of the Joint Legislative Committee on Government Operations, Appendix C*, pages 1–62.

87   "'It was DeSimone's job . . .'": "When Everything Was Lost," by Judith Moore, *San Diego Reader*, March 18, 1999.

88   "Russell Bufalino, a Scranton racketeer . . .": "Federal Judge Rules State Police 'Altogether Proper' at Apalachin," *Utica Observer-Dispatch*, December 2, 1959.

88   "He would be Charlie Lucky's . . .": *New York Journal-American*, page 4, November 22, 1957.

88   "He had a brace . . .": "Bird's Eye View," by Vince Bird, *The Scrantonian* [Scranton, PA], August 10, 1958.

90   "'You want to know who really rules . . .'": "Apalachin Put Genovese in Spotlight," *New York Journal-American*, p. 13, August 7, 1958.

91   "'As a favor to Lansky . . .'": *Double Cross*, by Sam and Chuck Giancana, p. 253.

92   "Are you ashamed . . .": "New Mafia File on Luciano Kept Secret," *Utica Observer-Dispatch*, p. 1, July 2, 1958.

93   "The summit guest list bulged . . .": "Apalachin Barred Women, Jury Told," *New York Times*, November 26, 1959. See also "Trial Told of Large Barbara Guest List," *Utica Observer-Dispatch*, Nov. 25, 1959.

9. CROSWELL MAKES HIS MOVE

98   "They fled like ballet belles . . .": "Did Lucky Call Meeting of Mob?" *Newark Star-Ledger*, November 16, 1957.

99   "Glen Craig lived in a small trailer . . .": "Apalachin Presence Claimed," *Binghamton Press*, November 26, 1957.

101   "The sixty-four-year-old Montana had gotten . . .": "Apalachin Raider Said Barbed Wire Snagged Montana," AP (syndicated), *Binghamton Press*, November 14, 1959.

103   "It was horrendous . . .": *Man of Honor*, by Joe Bonanno, 2003, p. 214.

103   "The lid had been blown off . . .": *Bound by Honor*, by Bill Bonanno, 1999, p. 58.

103   "The correct tally . . .": "Harriman Calls More Agencies into Apalachin Mob Probe," *Binghamton Press*, Nov. 21, 1957.

105   "Some talk centered around . . .": "Police on Carpet Over Raid," *New York World-Telegram and Sun*, Nov. 20, 1957.

10. THE BIG ROUNDUP

109   "'We gave them a rough time' . . .": *The Outfit*, by Gus Russo, 2001, p. 328.

110   "Later in his checkered racketeering career . . .": *Mob Nemesis*, by Joe Griffin, p. 126.

112   " 'We first became aware of something' . . .": "Roundup Startles Apalachin," *The Daily Bulletin* [Endicott, Endwell, Vestal, Western Broome and Eastern Tioga Counties], November 15, 1957.

11. THE RACKETS COMMITTEE CONVENES

117   "The committee was largely Bobby's baby . . .": *Robert Kennedy: His Life,* by Evan Thomas, p. 76.

118   "Joe described the idea of targeting . . .": *The Presidency of John F. Kennedy,* by James N. Giglio, 1991, p. 144.

118   "He confronted his brother . . .": Thomas, *op. cit.,* pp. 110–11.

119   "Amato counted himself as a charter member . . .": *The Strength of the Wolf,* by Douglas Valentine, p. 58.

119   "Is there any organization . . .": *Hearings Before the Select Committee on Improper Activities in the Labor or Management Field,* first session, Part 17, p. 6,744.

120   " 'RFK didn't really become engaged' . . .": *Robert Kennedy: His Life,* by Evan Thomas, p. 404.

120   "To him, [Apalachin] was prima facie . . .": "The Day a Lone Trooper Shook Up the Underworld," by Jeffrey Stinson, *The Trooper* (magazine), Nov./Dec. 1987.

120   "The dramatic, marathon face-off . . .": *Perfect Villains, Imperfect Heroes,* by Ronald Goldfarb, p. 5.

120   "RFK 'appeared to lose all interest' . . .": Thomas, *ibid.,* p. 283.

121   "I saw him often . . .": Thomas, *ibid.,* p. 283.

121   "The greatest campaigner of them all . . ." *Estes Kefauver: A Biography,* by Charles L. Fontenay, 1980, p. 137.

123   "Impromptu campaign for the number two spot . . .": Thomas, *ibid.,* p. 73.

124   "Kissed very hard . . .": Thomas, *ibid.,* p. 65.

124   "RFK arranged an invitation . . .": *Perfect Villains, Imperfect Heroes,* by Ronald Goldfarb, p. 4.

125   "At the time, I thought there was a serious internal security threat . . .": quoted in *Robert Kennedy and His Times,* by Arthur Schlesinger, p. 106.

125   "Sin held a fascination . . .": Thomas, *ibid.,* p. 71.

125   "Theodore Roosevelt's daughter . . .": quoted in "Bobby, My Moral Beacon," by Gordon Brown, *The New Statesman,* April 30, 2007.

125   "Said one Justice Department official . . .": *The Presidency of John F. Kennedy,* by James N. Giglio, p. 145.

125   "The privileged kid with the Harvard education . . .": Thomas, *ibid.,* p. 71.

126   "The sheriff who could have been . . ." *Robert Kennedy and His Times,* by Arthur Schlesinger, p. 816.

126   "James M. Landis, a legal advisor . . .": *Kennedy Justice,* by Victor Navasky, 1971, p. 6.

12. HOOVER DENIES THE MAFIA

128   "'After the meeting at Apalachin . . .'": *Robert Kennedy and His Times,* by Arthur Schlesinger, p. 168.

128   "The FBI, in an official revisionist history . . .": "Turning Point: Using Intel to Stop the Mob, Part 2," posted August 9, 2007, accessed May 21, 2011. (http://www.fbi.gov/news/stories/2007/august/mobintel2 _080907/).

128   "The file on Frank Costello's shooting . . .": *Bringing Down the Mob,* by Thomas Repetto, p. 71.

129   "'They had something . . .'": Schlesinger, *ibid.,* p. 168.

129   "Boiled through the building . . .": *Inside Hoover's FBI: The Top Field Chief Reports,* by Neil J. Welch and David W. Marston, 1984, p. 87.

130   "'For pretty much close to twenty-five years' . . .": *Kennedy Justice,* Navasky, p. 63–64.

131   "George E. Allen . . . said he was present . . .": *J. Edgar Hoover: The Man and the Secrets,* by Curt Gentry, 1991, p. 329.

132   "I'm sure he would have been the chief librarian . . .": *J. Edgar Hoover,* Gentry, p. 67.

133   "Heading up the group was Carlo Tresca . . .": *Young J. Edgar,* Ackerman, p. 283.

134   "Edgar began to see his anti-Red mission . . .": *Young J. Edgar: Hoover, the Red Scare and the Assault on Civil Liberties,* by Kenneth D. Ackerman, 2007, p. 86.

134   "A slender bundle of high-charged electric wire . . .": *ibid.,* p. 159.

135   "The card index multiplied . . .": *The Boss: J. Edgar Hoover and the Great American Inquisition,* by Athan G. Theoharis, and John Stuart Cox, 1988, p. 5; and *Young J. Edgar,* Ackerman, pp. 66, 341.

135 "Hoover had evolved into . . .": *Bobby and J. Edgar: The Historic Face-off Between the Kennedys and J. Edgar Hoover That Transformed America,* by Burton Hersh, 2004, p. 340.

136 "'We are delighted . . .'": *The Boss,* Theoharis, p. 339.

13. THE MYSTERY OF APALACHIN

138 "Sixty-two top leaders of the dreaded Mafia . . .": "Seize 62 Mafia Chieftains In Upstate Raid," by Howard Wantuch and Sidney Kline, New York *Daily News,* November 15, 1957.

139 "The *World-Telegram* blasted Croswell . . .": "Police on Carpet Over Raid," by Fred J. Cook and Walter MacDonald, *New York World-Telegram and Sun,* November 20, 1957; "Harriman Reported Furious Over Conduct of Mafia Raid," by Richard J. Roth, *New York World-Telegram and Sun,* November 21, 1957.

139 "Harriman went out of his way to praise . . .": "Harriman Praises Croswell for Raid," Associated Press (syndicated), *Binghamton Press,* November 22, 1957.

139 "'[Croswell] should be given a pat' . . .": "Trooper's Raid 'Error' Paying Off," by Frances Segrue, *New York Herald Tribune,* November 24, 1957.

139 "Along with its front page . . .": "The Mafia: Folklore or Death Syndicate?" by Sid Friedlander, *New York Post,* November 15, 1957.

139 "The next day . . .": "Mafia's Existence a Police Mystery," by David Lyle, *New York Herald Tribune,* November 16, 1957.

139 "Likewise, the Associated Press offered . . .": "Mafia: Myth or Menace?" by Jack Hand, *The Sunday Press* [Binghamton], January 8, 1958.

140 "Louis B. Nichols, Hoover's official flack . . .": "No Mafia at Barbara's, None in U.S., Says FBI," by John Kelso, *Binghamton Press*, November 21, 1957, p. 3.

142 "For Hoover, as one commentator . . .": *The Mafia Encyclopedia,* by Carl Sifakis, 1987, p. 89.

142 "In FBI memos, the mob became . . .": *Mobs and the Mafia,* by Hank Messick and Burt Goldblatt, 1972, p. 188.

142 "The last word on the name game . . .": *Bringing Down the Mob,* by Thomas Repetto, 2006, p. 71.

142 "'Steak-eaters' was jocular . . .": "Anastasia Probers Seek Steak-Eater," *Binghamton Press,* January 8, 1958.

142 "Associated Press reports . . .": For example, "Riddle of Apalachin Still Unsolved 2 Years After Raid," by George W. Cornell, Associated Press, *Utica Observer-Dispatch,* November 13, 1959.

143 "On Monday, November 18 . . .": *Mob Nemesis,* by Joe Griffin with Don DeNevi, p. 34.

143 "In 1953, agents in the New York office . . .": "Turning Point: Using Intel to Stop the Mob, Part 2" (http://www.fbi.gov). For the Top Hoodlum program beginning only after Apalachin, see another internal FBI text, "Organized Crime and 'Joe's Barbecue,'" *A Byte Out of History,* posted November 14, 2003, at http://www2.fbi.gov/page2/nov03/crime111403.htm.

144 "The Mafia had 5,000 core members . . .": *Honor Thy Father,* by Gay Talese, 1971, p. 181.

144 "But the mob knocked down an estimated $7 billion . . .": *Five Families,* by Selwyn Raab, p. ix; for the Soviet subsidy, see Harvey Klehr, John Earl Haynes, and Kyrill M. Anderson, *The Soviet World of American Communism,* Yale University Press (1998), p. 155.

146 "'An FBI wiretap' . . .": *J. Edgar Hoover, Sex, and Crime: An Historical Antidote,* by Athan G. Theoharis, 1995, p. 141.

14. THE WATCHDOGS

149 "They kicked things off with Croswell . . .": "Had To Free Mob: Croswell," by Arvis Chalmers, *The Knickerbocker News* [Albany], November 12, 1957.

150 "Some of the witnesses were less . . .": "Didn't Tip Hoods, Just Forget Fish Order," *Binghamton Press,* November 13, 1958.

151 "By their own tally they combed through . . .": *The Crime Confederation: The Cosa Nostra and Allied Operations in Organized Crime,* by Ralph Salerno and John S. Tompkins, 1969, p. 301.

152 "'The revolver has reposed'. . . .": "Buffalo's 'Man of Year' Loses His Pistol Permit," by James D. Horan and Edward Newman, *New York Journal-American,* December 10, 1957.

152 "Reporters asked Joe Profaci . . ." "Mafia Roundup Tipoff Charged," by Sam Crowther, *New York Journal-American,* Nov. 22, 1957. The

"frightened man" characterization and the Castellano quote are from the same article.

153 "Croswell and his fellow state police . . .": "Majuri's Presence Claimed," *Elizabeth Daily Journal,* December 3, 1957.

154 "Majuri's lawyer Ed Cohen posed . . .": "Majuri 'Unconvincing,' Given Prison Term," *Elizabeth Daily Journal,* December 5, 1957.

155 "'I just bought a horse' . . .": *The Sins of the Father: Joseph P. Kennedy and the Dynasty He Founded,* by Ronald Kessler, 1996, p. 1.

000 "The day of the summit, when reporters . . .": "Mafia's Existence a Police Mystery," by David Lyle, *New York Herald Tribune,* November 16, 1957.

155 "'Facets of the information gleaned thus far' . . .": "New Senate Probe to Cover Apalachin Mob-Union Links," *Times-Union* [Albany, NY], December 22, 1957.

156 "'If I were governor of a large state' . . .": "The Democratic Whiz of 1957," *Time,* December 2, 1957.

157 "*Look* magazine alone took some eight thousand . . .": *Ultimate Sacrifice,* by Lamar Waldron, 2006, p. 302.

157 "'As a starting point for our hearings,' . . .": *Proceedings of the Permanent Subcommittee on Investigations,* pp. 12, 193. Subsequent quotes from the Rackets Committee proceed from there.

160 "With hundreds of lawyers . . .": *Kennedy Justice,* by Victor Navasky, p. xiv.

160 "The Apalachin debacle provided Robert Kennedy . . .": *The Strength of the Wolf,* by Douglas Valentine, p. 176.

161 "'He had a coronary thrombosis' . . .": "U.S. to Act on Mafia Mob," by Harry Altshuler, *New York Daily Mirror,* September 17, 1957.

162 "On September 20, 1958, a Saturday, Benenati . . .": details from author interview, Joseph Benenati; see also "Apalachin Host Hard to Get," *New York Tribune,* November 7, 1958.

15. THE FEDS TAKE DOWN VITO

164 "He rattled off his bailiwick . . .": "Thorough Ferreter," *The New Yorker,* June 9, 1956, p. 24.

165 "Genovese's narcotics trafficking charge . . .": *The Strength of the Wolf,* by Douglas Valentine, p. 178–180. The "musk melon" characterization

is from "Get 'The Right Man': How the FBN Nailed Vito Genovese," by Thom L. Jones, accessed May 12, 2011, at MobCorner.com.

166 "Author Douglas Valentine interviewed . . .": *The Strength of the Wolf,* by Douglas Valentine, p. 180.

167 "Williams took pains to connect Genovese . . .": *Five Families,* by Selwyn Raab, p. 536.

167 "Not everyone was convinced . . .": *The Strength of the Wolf,* by Douglas Valentine, pp. 241, 247, 253.

167 "Enraged and jealous at the FBN . . .": *Crusade: Undercover Against the Mob and KGB,* by Tom Tripodi with Joseph P. DeSario, 1993, p. 60.

169 "The Cosa Nostra's variegated crimes . . .": *Five Families,* by Selwyn Raab, p. 114.

169 "In the mid-fifties, a kilo . . .": "The Rap Gangsters Fear Most," by Stanley Frank, *Saturday Evening Post,* September 13, 1958.

169 "Vito Genovese helped kill . . .": *Wishing on the Moon: The Life and Times of Billie Holiday,* by Donald Clarke, 1994, pp. 226–28; *Billie Holiday,* by Stuart Nicholson, 1995, pp. 141–42, 147–48.

170 "Genovese himself instituted . . .": *The Strength of the Wolf,* by Douglas Valentine, p. 241.

170 " 'What the edict against narcotics' . . .": Ralph Salerno quoted in *Five Families,* by Selwyn Raab, p. 119.

170 "Some of Williams's targets managed . . .": "Galante Denies Narcotics Charge, Held In Default of $100,000 Bail," *Binghamton Press,* June 4, 1959.

171 "The day after his office indicted . . .": "On the Washington Merry-Go-Round," by Drew Pearson, syndicated, *Binghamton Press,* July 7, 1958.

172 "Recalled New York narcotics agent . . .": *The Strength of the Wolf,* by Douglas Valentine, p. 181.

172 "Testifying before Congress, Hoover . . .": *The Crime Confederation,* by Ralph Salerno and John S. Tompkins, p. 300.

173 " 'Under the interpretation' . . .": "How the Big Roundup Was Run," by John Brean, *Life,* June 1, 1959.

16. THE BROTHER WITHIN

175 "A picture of downward mobility . . .": "Barbaras Move to Vestal Home," *Binghamton Press,* September 23, 1959.

175 "That spring, after seventeen months . . .": "Flashbulbs Signal End of Joe Barbara's Long Seclusion," *Binghamton Press,* April 28, 1959.

176 "The man himself didn't last long enough . . .": "Apalachin Secrets Die with Barbara," *Binghamton Sun,* June 18, 1959; "Sicilian Immigant's Dream Was Smashed by Headlines," *Binghamton Press,* June 18, 1959.

176 "Nineteen-year-old Angie did not allow . . .": "Barbara's Body at Endictoo Home in Silver-Plated Casket," *Binghamton Press,* June 19, 1959.

177 "In a will dated March 24, 1957 . . .": "Barbara Estate Guess $300,000," *Binghamton Press,* June 27, 1959.

177 "There'll be fifty-eight for tea . . .": *The Enemy Within,* by Robert F. Kennedy, p. 239.

178 "It was not a chance meeting . . .": *ibid.,* pp. 239–40.

178 "It seemed to me rather funny at the time . . .": *ibid.,* p. 81.

179 "They have the look of Capone's men . . .": *ibid.,* p. 75.

182 "Staten Island boss Joe Riccobono triggered laughter . . .": "Apalachin Jury Hears New Tales of Parley," AP (syndicated), *Binghamton Press,* December 2, 1959.

182 "Defense attorney Henry G. Singer questioned . . ." "Kennedy Presidential Ambition Brought Up at Apalachin Hearing," AP (syndicated), *Binghamton Press,* December 4, 1959.

183 "He provided a series of thumbnail portraits . . .": "Apalachin Guests Given Stiff Terms," *New York Times,* January 14, 1960; "Excerpts from the Judge's Ruling," *New York Times,* January 13, 1960.

17. GENERAL KENNEDY GOES AFTER THE MOB

186 "On January 17, 1960, immediately after . . .": " 'Meeting at Apalachin' Desilu Playhouse Story," *Binghamton Press,* January 17, 1960. See also, "TV Heeds Uncle Sam's Apalachin Appeal," *Binghamton Press,* September 23, 1959.

186 "Ed Croswell got a little taste of media . . .": "Croswell Fools Only 1 of 4," *Binghamton Press,* January 15, 1960.

188 " 'After all these years,' Clark said . . .": "Apalachin Free in Court Upset," New York *Daily News,* January 26, 1960; "No Apologies for Apalachin Roundup Says Croswell After Court Reverses Barbara's Pals' Convictions," *Binghamton Press,* January 26, 1960.

188 "Croswell reacted to Clark's Javert slur . . .": " 'Javert? I've Been Called Many Things,' " *Binghamton Press,* January 26, 1960.

189   "Notre Dame law professor G. Robert Blakey . . .": "RICO: The Gene-
       sis of an Idea," by G. Robert Blakey, *Trends in Organized Crime*, vol-
       ume 9, summer 2006.

189   "The nomination of the president's little brother . . .": *Robert Kennedy:
       His Life*, by Evan Thomas, p. 109–10.

190   "I have now watched . . .": *An Unfinished Life: John F. Kennedy, 1917–
       1963*, by Robert Dallek, p. 316.

190   "All of us worked our tails off . . .": *Counsel to the President: A Memoir*,
       by Clark Clifford with Richard Holbrooke, 1992, p. 337. "To my pleas-
       ant surprise . . .": *ibid*, p. 338.

192   "'Mr. Hoover became the Director of the Bureau' . . .": *The Presidency
       of John F. Kennedy*, by James N. Giglio, p. 145.

192   "And he brought his dog to work . . .": *Robert Kennedy: Brother Protec-
       tor*, by James W. Hilty, p. 195.

192   "It was apparent that if Robert Kennedy . . .": *Kennedy Justice*, by Vic-
       tor Navasky, p. 45.

18. BOBBY GOES TOO FAR

195   "The old Harvard crowd voiced concern . . ." *A Common Good: The
       Friendship of Robert F. Kennedy and Kenneth P. O'Donnell*, by Helen
       O'Donnell, 1998, pp. 146–47.

195   "The year before RFK took up the reins . . .": *Official and Confidential:
       The Secret Life of J. Edgar Hoover*, by Anthony Summers, 1993, p. 282.

196   "'I wouldn't characterize Bobby' . . .": *Perfect Villains, Imperfect He-
       roes*, by Ronald Goldfarb, p. 25.

196   "On the morning of April 4, 1961 . . .": *Perfect Villains, Imperfect He-
       roes*, by Ronald Goldfarb, pp. 74–76; *Mafia Kingfish: Carlos Marcello
       and the Assassination of John F. Kennedy*, by John Davis, pp. 90–99.
       "No Mafia figure . . .": *The Road to Dallas: The Assassination of John F.
       Kennedy*, by David Kaiser, p. 332.

198   "A morose RFK told his aide . . .": *Robert Kennedy*, by Evan Thomas,
       p. 337.

199   "When Bob Kennedy left . . .": *Kennedy Justice*, by Victor Navasky,
       p. 240.

199   "No single individual or coalition of racketeers dominates . . .":
       Kennedy Justice, by Victor Navasky, pp. 8–9.

19. NOVEMBER 14, 1957

200 "The wholesale meat truck violates . . .": *Treasury Agent: The Inside Story,* by Andrew Tully, 1958), p. 61; *Binghamton Press,* "Bar-B-Q Meat Was Charged to Canada Dry," *Daily Bulletin,* November 25, 1957.

200 "A pair of illuminated Gibbons Beer . . .": "First Look Inside Barbara's Hillside Hideout," *Sunday Press* (Binghamton), May 31, 1959. Further details regarding interior furnishings are generally from this source.

201 "Joe and his Endicott subordinate . . .": "6 Apalachin delegates, 2 from Endicott, Plead Innocent," by Woody Fitchette, *Binghamton Press,* May 22, 1959.

201 "Barbara telephones Russell Bufalino . . .": "Apalachin Confab Like a Clambake," *Binghamton Press,* November 20, 1959; for Osticco account from Bufalino deportation proceedings, see "Bufalino Hearing Set to End In Afternoon," *Scranton Tribune,* January 27, 1958; further details, including "he visits his beef," from author interview, Joseph Benenati.

202 "Joe doesn't think he can sleep . . .": "It Was Self-Service—Turrigiano," *Binghamton Press,* November 14, 1959; "Apalachin Jury Hears Turrigiano Testimony," Associated Press (syndicated), November 18, 1959.

203 "Nervous, Joe makes a few runs . . .": *Interim Report of the Joint Legislative Committee on Government Operations, Appendix C,* p. 49.

203 "The newly arrived Profaci greets . . .": "'Wrong Way' Profaci Talks of Apalachin," New York *Daily News,* January 21, 1959.

204 "Joe the host announces . . .": "It Was Self-Service—Turrigiano," *Binghamton Press,* November 14, 1959.

205 "His cohost Bufalino describes him . . .": "Barbara Was Host to Judges," *Binghamton Press,* Nov. 23, 1959; also "Bufalino Hearing Set to End in Afternoon," *Scranton Tribune,* Jan. 27, 1958.

206 "Lombardozzi is under a sentence . . .": "Condemned Hood Reprieved at Apalachin," *Binghamton Press,* Feb. 12, 1959.

206 "That small matter taken care of . . .": "Topic A at Apalachin Was Dope Racket Feds Reveal," New York *Daily News,* Feb. 28, 1960. See also, "Narcotics 'Definitely' Apalachin Topic," an account by FBN chief Harry Anslinger at the House Appropriations Subcommittee, *Binghamton Press,* Feb. 7, 1958; *Five Families,* by Selwyn Raab, pp. 118–19; *Havana Nocturne,* by T. J. English, p. 239; further details from author interview, Joseph Benenati.

EPILOGUE: APALACHIN IN THE AMERICAN IMAGINATION

212 "The 'Kennedy stomach,' the tranquilizers . . .": *The Sins of the Father*, by Ronald Kessler, p. 428.

BIBLIOGRAPHY

Ackerman, Kenneth D. *Young J. Edgar: Hoover, the Red Scare, and the Assault on Civil Liberties.* New York: Carroll & Graf Publishers, 2007.

Agar, Michael. *Ripping and Running: A Formal Ethnography of Urban Heroin Addicts.* New York: Academic Press Inc., 1973.

Alvarez, Josephine Nesline. *Lucky "325."* New York: Lucky 325, Inc., 2009.

Ambrose, Stephen E. *Eisenhower.* New York: Simon & Schuster, 1983, 1984.

America's Habit: Drug Abuse, Drug Trafficking, and Organized Crime: Report to the President and the Attorney General. Washington, D.C.: The Commission, 1986.

Anastasia, George. *Blood and Honor: Inside the Scarfo Mob, the Mafia's Most Violent Family.* New York: William Morrow, 1991.

Anslinger, Harry J. *The Protectors, Narcotics Agents, Citizens and Officials Against Organized Crime in America.* New York: Farrar, Straus & Co., 1964.

Arlacchi, Pino. *Mafia Business: The Mafia Ethic and the Spirit of Capitalism.* London: Verso, 1986.

Balsamo, William, and John Balsamo. *Young Al Capone: The Untold Story of Scarface in New York, 1899–1925.* New York: Skyhorse Publishing, 2011.

Bari, Frank, and Mark C. Gribben. *Under the Williamsburg Bridge: The Story of an American Family.* British Columbia, Canada: Trafford Publishing, 2009.

Barnes, Charles B. *The Longshoremen.* New York: Survey Associates, 1915.

Bauder, Julia. *Drug Trafficking.* New York: Greenhaven Press, 2008.

Becker, Ed, and Charles Rappleye. *All American Mafioso: The Johnny Rosselli Story.* Fort Lee: Barricade Books, 1995.

Bell, Graham. *Murder, Inc.: The Mafia's Hit Men in New York City.* Charleston, SC: History Press, 2010.

Beran, Michael Knox. *Last Patrician: Bobby Kennedy and the End of American Aristocracy.* London: Griffin, 1999.

Bergreen, Laurence. *Capone: The Man and the Era.* New York, NY: Simon & Schuster, 1994.

Berson, Fred. *After the Big House: The Adventures of a Parole Officer.* New York: Crown Publishers, 1952.

Blakey, G. Robert, and Richard N. Billings. *Fatal Hour: The Assassination of President Kennedy by Organized Crime.* New York: Berkley Books, 1992.

Blakey, G. Robert, Ronald Goldstock, and Charles H. Rogovin. *Rackets Bureaus: Investigation and Prosecution of Organized Crime.* Washington: National Institute of Law Enforcement and Criminal Justice, Law Enforcement Assistance Administration, U.S. Dept. of Justice, 1978.

Blakey, G. Robert. *The RICO Option: Criminal and Civil Remedies for the Unlawful Operation of Enterprises.* Philadelphia, Pa.: Temple Law School, 1986.

Blakey, G. Robert. *Techniques in the Investigation and Prosecution of Organized Crime: Materials on RICO: Criminal Overview, Civil Overview, Individual Essays.* Ithaca, N.Y.: Cornell Institute on Organized Crime, 1980.

Block, Alan A. and William J. Chambliss. *Organizing Crime.* New York, N.Y.: Elsevier, 1981.

Block, Alan A. *East Side, West Side: Organizing Crime in New York, 1930–1950.* New Brunswick, NJ.: Transaction Books, 1983.

Bonanno, Bill, and Gary B. Abromovitz. *The Last Testament of Bill Bonanno: The Final Secrets of a Life in the Mafia.* New York: HarperCollins Publishers, 2011.

Bonanno, Bill. *Bound by Honor: A Mafioso's Story.* New York: St. Martin's Press, 1999.

Bonanno, Joseph, and Sergio Lalli. *A Man of Honor: The Autobiography of Joseph Bonanno.* New York: Simon & Schuster, 1983.

Brandt, Charles. *"I Heard You Paint Houses": Frank "The Irishman" Sheeran and Closing the Case on Jimmy Hoffa.* Hanover, NH: Steerforth Press, 2005.

Brashler, William. *The Don: The Life and Death of Sam Giancana.* New York: Harper & Row, 1977.

Calderone, Carmen. *The Geneaology of American Organized Crime: The First One Hundred Years, the 20th Century.* Seattle: CreateSpace: 2010.

Capeci, Jerry. *The Complete Idiot's Guide to the Mafia*. Indiannapolis: Alpha Books, 2004.

Carter, David. *Stonewall: The Riots That Sparked the Gay Revolution*. New York: St. Martin's Press, 2004.

Charbonneau, Jean. *The Canadian Connection*. Ottawa: Optimum, 1976.

Chein, Isidor, et al. *The Road to H: Narcotics, Delinquency, and Social Policy*. New York: Basic Books, 1964.

Chepesiuk, Ron. *The Trafficantes: Godfathers from Tampa, Florida: the Mafia, the CIA, and the JFK Assassination*. La Vergne, TN: Strategic Media Books Inc., 2010.

Cirules, Enrique. *The Mafia in Havana: A Caribbean Mob Story*. Melbourne: Ocean Press, 2004.

Clarke, Donald. *Wishing on the Moon: The Life and Times of Billie Holiday*. New York: Viking, 1994.

Clifford, Clark M., and Richard C. Holbrooke. *Counsel to the President: A Memoir*. New York: Random House, 1991.

Cockburn, Alexander, and Jeffrey Clair. *Whiteout: The CIA, Drugs, and the Press*. London: Verso, 1998.

Cohen, Rich. *Tough Jews*. New York: Simon & Schuster, 1998.

Cook, Fred J. *The FBI Nobody Knows*. New York: Macmillan, 1964.

Cook, Fred J. *The Secret Rulers: Criminal Syndicates and How They Control the U.S. Underworld*. New York: Duell, Sloan and Pearce, 1966.

Costanzo, Ezio. *The Mafia and the Allies: Sicily 1943 and the Return of the Mafia*. New York: Enigma, 2007.

Courtwright, David, Don Des Jarlais, and Herman Joseph. *Addicts Who Survived: An Oral History of Narcotic Use in America, 1923–1965*. Knoxville: University of Tennessee Press, 1989.

Courtwright, David T. *Dark Paradise: A History of Opiate Addiction in America*. Cambridge: Harvard University Press, 2001.

Courtwright, David T. *Forces of Habit: Drugs and the Making of the Modern World*. Cambridge: Harvard University Press, 2002.

Cressey, Donald R. *Theft of the Nation: The Structure and Operations of Organized Crime in America*. New York: Harper & Row, 1969.

Critchley, David. *The Origin of Organized Crime in America: The New York City Mafia, 1891–1931*. New York: Routledge, 2009.

Dallek, Robert. *An Unfinished Life: John F. Kennedy, 1917–1963*. Boston: Little, Brown, and Co., 2003.

Davis, John. *Mafia Kingfish: Carlos Marcello and the Assassination of John F. Kennedy*. New York: New American Library, 1989.

Deitche, Scott. *The Silent Don: The Criminal World of Santo Trafficante, Jr.* Fort Lee, New Jersey: Barricade Books, 2007.

Demaris, Ovid. *The Director: An Oral Biography of J. Edgar Hoover.* New York: Harper's Magazine Press, 1975.

Dennis, Uri Dan, and Eli Landau Eisenberg. *Meyer Lansky: Mogul of the Mob.* New York: Paddington Press Ltd., 1979.

De Stefano, George. *An Offer We Can't Refuse: The Mafia in the Mind of America.* Oxford: Faber & Faber, 2007.

Devico, Peter J. *The Mafia Made Easy: The Anatomy and Culture of La Cosa Nostra.* Mustang, OK.: Tate Publishing & Enterprises, 2007.

DiMona, Joseph, and George Wolf. *Frank Costello: Prime Minister of the Underworld.* New York: Hodder & Stoughton Ltd, 1975.

Dickie, John. *Cosa Nostra: A History of the Sicilian Mafia.* New York: Palgrave Macmillan, 2004.

Donati, William. *Lucky Luciano: The Rise and Fall of a Mob Boss.* Jefferson: McFarland & Co., 2010.

Downey, Patrick. *Gangster City: The History of the New York Underworld, 1900–1935.* Fort Lee: Barricade Books, 2004.

Dunar, Andrew J. *America in the Fifties.* Syracuse, N.Y.: Syracuse University Press, 2006.

Eig, Jonathan. *Get Capone: The Secret Plot that Captured America's Most Wanted Gangster.* New York, NY: Simon & Schuster, 2010.

Eisenhower, Dwight D. *Public Papers of the Presidents of the United States: Dwight D. Eisenhower.* Washington: Office of the Federal Register, National Archives and Records Service, General Services Administration, 1960.

Elmaleh, Edmund. *The Canary Sang but Couldn't Fly: The Fatal Fall of Abe Reles, the Mobster Who Shattered Murder, Inc.'s Code of Silence.* New York: Sterling Pub., 2009.

English, T. J. *Havana Nocturne: How the Mob Owned Cuba—and Then Lost It to the Revolution.* New York: William Morrow, 2008.

Feder, Sid, and Burton B. Turkus. *Murder, Inc.: The Story Of the Syndicate.* New York and Washington D.C.: Da Capo Press, 2003.

Fiddle, Seymour. *Portraits from a Shooting Gallery: Life Styles from the Drug Addict World.* New York: HarperCollins, 1967.

Finkelstein, Monte S. *Separatism, the Allies and the Mafia: The Struggle for Sicilian Independence, 1943–1948.* Bethlehem, Pa.: Lehigh University Press, 1998.

Fischer, Steve. *When the Mob Ran Vegas: Stories of Murder, Mayhem, and Money*. Omaha: Berkline Press, 2005.

Fontenay, Charles L. *Estes Kefauver, a Biography*. Knoxville: University of Tennessee Press, 1980, 1991.

Fox, Stephen R. *Blood and Power: Organized Crime in Twentieth-Century America*. New York: William Morrow, 1989.

Frasca, Dom. *Vito Genovese: King of Crime*. New York: Avon Books, 1963.

Friedman, John S. *The Secret Histories: Hidden Truths that Challenged the Past and Changed the World*. New York: Picador, 2005.

Gage, Nicholas. *The Mafia Is Not an Equal Opportunity Employer*. New York: McGraw-Hill, 1971.

Gallagher, Dorothy. *All the Right Enemies: The Life and Murder of Carlo Tresca*. New Brunswick, N.J.: Rutgers University Press, 1988.

Gaspairini, Marco. *The Mafia: History and Legend*. Milan, Italy: Flammarion, 2011.

Gentry, Curt. *J. Edgar Hoover: The Man and the Secrets*. New York: W. W. Norton & Company, 1991.

Giancana, Antoinette. *Mafia Princess: Growing Up in Sam Giancana's Family*. New York: Avon Books, 1985.

Giancana, Antoinette, John R. Hughes, and Thomas H. Jobe. *JFK and Sam: The Connection Between the Giancana and Kennedy Assassinations*. Nashville: Cumberland House Publishing, 2005.

Giglio, James N. *The Presidency of John F. Kennedy*. Lawrence, Kansas: University Press of Kansas, 1991.

Gillers, Stephen and Pat Watters. *Investigating the FBI*. New York: Doubleday, 1973.

Goettel, Gerald. "Why the Crime Syndicates Can't be Touched." *Harper's*, Nov. 1960.

Goldfarb, Ronald L. *Perfect Villains, Imperfect Heroes: Robert F. Kennedy's War Against Organized Crime*. New York: Random House, 1995.

Goodwin, Doris Kearns. *The Fitzgeralds and the Kennedys*. New York: Simon & Schuster, 1987.

Gosch, Martin A., Richard Hammer. *The Last Testament of Lucky Luciano*. Boston: Little, Brown, 1975.

Griffin, Joe and Don DeNevi. *Mob Nemesis: How the FBI Crippled Organized Crime*. Buffalo, NY: Prometheus Books, 2002.

Hack, Richard. *Puppetmaster: The Secret Life of J. Edgar Hoover*. Beverly Hills: New Millennium Press, 2004.

Halberstam, David. *The Coldest Winter: America and the Korean War*. New York: Hyperion, 2007.

Halberstam, David. *The Fifties*. New York: Villard Books, 1993.

Hammer, Richard. *Gangland, U.S.A.: The Making of the Mob*. Chicago: Playboy Press, 1975.

Hammer, Richard. *Playboy's Illustrated History of Organized Crime*. Chicago: Playboy Press, 1975.

Hanson, Bill. *Life With Heroin: Voices from the Inner City*. New York: Lexington Books, 1985.

Hersh, Burton. *Bobby and J. Edgar: The Historic Face-off Between the Kennedys and J. Edgar Hoover That Transformed America*. New York: Basic Books, 2008.

Hersh, Seymour M. *The Dark Side of Camelot*. Boston: Little, Brown, 1997.

Heymann, C. David. *RFK: A Candid Biography of Robert F. Kennedy*. New York: Dutton, 1998.

Hibbert, Christopher. *Mussolini: The Rise and Fall of Il Duce*. New York: Palgrave Macmillan, 2008.

Hilty, James W. *Robert Kennedy: Brother Protector*. Philadelphia, PA.: Temple University Press, 1997.

Investigation of Improper Activities in the Labor or Management Field. Washington, D.C.: U.S.G.P.O, 1957.

Jacobs, James B. *Mobsters, Unions, and Feds: The Mafia and the American Labor Movement*. New York: New York University Press, 2007.

Jennings, Dean Southern. *We Only Kill Each Other: The Life and Bad Times of Bugsy Siegel*. Englewood Cliffs, N.J.: Prentice-Hall, 1967.

Joselit, Jenna Weissman. *Our Gang: Jewish Crime and the New York Jewish Community, 1900–1940*. Bloomington: Indiana University Press, 1983.

Josephson, Barney, and Terry Josephson. *Cafe Society: The Wrong Place for the Right People*. Urbana: University of Illinois Press, 2009.

Kaiser, David E. *The Road to Dallas: The Assassination of John F. Kennedy*. Cambridge, Mass.: Belknap Press of Harvard University Press, 2008.

Katz, Leonard, and Frank Costello. *Uncle Frank: The Biography of Frank Costello*. New York: Pocket Books, 1975.

Katzenbach, Nicholas de B. *The Challenge of Crime in a Free Society: A Report by the President's Commission on Law Enforcement and Administration of Justice*. Washington, D.C.: U.S. Govt. Off., 1967.

Kavieff, Paul R.. *The Life and Times of Lepke Buchalter: America's Most Ruthless Labor Racketeer*. Fort Lee, N.J.: Barricade, 2006.

Keating, William J., and Richard Carter. *The Man Who Rocked the Boat.* New York: Harper, 1956.

Keating, William J., and Richard Carter. *Slaughter on 10th Avenue.* New York: Paperback Library, 1956.

Kefauver, Estes. *Crime in America.* Garden City, N.Y.: Doubleday, 1951.

Kelly, Robert J., Ko Chin, and Rufus Schatzberg. *Handbook of Organized Crime in the United States.* Westport, Conn.: Greenwood Press, 1994.

Kennedy, Robert F. *The Enemy Within: The McClellan Committee's Crusade Against Jimmy Hoffa and Corrupt Labor Unions.* New York: Da Capo, 1994.

Kennedy, Robert F. *The Pursuit of Justice.* New York: Harper & Row, 1963.

Kennedy, Robert F., Edwin O. Guthman, and Jeffrey Shulman. *Robert Kennedy, in his Own Words: The Unpublished Recollections of the Kennedy Years.* Toronto: Bantam, 1988.

Kessler, Ronald. *The Bureau: The Secret History of the FBI.* New York: St. Martin's Press, 2002.

Kessler, Ronald. *The Sins of the Father: Joseph P. Kennedy and the Dynasty He Founded.* New York: Warner Books, 1996.

Kraft, Joseph. *Profiles in Power: A Washington Insight.* New York: New American Library, 1966.

Lacey, Robert. *Little Man: Meyer Lansky & the Gangster Life.* New Jersey: Random House Value Publishing, 1993.

Lamothe, Lee, and Adrian Humphreys. *The Sixth Family: The Collapse of the New York Mafia and the Rise of Vito Rizzuto.* New York: J. Wiley & Sons Canada, 2006.

Larner, Jeremy. *The Addict in the Street.* New York: Grove Press, 1971.

Lewis, Norman. *The Honored Society: A Searching Look at the Mafia.* New York: Putnam, 1964.

Lindesmith, Alfred R. *Drug Addiction: Crime or Disease? Interim and Final Reports of the Joint Committee of the American Bar Association and the American Medical Association on Narcotic Drugs.* Bloomington: Indiana University Press, 1967.

Lopate, Phillip. *Seaport: New York's Vanished Waterfront: Photographs from the Edwin Levick Collection.* Washington, D.C.: Smithsonian Books, 2004.

Lunde, Paul. *Organized Crime: An Inside Guide to the World's Most Successful Industry.* London, UK: DK, 2004.

Lupo, Salvatore. *History of the Mafia.* New York: Columbia University Press, 2009.

Maas, Peter. *The Valachi Papers.* New York: G.P. Putnam, 1968.

Madinger, John. *Confidential Informant: Law Enforcement's Most Valuable Tool.* Boca Raton, FL: CRC Press, 2000.

Martin, Ralph G. *Seeds of Destruction: Joe Kennedy and His Sons.* New York: G.P. Putnam's Sons, 1995.

Martin, Raymond V. *Revolt in the Mafia.* New York: Duell, Sloan and Pearce, 1963.

Mastantuono, Michel, and Michel Auger. *The Heroin Triangle: Marseilles . . . Montreal . . . New York.* Markham, Ont.: Paperjacks, 1978.

May, Allan R. *Gangland Gotham: New York's Notorious Mob Bosses.* Santa Barbara, Calif.: Greenwood Press, 2009.

Mayer, Michael S. *The Eisenhower Years.* New York: Facts on File, 2010.

Mayo, Katherine. *Justice to All: The Story of the Pennsylvania State Police.* New York: G.P. Putnam's Sons, 1917.

McClellan, John L. *Crime Without Punishment.* New York: Duell, Sloan and Pearce, 1962.

Mccoy, Alfred W. *The Politics of Heroin: CIA Complicity in the Global Drug Trade.* Chicago, Illinois: Lawrence Hill Books, 2003.

McWilliams, John C. *The Protectors: Harry J. Anslinger and the Federal Bureau of Narcotics, 1930–1962.* Newark: University of Delaware Press, 1990.

Messick, Hank. *Lansky.* London: Robert Hale Ltd, 1973.

Messick, Hank and Burt Greenblatt. *Mobs and the Mafia.* New York: Thomas Crowell, 1972.

Messick, Hank. *The Silent Syndicate.* New York: Macmillan, 1967.

Messick, Hank. *Syndicate Abroad.* New York: Macmillan, 1969.

Moore, James. *Very Special Agents: The Inside Story of America's Most Controversial Law Enforcement Agency—The Bureau of Alcohol, Tobacco, and Firearms.* Champaign, Illinois: University of Illinois Press, 2001.

Moore, Robin. *The French Connection.* London: Bloomsbury, 2000.

Morgan, John. *Prince of Crime.* Lanham, Maryland: Madison Books, 1986.

Moscow, Alvin. *Merchants of Heroin.* St. John's Hill, London: Littlehampton Book Services Ltd, 1968.

Moynihan, Daniel P. "The Private Government of Crime." *Reporter,* July 6, 1961.

Musto, David F. *The American Disease: Origins of Narcotic Control.* New York: Oxford University Press, 1999.

Nash, Arthur. *New York City Gangland (Images of America Series)*. Charleston: Arcadia Publishing, 2010.

Navasky, Victor S. *Kennedy Justice*. New York: Atheneum, 1971.

Newark, Timothy. *Lucky Luciano: The Real and Fake Gangster*. New York: Thomas Dunne Books, 2010.

Newark, Timothy. *Mafia Allies: The True Story of America's Secret Alliance with the Mob in World War II*. St. Paul, Minn.: Zenith Press, 2007.

Newfield, Jack. *Robert F. Kennedy: A Memoir*. New York: Berkley Pub Group, 1978.

Nicholson, Stuart. *Billie Holiday*. Boston: Northeastern University Press, 1995.

O'Donnell, Helen. *A Common Good: The Friendship of Robert F. Kennedy and Kenneth P. O'Donnell*. New York: William Morrow, 1998.

Oakley, J. Ronald. *God's Country: America in the Fifties*. New York: Dembner Books, 1986.

Olla, Roberto. *Godfathers: Lives and Crimes of the Mafia Mobsters*. Korea: Alma, 2007.

Organized Crime and Heroin Trafficking: Record of Hearing V, February 20–21, 1985, Miami, Florida. Washington, D.C.: The Commission, 1985.

Organized Crime 25 Years After Valachi: Hearings Before the Permanent Subcommittee on Investigations of the Committee on Governmental Affairs, United States Senate, One Hundredth Congress, Second Session, April 11, 15, 21, 22, 29, 1988. Washington, D.C.: U.S. G.P.O., 1988.

Pantaleone, Michele. *The Mafia and Politics*. New York: Coward-McCann, 1966.

Peterson, Virgil W. *The Mob: 200 Years of Organized Crime in New York*. Ottawa, Ill.: Green Hill Publishers, 1983.

Pokorski, Douglas. *Frank Zito: Springfield's Godfather*. Springfield, IL: Sangamon County Historical Society Publications, 2002.

Pope, Paul David. *The Deeds of My Fathers: How My Grandfather and Father Built New York and Created the Tabloid World of Today*. Maryland: A Philip Turner Book, Rowman & Littlefield Publishers, 2010.

Powers, Richard Gid. *Secrecy and Power*. New York City: Free Press, 1988.

Raab, Selwyn. *Five Families: The Rise, Decline, and Resurgence of America's Most Powerful Mafia Empires*. New York: St. Martin's Griffin, 2006.

Ragano, Frank. *Mob Lawyer*. New York: Random House, 1996.

Reid, Ed, and Ovid Demaris. *Green Felt Jungle*. New York: Simon & Schuster, 1963.

Reid, Ed. *The Grim Reapers: The Anatomy of Organized Crime in America, City by City*. New York: Bantam Books, 1972.

Reid, Ed. *Mafia: The History of the Ruthless Gang that Runs the Nationwide Crime Syndicate.* New York: Ishi Press International, 2010.

Reppetto, Thomas. *American Mafia: A History of Its Rise to Power.* New York: Holt Paperbacks, 2005.

Reppetto, Thomas. *Bringing Down the Mob: The War Against the American Mafia.* New York: Henry Holt & Company, 1980.

Riebling, Mark. *Wedge: From Pearl Harbor to 9/11—How the Secret War between the FBI and CIA Has Endangered National Security.* New York: Touchstone, 2002.

Roemer, Jr., William F. *Roemer: Man Against the Mob: The Inside Story of How the FBI Cracked the Chicago Mob by the Agent Who Led the Attack.* New York: Donald I. Fine, 1989.

Roemer, William F. *War of the Godfathers: The Bloody Confrontation Between the Chicago and New York Families for the Control of Las Vegas.* New York: Donald I. Fine, 1990.

Rudolph, Robert. *The Boys from New Jersey: How the Mob Beat the Feds.* New York: William Morrow, 1992.

Russo, Gus. *Brothers in Arms.* London: Bloomsbury, 2010.

Russo, Gus. *Live By the Sword: The Secret War Against Castro and the Death of JFK.* Baltimore: Bancroft Press, 1998.

Russo, Gus. *The Outfit.* New York: Bloomsbury USA, 2003.

Russo, Gus. *Supermob: How Sidney Korshak and His Criminal Associates Became America's Hidden Power Brokers.* New York: Bloomsbury USA, 2007.

Salerno, Ralph, and John S. Tompkins. *The Crime Confederation: Cosa Nostra and Allied Operations in Organized Crime.* Garden City, N.Y.: Doubleday, 1969.

Sceurman, Mark, and Mark Moran. *Weird N.J.: Your Travel Guide to New Jersey's Local Legends and Best Kept Secrets.* New York: Barnes & Noble, 2003.

Schlesinger, Arthur M. *Robert F. Kennedy: His Time.* Boston: Houghton Mifflin, 1978.

Schlesinger, Arthur M. *A Thousand Days: John F. Kennedy in the White House.* Boston: Houghton Mifflin, 1965.

Schneider, Eric C. *Smack: Heroin and the American City (Politics and Culture in Modern America).* Philadelphia: University of Pennsylvania Press, 2008.

Schoenberg, Robert J. *Mr. Capone.* New York: Morrow, 1992.

Scorza, S. E. *Mafia: The Government's Secret File on Organized Crime*. New York: HarperCollins, 2007.

Scott, James Maurice. *The White Poppy: A History of Opium*. Mahwah: Funk & Wagnalls Co, 1969.

Selvaggi, Giuseppe, and William A. Packer. *The Rise of the Mafia in New York: From 1896 Through World War II*. Indianapolis: Bobbs-Merrill, 1978.

Shawcross, Tim, and Martin Young. *Men of Honour: The Confessions of Tommaso Buscetta*. London: Collins, 1987.

Siragusa, Charles, and Robert Wiedrich. *The Trail of the Poppy: Behind the Mask of the Mafia*. Englewood Cliffs, N.J.: Prentice-Hall, 1966.

Sloman, Larry. *Reefer Madness: Marijuana in America*. New York: Grove Press, 1983.

Sondern, Frederic. *Brotherhood of Evil: The Mafia*. New York: Farrar, Straus and Cudahy, 1959.

Sterling, Claire. *Octopus: The Long Reach of the International Sicilian Mafia*. New York: Norton, 1990.

Sullivan, William C., and Bill Brown. *The Bureau: My Thirty Years in Hoover's FBI*. New York: Norton, 1979.

Summers, Anthony. *Official and Confidential: The Secret Life of J. Edgar Hoover*. New York: G.P. Putnam's Sons, 1993.

Super, John C. *The Fifties in America*. Pasadena: Salem Press, 2005.

Sutton, Willie, and Edward Linn. *Where the Money Was*. New York: Viking Press, 1976.

Talbot, David. *Brothers: The Hidden History of the Kennedy Years*. New York: Free Press, 2007.

Talese, Gay. *Honor Thy Father*. London: Sphere, 1973.

Theoharis, Athan G., and John Stuart Cox. *The Boss: J. Edgar Hoover and the Great American Inquisition*. Philadelphia: Temple University Press, 1988.

Theoharis, Athan G. *The FBI: A Comprehensive Reference Guide*. Phoenix, Ariz.: Oryx Press, 1999.

Theoharis, Athan G. *From the Secret Files of J. Edgar Hoover*. Chicago: Ivan R. Dee, 1991.

Theoharis, Athan G. *J. Edgar Hoover, Sex, and Crime: An Historical Antidote*. Chicago: Ivan R. Dee, 1995.

Thimmesch, Nick, and William O. Johnson. *Robert Kennedy at 40*. New York: W.W. Norton, 1965.

Thomas, Evan. *Robert Kennedy: His Life*. New York: Simon & Schuster, 2002.

Thompson, Craig, and Allen Raymond Thompson. *Gang Rule in New York: The Story of a Lawless Era*. New York: Dial Press, 1940.

Thompson, Robert E. *Robert F. Kennedy: The Brother Within*. New York: Macmillan, 1962.

Tosches, Nick. *Where Dead Voices Gather*. Boston: Little, Brown, 2001.

Tripodi, Tom, and Joseph P. DeSario. *Crusade: Undercover Against the Mafia & KGB*. Washington: Brassey's Inc., 1993.

Tully, Andrew. *Treasury Agent: The Inside Story*. New York: Simon & Schuster, 1958.

Tuohy, John William. *The Salerno Report: The Mafia and the Murder of President John F. Kennedy: The Report by Mafia Expert Ralph Salerno, Consultant to the Select Committee on Assassinations*. CreateSpace, 2011.

Turner, William W. *Hoover's FBI*. New York: Thunder's Mouth Press, 1993.

Tyler, Gus. *Combating Organized Crime*. Philadelphia: American Academy of Political and Social Science, 1963.

Tyler, Gus. *Organized Crime in America: A Book of Readings*. Ann Arbor: Univ. of Michigan Press, 1962.

Valentine, Douglas. *The Strength of the Wolf: The Secret History of America's War on Drugs*. New York: Verso, 2006.

Wagner, Rob Leicester. *Fabulous Fins of the Fifties*. New York: MetroBooks, 1997.

Waldron, Lamar. *Ultimate Sacrifice: John and Robert Kennedy, the Plan for a Coup in Cuba, and the Murder of JFK*. New York: Carroll & Graf, 2006.

Watters, Pat, and Stephen Gillers, eds. *Investigating the FBI*. New York: Doubleday, 1973.

Woodiwiss, Michael. *Organized Crime and American Power: A History*. Toronto: University of Toronto Press, 2001.

Zion, Sidney, and Pete Hamill. *Loyalty and Betrayal: The Story of the American Mob*. San Francisco, CA: Collins Publishers San Francisco, 1994.

INDEX